Sailing to the
Edge of Time

Sailing to the Edge of Time

The Promise, the Challenges, and the Freedom of Ocean Voyaging

JOHN KRETSCHMER

ADLARD COLES

LONDON · OXFORD · NEW YORK · NEW DELHI · SYDNEY

For Tadji—the love of my life and my true friend—it's our time now.

ADLARD COLES
Bloomsbury Publishing Plc
50 Bedford Square, London, WC1B 3DP, UK
29 Earlsfort Terrace, Dublin 2, Ireland

BLOOMSBURY, ADLARD COLES and the Adlard Coles logo are
trademarks of Bloomsbury Publishing Plc

First published in 2018
This edition published 2020

A catalogue record for this book is available from the British Library

Library of Congress Cataloguing-in-Publication data has been applied for

ISBN: PB: 978-1-4729-5166-3; ePDF: 978-1-4729-5164-9;
ePub: 978-1-4729-5163-2

2 4 6 8 10 9 7 5 3

Typeset in Minion Pro by Deanta Global Publishing Services, Chennai, India
Printed and bound in Great Britain by CPI Group (UK) Ltd, Croydon CR0 4YY

To find out more about our authors and books visit www.bloomsbury.com
and sign up for our newsletters

CONTENTS

CONTENTS

FOREWORD

Sometimes a sailor embodies two rare things coming together: the accomplishment of great voyages at sea, and the ability to write about them with intelligence, self-reflection and a high style.

In previous centuries the three masterful "sea-brothers"—Richard Henry Dana, Herman Melville, and Joseph Conrad—exemplified that experience and singular ability. Then, the first lone circumnavigator, Joshua Slocum, comes to mind, and others who could sail far and write well: Richard Maury, Hilaire Belloc, and Jack London. In our own time, the virtuoso French singlehander Bernard Moitessier, the square-rigger captain Alan Villiers, and small-boat sailors such as Eric Hiscock, Lin and Larry Pardey, and Hal Roth, have sailed the oceans and written about how to do it and what it means to them.

In their accounts, the reader learns about the voyage itself—the practical and mundane, yet essential, requirements for safely completing an open ocean passage under sail. But these writers often give us more: they reaffirm the role of the sea in our consciousness as a place of trial and courage, of honor and inspiration, and most of all, as the last great setting for untrammeled human freedom.

John Kretschmer fits easily into this distinguished coterie. I doubt that any living sailor has put in more miles at sea in small sailing vessels. His experience is astonishing in its variety, and in its relentlessness. By the latter I mean John's unparalleled—and profound—desire always to leave the land, to be at sea. He can't resist the call that "urges the heart to the whale's way over the stretch of the seas," as the Anglo-Saxon poem *The Seafarer* puts it. John exemplifies the dictum: life on land is complicated, cluttered, compromised; life at sea is clean, simple, honorable. "There's a blessed eternity to the sea, and time loses its greedy grip on our experiences," he writes.

But experience is nothing without the ability to describe it, to draw lessons from it, and to place it in the context of life on Planet Earth— which should be called Planet Ocean. And John Kretschmer is one of the chosen: he knows the sea and boats and he knows how to write about them. *Sailing to the Edge of Time* is a notable addition to his other fine books. Through the accretion of stories about his experiences at sea, how he handles crises, the mistakes he has made, we absorb his invaluable knowledge, and a sense of the skills such deep understanding brings. At the same time, he tells us what the sea means to him, and how it *feels* to sail it—the intense joys and satisfactions, or anxieties—to run swiftly and easily before trade winds or precariously before gales, to ghost in light air, to heave-to or to fore-reach in heavy weather when nothing else is possible.

I've had the privilege of sailing with John—just once (although I very much hope to again). It's an experience like no other at sea: an extended seminar by an intelligent, well-read and good man (in both the practical and the moral sense) who can teach you anything about a sailing vessel, and then can talk about Kierkegaard or Conrad, and then, not least, can cook an excellent chicken stew in any conditions and mix up a dynamite rum punch for his sacred Captain's Hour.

We sailed around the Caribbean for ten days aboard the handsome and sea-kindly *Quetzal*. I learned a lot I didn't know, and, of equal value, it was confirmed for me that some of the *ad hoc* things I was doing on my own boat were all right. For example: I'd always thought there must be a better way, besides a sheet of plastic and duct tape, of securing a forehatch from leaking during a hard beat to windward. Then, before *Quetzal* departed English Harbour bound for Barbados, I saw John go up on the foredeck with a sheet of plastic and a roll of duct tape and wrap his troublesome hatch as if it was going to be mailed somewhere.

His ceaseless and wide-ranging travels at sea and his landfalls in exotic ports anywhere in the world create, for me, a sense of John as a kind of classical hero. There's a whiff of wandering Odysseus about him. The hero goes to sea and endures trials and dangers and then returns to tell us about his adventures and what they taught him about himself and, therefore, about all of humanity. But it's his life at sea and what he experiences there that have meaning. There is always a destination, but the voyage is everything.

Sooner or later, we all arrive at the same port—a kind of Ithaca. The poet Constantine Cavafy wrote: "With the great wisdom you have gained, with so much experience, you must surely have understood by then what Ithacas mean." So let the voyage go on for as long as possible. There's no need to hurry to its end. *Sailing to the Edge of Time* will be an excellent companion along the way.

Derek Lundy
Derek Lundy is the author of five books, including *Godforsaken Sea: The True Story of a Race Through the World's Most Dangerous Waters*, and *The Way of a Ship: A Square-Rigger Voyage in the Last Days of Sail*. He lives on Salt Spring Island, British Columbia, and sails a Bristol Channel Cutter in the Salish Sea.

THE OLD NEIGHBORHOOD

*Discerning Lights at Night • Solo Watch in the
Gulf Stream • Washed Overboard*

"*There is always a certain risk in being alive, and if you are more
alive, there's more risk.*"

—Henrik Ibsen, *A Doll's House*

"*A man needs a little madness, or else... he never dares cut the rope
and be free.*"

—Nikos Kazantzakis, *Zorba the Greek*

The Atlantic, South of Bermuda, November 2015

My weary brain was taking its sweet time processing the fast-approaching
lights. We were a long way from anywhere, at least anywhere hard,
anywhere with a name that broke the surface of the stirred-up sea.
The tall grasses of tidewater Georgia were 1,000 rhumb-line miles to
starboard. The overgrown, overpriced, but always welcoming spits
that make up the Bermuda Islands were at least two tough days astern.
Quetzal, our well-traveled cutter, was sashaying across a stretch of the

ocean that's usually blissfully dark and soul-cleansingly lonely. It was breezy and we were sailing on a tight reach. It was a fast but lively point of sail, a balancing act that at times seemed like a ballet as *Quetzal* slipped gracefully between frothy breakers, and at other times a forced march as we punched into stern-faced waves that lacked any charity. Random buckets of spray launched over the port bow made peering over the dodger for a look about the horizon a risky gambit. If you tarried you were likely to be soaked, but if you remained huddled beneath the fraying canvas sanctuary you might miss something interesting, like fast-approaching lights. There was no denying that the lights were dangerously close.

Alone on watch, I wriggled past the wheel and made my way to the helm. As on most passages, the autopilot was doing the real work, and we were along for the ride. The instruments were perched in a housing just above *Quetzal*'s giant wheel and I dimmed the lights to preserve my night vision. The soft green glow of the radar confirmed that we were less than half a mile from an approaching target, and the screen was alight with ill-defined splotches suggesting additional targets nearby. There was no signal from the AIS receiver, though. An acronym for Automatic Identification System, AIS is a magical network that identifies vessels by name, gives important navigational information, and is quite useful when ships bother to transmit data. As with most electronic devices, you can never count on it when you really need it.

I searched for red and green navigation lights that would help determine the vessel's heading but they weren't readily visible. The lights I could see seemed out of focus and loomed in and out of view. The vessel was being tossed about in the jumbled seas and its heading was erratic, like a drunk swaying to the bar for one last drink. I wanted to be certain of its intentions before I altered *Quetzal*'s course. At night it's all too easy to make an uncertain situation worse by making a hasty course change.

Finally I made out two vertical lights. "Green over white," I mumbled, "what the hell is green over white?" Then a synapse fired. "Of course, you idiot, green over white—fishing at night." A silly mnemonic phrase from when I first studied for my captain's license—a lifetime ago—and lodged in my mind's cluttered attic ever since was suddenly quite handy. Although I was surprised to encounter a fishing fleet so far offshore, it was brain-numbingly obvious—we were passing through a fleet of offshore stern trawlers and one was closing fast on a collision course with *Quetzal*. The heavy tackle trailing astern came into view as I hit the standby button on the autopilot and took the wheel. I made a significant course correction, falling off the wind to pass well astern of the lumbering fishing boat. The stern deck was well lit and I could see one crew on deck, nonchalantly smoking, and seemingly unaware of us. An insatiable and cruelly efficient working vessel, plying ever more remote longitudes, it was intent on harvesting every unfortunate sea creature that strayed near its deadly trawls. Its crew simply didn't give a damn about a wayward sailboat on a self-inflicted adventure. They had right of way after all.

My watchmate was a week into an unrelenting bout of gut-heaving seasickness, and I didn't have the heart to rouse him from his first good sleep of the passage. The 0200–0500 watch is hard enough when you're feeling well, so I let him sleep. While I was happy for some alone time in the cockpit I was also bone tired. It had been a challenging passage and we had at least four days to go before making landfall in St. Martin. I wanted a cup of coffee. I always want a cup of coffee on watch. It's part of my nightly ritual, along with taking the helm for a few minutes, or sometimes a few hours, to have a chat with my beautiful boat and listen to any secrets she wants to share. I confess I was a bit shaken by the close encounter with the trawler, something that hadn't happened in many years and a reminder that experience is only as valuable as your last bad decision. I was wary of leaving the cockpit for even a few minutes. But caffeine is a powerful drug and the desire for coffee won out, especially with a clear path opening up between the fishing boats and uncluttered seas ahead.

I switched the autopilot back on and conjured a brilliant, multistage scheme to make a cup without disturbing the slumbering crew or taking my eyes off the horizon for too long. The plan looked like this: One—dash below, fill the kettle, turn on the stove and heat the water, then return to the companionway for a quick look about. Two—dash below again, spoon three heaping scoops of coffee into the French press, then intercept the kettle before it whistled. Fill the press with boiling water and carefully balance it in the sink wedged between the sponge and soap container, before returning to the companionway for another look about while the coffee steeped. Three—slip below one final time, plunge the press, fill the cup, add a splash of milk and silently but triumphantly return to the cockpit without any of the below-deck crew being the wiser.

I was done in by one wave. It's always just one wave, a sneaky curl of dark Atlantic marauding over the prevailing swell with sinister intentions. I was already on to stage three when it slapped the hull and sent my just-filled coffee cup skidding across the galley counter. Impressed with my own quick reactions, I snatched it in midslide, but not before most of it spilled. As I whirled around to balance the half-drained cup, my elbow smacked the stainless steel French press and it spiraled off the counter and onto the sole. The metallic clang ricocheted around the cabin like a Gatling gun and hot coffee grounds took flight. My beautiful plan had become a colossal mess and I expected the sleeping crew, scattered around the boat like half-read books, to glare up at me in complete disgust. Luckily for me, the combination of a relentless wind groaning in the rigging, a rhythmic if rocky motion, and near total exhaustion seven days into an offshore passage meant that nobody stirred. I hastily cleaned up the mess, settled for a miserable cup of cowboy coffee—half liquid, half grounds—and returned to the cockpit, not entirely unhappy and actually quite amused by my escapade. I am a simple and messy man.

A few sips later I spat the grounds overboard and lodged the cup so it wouldn't fall. I took the helm again and felt *Quetzal* surge as I cheated the course to ride down the backside of a cresting wave. We touched 10 knots, which is almost speeding in a cruising boat, then 10.2, fleeting digital glory complete with the immediate feedback that we've come to expect in the GPS age. The fishing boats had been an unwelcome intrusion and I wanted to reclaim the splendid isolation of the ocean and leave them behind. I decided to fall off the wind, ease the sheets, and spend the last two hours of my watch reaching for speed instead of being a slave to a distant waypoint and an electronic course line. Glancing at the chartplotter, I noted that the new heading would take us very close to a fateful address, a set of coordinates that to this day hang like a specter over my subconscious.

It was many years before—OK, I'll admit it, 31 years before. I was a young man with an age-old dream—to go to sea. I mean really go to sea, to the far reaches of the sea. I was bound for Cape Horn, a game but woefully inexperienced skipper of a sailing expedition that naively but bravely set out to retrace the route of the famed clipper ships from New York to San Francisco in a tiny sloop named *Gigi*. It was early in the voyage. We had sailed to Bermuda as a shakedown, and despite a troubling forecast, shoved off for Rio de Janeiro on Leg One of a 12,000-mile voyage. Leg Two would later take us around Cape Horn, and Leg Three from Valparaíso, Chile, to San Francisco. My crew on Leg One, my girlfriend Molly, really didn't want to be there. She was swept along in the torrent of my selfish dreams and didn't know how to free herself.

You need to maintain a sense of awe leavened with irony to survive at sea, or maybe to survive at all. Skidding over dark seas in an effort to embrace the moment and blot out the past, I drove *Quetzal* hard, steering instinctively, by the seat of my pants and the slant of the waves. But I couldn't help but smile when I realized that it was not just the same stretch of ocean that we were sailing over, it was also the very same day, November 1, and almost the same time, 2200 Atlantic standard, that *Gigi* capsized and I was washed overboard. I've written about this incident in all my books and in countless articles, and described it in many lectures. I've relived those fateful 15 seconds, maybe it was 30, or even 60, over and over again.

I heard the wave before I saw it. It broke with a deep-throated roar that I'll never forget. I've since learned that the sense of hearing is as vital, maybe more so, than keen vision for a sailor. Dangerous seas are clumsy assailants, they always give you fair warning if you're listening, especially on dark nights when your eyes can deceive you. *Gigi* was beating into the wind with just a deep-reefed mainsail. We were undercanvassed and out of balance, not a good combination afloat or ashore. The boat was sluggish in the water, vulnerable to the vagaries of breaking waves. I recognized the danger but I was too exhausted to address the situation. As I said, it's always just one wave. The wave that crushed us that storm-tossed night years ago did more than dislodge a coffee pot. It came within a razor's edge of sending me to a watery grave.

Gigi, one of the surest-footed sailboats ever built, was caught off guard. It was not her fault, it was her inexperienced skipper's fault. The wave was out of sequence with the others and broke at precisely the wrong moment, completely engulfing the boat. The raging torrent swept me overboard as *Gigi* rolled over violently on her port side. I didn't have time to be frightened, and remember thinking that the water was surprisingly warm. I was completely submerged and thoroughly

6

entangled in the excess coils of the mainsheet. I realized that I had to free myself if I was going to survive but I was not sure where to start. Time stopped, or at least screeched to a crawl. There's actually a phrase for this mental state which seems to occur during life-threatening situations: "slow-motion perception." David Eagleman, a neuroscientist at Baylor College of Medicine, believes that while time doesn't change, our memories of the events do. "Frightening events are associated with richer and denser memories," he explained in an online interview with *Live Science*. "The more memory you have of an event, the longer you believe it took." I have no idea how much time actually passed while I was in the water but my memory of it keeps expanding. I do know that a lifetime yet to come hung in the balance.

Gigi had too much pride and ballast; she refused to roll completely over. Once the wave passed she did a weird underwater pivot and righted herself with astonishing force. When she settled on the surface she was facing north, a full 180-degree change of direction. I was attached to the boat via an old-fashioned harness and ripped back to the surface like a fish on a line. Still ensnared in the mainsheet, I was just a few feet from the boat as she bobbed in the hissing slick that formed in the wake of the destructive wave. I finally shed the mainsheet and managed to climb over the crushed lifelines, throwing myself into the cockpit. I remember being amazed that the mast was still standing.

I have often wondered if I would have survived if I'd been wearing a modern harness with an inflatable PFD. Would I have been able to free myself from the mainsheet with a bulky inflated necklace restricting my movements? Would I have been able to dive as *Gigi* rolled over or would I have been crushed, helplessly stuck on the surface as 5 tons of fiberglass came crashing my way? Would the cushion of air have made it impossible to pull myself up over the side of the boat? I know from conducting many life-raft training and safety drills that with an inflated

PFD it's nearly impossible to climb into a low-sided life raft in moderate seas, much less climb back into a boat in a gale.

Aboard *Quetzal* I tried to delete the image of floundering in the water from my mind but I wasn't very successful. Although getting washed overboard *Gigi* was long ago, literally hundreds of thousands of bluewater miles ago, it's seared into my cortex. It's a part of my DNA and it has shaped me as a sailor as surely as the chromosomes I inherited from my parents. I remember the incredible relief to learn that Molly, who was below, was OK, and I remember the deep fear and fatigue that gripped me afterward, through the longest and blackest of nights. And I remember the sheer deliverance of dawn's light. I survived. My dreams survived. The moment survived. It transcends time and revisits me whenever I am in the old neighborhood south of Bermuda. It doesn't terrify me. It invigorates me and reminds me of my sweet but fleeting existence. I've been dancing one step, or maybe one wave, ahead of disaster for a long time. Against the odds we put *Gigi* back to together and she and I carried on around Cape Horn, a voyage that blended misery and revelation in equal parts. I was the lucky soldier who survived his first hour of battle, saved from a bullet with his name on it by the whiskey flask in his breast pocket. My flask was an amazing little boat.

ONE

REUNION

Contessa 32s • Fastnet • Sailboat Failures • Ulysses Generation • Dreams of a Young Sailor • Landfall in Antigua • Gigi's Resurrection • Whisky Windfall in the Outer Hebrides • Eudaemonia

"There are stars whose radiance is visible on Earth though they have been long extinct. There are people whose brilliance continues to light the world though they are no longer among the living. These lights are particularly bright when the night is dark. They light the way for human kind."

—Hannah Senesh, poet, playwright, paratrooper (1921–1944)

"Due to the time required for light traveling through the cosmos to reach Earth, astronomic observers are always viewing the past—an effect known as 'look-back time.' The sun has a look-back time of eight minutes, while the Andromeda Galaxy is two million years."

—Lapham's Quarterly

"In a sense, it is always too late to talk about time."

—Jacques Derrida, philosopher (1930–2004)

The Sea of the Hebrides, June 2016

The opportunity to sail *Gigi* again, more than three decades after I had gone overboard south of Bermuda, was a dreamlike experience that filled me with joy but also left me feeling vulnerable and fully exposed to my past. I confess, I was having a difficult time corralling my emotions as we glided over gray Scottish seas. I shouldn't have been surprised because I knew that *Gigi* is a sorceress. She defies physics in the way she knifes through waves and keeps her composure when the ocean turns ugly. But like any good witch, she takes you by the chin when your mind starts to wander and demands your full attention, chaining you to the moment.

I was at the helm, steering a desultory course toward a dark stain of an island where the lumpy horizon merged with the leaden Hebridean sky. I wasn't concentrating on our heading and had drifted back in time. I wanted to feel the warm embrace of memory and find a connection to that long-ago voyage. I hoped to conjure the spirit of that brash 25-year-old who had a full beard and head of hair but no business sailing from New York to San Francisco in a pint-sized sloop. But those memories were elusive, seemingly in reach one moment and then vanishing with the rush of each wave beneath the hull.

I did remember that *Gigi* had a fair bit of weather helm—the tendency to head into the wind in strong gusts. She required coaxing, and I pulled the tiller up to ride down the face of a breaking sea but reacted slowly. "Come on, John," I mumbled to myself, "pay attention." I was out of practice steering with a tiller, my biceps softened by years of sailing with the mechanical advantage of a wheel and quadrant. A sudden thud on the hull was an unmistakable warning, a tracer shot from Neptune. I flinched, instinctively, bracing for the cold sea that was sure to follow and find its way into the cockpit. Somehow *Gigi* sidestepped the incoming soaker and I pushed the tiller away as we surged ahead, leaving a trail of foam in our wake.

"It's the same tiller," François explained proudly, pointing to the weathered sweep of laminated mahogany I was wrestling with, "the same one that went around Cape Horn." His accented English was precise; he was determined to find the right words. He wanted to explain that he sees himself as *Gigi*'s steward as much as her owner, a difficult concept in any language but something sailors understand intuitively. While you definitely throw money at them, sometimes lots of money, you don't really own sailboats, you have relationships with them, and some are definitely better than others. He tilted his head gently from side to side, no doubt silently cursing me for not understanding more than rudimentary French, and said simply, "I am so grateful to be able to sail *Gigi*."

François is a retired insurance executive from Brittany with a long sailing résumé. "Is it strange for a Frenchman to want an English boat?" he asked with a wry grin and Gallic shrug. "I wanted a Contessa, and to find *Gigi*, the most famous Contessa of all, was a dream for me." He knew every detail of *Gigi*'s proud history before he bought the boat in 2009. He has spent each summer since exploring the rugged Scottish coast, gamboling from one anchorage to another, motoring only when completely becalmed. He moves as gracefully as his beloved boat. Defying his 64 years, he agilely shifted forward and propped himself in the companionway. Smiling back at me, he said, "This was your favorite spot, that's what you wrote in your book. It's good to have you back aboard *Gigi*."

It began to drizzle and the biting north wind settled in at 25 knots. A cocktail of rain and salt spray blowing sideways down the back of my jacket seemed appropriate as I recalled how *Gigi*, with her low freeboard and pugilistic approach to head seas, subjected you to an intimate relationship with weather. I tightened my grip on the tiller with one hand and the drawstrings on my hood with the other. Yes, that was my favorite spot, huddled in the companionway beneath the dodger and the only spot in the cockpit remotely protected from the elements. And yes, it was good to be back aboard *Gigi*. "Now pay attention," I reminded myself.

I was between voyages on *Quetzal* when I leapt at François' generous offer to reunite with *Gigi*. I made my way to Oban, Scotland, with my dear friend Alan. Alan lives in a world without strangers and is the best of travel companions. We've shared adventures, afloat and ashore, all over the world and have been accused by my daughters of having a bromance. So be it. When Alan's your friend you're always better for it. He had met François a few years before when they both signed aboard *Quetzal* for a cruise of Alan's home waters, the craggy south shore of Nova Scotia. That's when we first discussed the possibility of a *Gigi* reunion voyage. These days Alan manages the affairs of Canada's famous tall ship, the schooner *Bluenose*, but as a frequent shipmate he has suffered through many stories about the intrepid sloop *Gigi*. He was curious to see if the boat squared with the legend. I knew I had to sail *Gigi* again—it was as close to a calling as I've ever had. I wasn't sure what I was looking for but hoped there would be enough time to pry open the vault of memories and see what remained inside. The last time I'd sailed her was the spring of 1984 when we arrived in San Francisco after the Cape Horn voyage mentioned in the Prologue.

Anyone who has ventured into my previous books knows that *Gigi*, a 1982 Contessa 32, is the boat I hold closest to my heart. I've sailed many different boats through a long career as a professional skipper, sailing journalist, and almost full-time ocean voyager, ranging from an 80´ classic ketch to my first boat, a sprightly 27´ sloop. I've crisscrossed the Atlantic in *Quetzal*, conducting training passages and cruising, and I love the boat in a way that makes land people uncomfortable. But *Gigi*'s place at the head of the class is unchallenged. She carried me to the bottom of the world and back when I had no right to undertake such an audacious voyage. I was trespassing in the Southern Ocean and *Gigi* stood watch, keeping an eye on her young skipper. She was that one teacher who believed in you and changed your life. I know that chasing history, especially your own, is a field mined with disappointment, but I was willing to chance disillusionment for the slightest dash of enlightenment. Not surprisingly, I chose to sail *Gigi* instead of attending my fortieth high-school reunion that was also scheduled for the summer of 2016.

I began to find my way with the tiller, reading the wind in the face of the waves and anticipating stronger puffs as *Gigi* stretched her wings, skimming low over charcoal seas like the fulmars gliding purposely nearby. Alan and François eased the sheets with the clocking wind and *Gigi* surged in gratitude. It was coming back to me, that sense of confidence that *Gigi* inspired in her crew, the pact she offered those willing to accept all the consequences of ocean sailing. She was in her element and I was trying to join her, knowing full well that neither one of us was bound by the horizon. I realized then that I wasn't searching for an elixir or yearning to slurp at the fountain of youth. I wasn't looking to go home again, I wasn't, in the words of Thomas Wolfe, looking to go back "to a young man's dreams of glory and fame." I wanted to revisit—not relive—the reasons why as a young man I rejected the security of life ashore for an itinerant, and at times dangerous—but always inspiring—life afloat. I had come to Scotland to pay homage to *Gigi*, my mentor, a boat limited only by the imagination and moxie of her crew, and always willing to do her part. She was there when I needed her most, welcoming me back aboard on that stormy night south of Bermuda long ago, and giving me a second chance to prove myself worthy of my own dreams. She introduced me to the promise of the demanding but ultimately good life at sea, to hard-edged truths and moments of clarity that can be found only on a seaworthy sailboat far from the distractions of land. I've tried to do my part by sharing this abundance with those who choose to sail with me.

Joseph Conrad, the sea's most prescient chronicler, would have scoffed at applying this sanguine Stoic concept to the hostile ocean. "The sea is impenetrable and heartless," he wrote in his aptly titled memoir, *The Mirror of the Sea*. Adding, "most sailors harbor more hate than love for the sea." Captain Joe might have felt differently if he'd been able to sail *Gigi*. She was the perfect boat for a kid from the suburbs, a college dropout impersonating an old salt and determined to become an offshore sailor. Nimble, forgiving, and deceptively capable, *Gigi* liberated my ocean dreams. Designed by David Sadler and built by Jeremy Rogers on the south coast of England, the Contessa 32 was well respected by serious sailors before the infamous 1979 Fastnet Race disaster—and a legend afterward.

Even for devout landlubbers the word "Fastnet" is associated not with a weathered lighthouse atop a rocky outcropping a few miles off the coast of Ireland, but with the setting for a terrible storm. Almost 40 years later it's still the benchmark when it comes to yachting disasters. Tragedy struck when unpredicted Force 10 conditions overwhelmed the fleet of 303 sailboats participating in Europe's oldest, largest, and best-known offshore sailing regatta. The Beaufort scale quantifies sea conditions in 12 forces, the higher the number the more desperate the conditions. Anything over Force 7 is considered a gale. Force 10 is a full storm and includes winds from 48 to 55 knots, and seas from 30 to 40 feet. Named after the Royal Navy admiral who devised the system in 1758, and still in use today, the Beaufort scale also includes surreal written descriptions of conditions. Here's the definition of Force 10: "*Very high waves with large patches of foam from wave crests that give the sea a white appearance. There is considerable tumbling of waves with heavy impact. Large amounts of airborne spray reduce visibility."* This is weirdly dispassionate and not nearly scary enough. My addendum would include, *"those unfortunate souls on small sailboats are terrified, fighting for survival, and hoping their wills are up to date."*

The violent winds and lethal seas that raked the Irish Sea on that fateful August day left a trail of carnage. More than 100 boats were knocked down, meaning their masts were laid horizontal to the sea or beyond, and many were completely capsized. Some were dismasted and others swamped. Twenty-four crews abandoned ship during the height of the storm. The Royal Navy performed heroically and managed to rescue scores of stricken sailors, plucking them from life rafts and sinking boats, but 15 did not survive. Three rescuers also perished. Of the 58 boats in the smallest and most vulnerable class, those between 28 and 32 feet, only one managed to finish the race, a Contessa 32 named *Ascent.*

Most of the lightweight production boats in the race were not designed or built to cope with survival conditions and were simply overwhelmed by the naked power of the sea. The official inquiry after the race commissioned by the Royal Yachting Association came down hard on designers, manufacturers, and the race sponsor, the Royal Ocean Racing Club, but ultimately left the blame where it belonged, with nature. The report concluded, "The sea showed that it can be a deadly enemy and that those who go to sea for pleasure must do so in full knowledge that they may encounter dangers of the highest order." That this was a revelation to any sailor was also a tragedy.

To modern sailors the Contessa 32, which was first launched in 1971, seems a bit quaint and woefully out of date. She has a short waterline—meaning that her rakish bow has a steep overhang—and she needs to be heeled hard over to maximize speed. The rig, with a stubby boom, was inspired by a silly and now obsolete rating rule called the IOR (International Offshore Rule). These guidelines were devised as a method of handicapping different boats to make racing more competitive but resulted instead in quirky design features that skirted the rules. The Contessa 32 has so little freeboard—the area between the sea and the deck—that she's sometimes referred to as a submarine with sails for the amount of spray she kicks up. She's certainly not roomy either, another memory that came back instantly after I stepped aboard in Oban and promptly smacked my head on the companionway hatch.

But these limitations pale when compared with her virtues. To me, she's a work of art, a Cézanne in particular. He's the painter who bridged impressionism and modernism. With her deep fin keel and racy low profile, the fresh thinking of the Contessa 32 served as a bridge between the narrow, traditional-looking, long-keeled boats of the early fiberglass age and the flat-bottomed, bluffbowed, broad-beamed boats of today. This analog may seem stretched, but art history was my last major before I dropped out for the last time. The Contessa 32 is one of many seagoing boats designed in the '70s and '80s—call them post-Impressionist masterpieces. They have not only aged well, but ocean voyagers like me appreciate their capability and beauty. All sailors agree that despite her diminutive stature, the Contessa 32 is remarkably seaworthy. With an angle of vanishing stability of 155°—meaning that she'll continue to right herself even when knocked over to that extreme angle (180° would have the mast pointing straight down)—the Contessa 32 is the epitome of seaworthiness. I can personally vouch for the accuracy of these statistics.

Sadly, the word "seaworthy" also seems a bit quaint these days. Instant access to weather forecasts and navigational data has fostered an unhealthy belief that heavy weather can be avoided and modern boats don't need to be designed to contend with severe conditions. I know that it's easy to fall backward, to insist that old boats, the ones we know by heart, like old songs, are better than today's boats. Despite my love for old boats, I recognize that this is almost always flawed thinking. I am not sure if Machiavelli was a sailor, but in his *Discourses on Livy*, he sums up this tendency perfectly: "Men do always, but not always with reason, commend the past and condemn the present ... [and] extol the days when they remember their youth to have been spent." From the freakishly fast-foiling America's Cup catamarans, to the 100´ trimaran that was recently sailed singlehanded around the world in 42 days, to luxurious and capable world-class yachts, to purposely built, high-quality cruising sailboats that are voyaging all over the planet, including the high latitudes, sailing is experiencing a golden age. At the top end of the market, the fusion of innovative design, material advances, and high-tech manufacturing is combining to produce the most capable and comfortable yachts ever built.

But as in most golden ages, the common person, or, in this case, the common sailor, is not sharing in all the fun. Almost all of us sail in quasi-affordable production boats of one kind or another and it's folly to deny that some modern designs are not oceanworthy, despite hyperbolic claims that every boat is built for blue water. Builders know that few sailors actually venture offshore, but they need to pay obeisance to the idea—it's an essential dream that sailors harbor deep in their souls. Let's be clear, many of today's boats are perfect for the ways in which they're used: afternoon sails on flat seas followed by drinks in a spacious cockpit with steaks grilling on the stern rail barbecue. The mushrooming bareboat charter industry represents this trend. Today's sailboats often double as dockside villas, vital weekend escape pods for these frenzied times, and there's not a damn thing wrong with that—unless you also plan to take them to sea.

There has been a spate of well-documented sailboat disasters over the past few years, invariably followed by dramatic YouTube videos of incredibly brave Coast Guard swimmers and chopper pilots coming to the rescue. The sailors are portrayed as feeble amateurs waiting for deliverance from the perils of the deep by steely professionals who reel them to safety as if they're landing giant tuna. And those are the lucky ones. Some are not rescued, like the four ill-fated crewmembers of the 41′ sloop *Cheeky Rafiki* who perished in 2014 when the keel fell off the hull of the production boat—and former charter boat—they were delivering across the Atlantic. Rarely mentioned is the fact the most of these unfortunate sailors who run into danger left port in boats that were not meant for ocean sailing and assumed they'd be able to use real-time data to dodge dangerous conditions. It just doesn't work that way—storms are as much a part of ocean sailing as calms and steady trade winds, especially today in these uncertain times of climate change. I fervently hope that it does not take another disaster of Fastnet proportions for us to remember the importance of seaworthiness. More selfishly, I don't want to see the untamed wilderness that is the ocean subjected to seatbelt and helmet laws, regulated by well-meaning but landlubbing overseers determined to whittle away the essential element of self-reliance that has always defined the meaning of going to sea.

Gigi was commissioned by my friend Ty, and somewhat disingenuously named after his wife, a sensible woman who instinctively recognized that a sailboat as alluring as a Contessa 32 would do little to help an already challenging marriage. To put it gently, the human Gigi was not an enthusiastic mariner and she never set foot aboard her fiberglass namesake. Ty asked me to help him sail *Gigi* from England to the Caribbean, my first Atlantic crossing, my first big job as a professional skipper and one for which I was woefully unqualified but which I enthusiastically accepted. It was the first of many opportunities Ty would throw my way.

I met Ty in a celestial navigation class in Fort Lauderdale. I owned a school, a fledgling enterprise that any sensible businessperson could see was destined to fail. Never much of a capitalist, I did have a lot of fun and met intriguing characters, from cocaine smugglers (who wanted to learn to navigate to one set of coordinates), to Cuban freedom fighters (who patrolled the Straits of Florida looking for *balseros*, or rafts), to aspiring bluewater sailors, and made lifelong friends in the process of going broke. In 1982 I was 23 years old and celestial navigation was the single marketable skill I possessed. Fortunately it was still a necessary evil for sailors, a dreaded process you had to master if you hoped to cross an ocean. There was little romance in using a sextant and the time-honored process was squarely in the crosshairs of rapidly advancing satellite technology. Leave it to me to start a celestial navigation school at the dawn of the technological revolution. Remarkably, I've been sailing so long now that celestial navigation has made a well-deserved comeback and today my celestial and natural navigation workshops attract sailors from all over the world, selling out well in advance.

Back then, however, the exhausted folks who turned up after work for my torturous four-hour night classes embraced the whiff of any gizmo promising to make navigation less of a headache. The transit system, better known as SatNav, was just beginning to find its way onto cruising boats, but it was unreliable at best and never produced a fix when you really needed one. LORAN-C, the more common electronic navigational system, was the ultimate tease. An acronym for Long Range Navigation, it was wickedly accurate—up to a point. It couldn't take you far enough offshore to actually get anywhere interesting. The 1962 Cuban Missile Crisis made sure that it couldn't even guide you from the east coast of the United States to the Caribbean. The U.S. military rebuffed future Soviet mischief by disabling several perfectly good LORAN towers in the Caribbean and Bahamas, effectively leaving sailors stranded a few hundred miles off the U.S. coast. Decca, a European radio system, never gained a foothold on this side of the Atlantic.

Ty was a quick student at celestial navigation but he was not interested in palm trees and tropical drinks—he didn't want to sail to the Caribbean. He wanted to cross the Atlantic and test himself in a storm. A successful businessman from Detroit, he was in his early 40s with a trim goatee and precisely arranged, slicked-back hair. Though small in stature, he had a penetrating gaze, a powerful grip, and a deep voice. He had a powerful presence, almost eerily so, and when he looked you in the eye it was hard to turn away. He tried to come across as a neophyte sailor, decked out in cargo shorts, bright Hawaiian shirts, and new snake-skinned deck shoes, but it didn't take long to realize that behind the kitschy wardrobe was a fiercely competitive guy with a five-gallon bucket list. Ty had a dark side too, and it fueled a fearlessness that bordered on recklessness. He was the toughest person I've ever known. Through many thousands of miles of bluewater sailing, some of it very hard going, he complained only once—the night a violent wave rocked *Gigi*, shattering both of his precious vodka bottles. It's always one damn wave that causes trouble.

Ty's sailing ambitions were freshly minted. He was done with skydiving, he'd set the Michigan amateur record for highest jump, and sailing was next on his to-do list. He liked the fact that offshore sailing, like skydiving, required complete commitment. "Once you step out of a plane there's no going back," he told an interviewer after our Cape Horn passage; "a storm at sea is the same thing, you either overcome or are overcome, you don't cry for help." Although I was 18 years his junior, my sailing dreams had been marinating for more than a decade when our wakes first crossed. I would never reduce an ocean passage to something as mundane as an item checked off a list. From a very young age I was thoroughly smitten with the romantic notion of sailing a small boat into the farthest reaches of the ocean. Peter Freuchen, the great polar explorer, wrote, "I discovered the ocean in my imagination." I discovered the ocean in books.

One of the first books I remember reading from cover to cover was *Call It Courage*. A Newbery Medal classic by Armstrong Sperry, it tells the tale of a Polynesian boy who is afraid of the sea. He eventually confronts his fears by sneaking away in his outrigger canoe with his dog and handy pet albatross. He encounters a storm and survives being shipwrecked before finding his way home with his demons slain. I can close my eyes and see the cover: a spindly outrigger surging before a towering sea and a small boy steering with a paddle, the dog perched on the outrigger looking oddly cheery, and the wise, drone-like albatross hovering overhead. I loved the book.

Years later I told many revised versions of this story to my young daughters. The bedtime tales always featured brave young girls, small and often sinking sailboats, uncharted islands, and bumbling parents who lost track of their kids. Some of the stories went on for months. They never wanted them to end and always extracted a promise for another adventure the following evening. I mentioned this to a psychologist who sailed with me a few years ago and she wondered, seriously, if the girls had abandonment issues, and that's why they wanted the stories to go on and on. I assured her that was not the case, that they were just really good stories, but the notion has haunted me ever since. Did I screw up my kids by having boats sink out from under them, stranding them on imagined islands, and leaving them to their wits to find their way home again?

We were gypsies during my own young years, and I attended six elementary schools in four states before my father became the director of a business college in Detroit. He worked tirelessly to turn the school around, and our fortunes changed too. We moved out of the city when

I was in middle school and followed the usual path of migration to the swanky suburbs northwest of Detroit. If that was the definition of the American Dream I wanted no part of it. I never fit in. The huge houses with manicured yards made me nervous—I was looking for a way out from the get-go.

I was never much of a student, at least in the conventional sense, but when it came to sailing literature I was a whiz kid. I would often skip class, sneak out of school, and steal away to the public library and devour sailing books. My vicarious adventures took me around the world with early voyagers Joshua Slocum, Alain Gerbault, and the boring but seamanlike Hiscocks. I waited impatiently for each issue of *National Geographic* magazine, hoping it had another episode of teenage circumnavigator Robin Lee Graham and his adventures aboard his 24′ sloop *Dove*. If the article included pictures of Patty, his exotic girlfriend, that was even better.

At some point I realized that celestial navigation was my ticket out of the suburbs. If I wanted to be an ocean sailor I had to learn how to navigate. I desperately needed a sextant. Miraculously, one snowy Christmas morning Santa delivered a cheap plastic Davis Mk15 complete with a short but bewildering set of instructions. It became my most cherished possession, though it would take years before I figured out how to use it and actually reduce a sight. Just knowing it was there, a talisman perched on my dresser, was reassuring.

Writer/sailor John Rousmaniere examines the motives of the "Ulysses Generation" in his brilliant book *After the Storm*. In the years directly after WWII a tiny but hell-bent group of sailors and mountaineers launched ambitious personal expeditions that scaled the highest peaks and crossed vast oceans in small boats. These mariners were not cruisers dropping out of society looking for island utopias. They were searching for profound challenges to test themselves against the dispassionate whims of nature and accept the consequences of their quests. Their idealism had been shattered by two monstrous world wars and they were driven by a desperate need for individual expression and personal freedom, to make their lives count amid the chaos that had come to define the modern age. I understood them intuitively; I was lusting for adventure, but adventure that spoke to my soul.

Rousmaniere chronicles the remarkable voyages of Miles and Beryl Smeeton, who were twice capsized in the Southern Ocean as they approached Cape Horn before finally succeeding in rounding that ornery headland on their third try. He marvels at the toughest voyager of them all, Bill Tilman, who was already in his sixties when he sailed his leaky 50-year-old pilot cutter from Greenland to Patagonia in a series of demanding voyages with ragtag crews for the express purpose of accessing remote mountains that he then scaled. Rousmaniere also describes William A. Robinson's legendary encounter with a Southern Ocean storm, a tempest he went in search of "to shake the malaise of the soft life out of his soul." Long before I came across Rousmaniere's book I knew all these accounts by heart, having lived through them in the library. The cruising life was alluring, but the ocean voyagers stirred me.

I devoured Francis Chichester's crotchety book about his record-breaking circumnavigation south of the great capes and spent many hours studying the aerial photo of his boat *Gypsy Moth* rounding Cape Horn in a full gale. The picture haunted me at night; I could feel the wind whistling through the rigging in my dreams. I pushed through Robin Knox-Johnston's plucky account of winning the *Sunday Times* Golden Globe Race in 1968/69, and in the process becoming the first person to sail nonstop around the world. I loved Vito Dumas's vivid narrative of sailing around the world in his 30′ double-ended ketch, *Leigh II*, named after his Buenos Aires mistress. Dumas was my idol until I discovered

Bernard Moitessier, and then my paradigm not only shifted, it did a full pirouette.

Moitessier is the legendary French voyager famous for turning his back on likely victory in the *Sunday Times* Golden Globe Race. He had discovered a sense of tranquility and fulfillment after more than six months at sea and was not ready to end his voyage. Instead of returning to Plymouth, England, where the prospect of wide acclaim and a nice financial award awaited him, Moitessier turned toward the bottom of Africa, opening the door for Knox-Johnston to win the race. He rounded the Cape of Good Hope a second time and retreated back to the solitude of the great Southern Ocean. He continued sailing another two-thirds of the way around the world before finally veering north and dropping anchor off Tahiti, the longest nonstop sailing voyage ever recorded at the time.

Although some modern French critics cynically suggest Moitessier's real motivation for carrying on was that after reaching for months on end, he had no stomach for beating—sailing into the wind—home, and just continued to sail with the wind at his back. This is nonsense. While it seems true that in many ways Moitessier was a difficult person, his vision of the ocean, and of man's place within its realm, was profound. He had come to realize that a sailboat race around the world was absurd, his fellow sailors were not competitors, and the ocean was not something to be conquered. His writings opened my eyes to the premise that the ocean is earth's most precious dominion, "a kingdom," as he put it, "still mercifully unclaimed by nation states." I flat out loved the notion that at sea we lowbrow voyagers are royalty and that the past and future hold no sway while every day matters equally. "How long will it last," Moitessier wrote in his book, *The Long Way*, "this peace I have found at sea? It is all of life that I contemplate—sun, clouds, time that passes and abides. Occasionally it is also that other world, foreign now, that I left centuries ago. The modern, artificial world where man has been turned into a money-making machine to satisfy false needs, false joys."

Moitessier combined the spirit of the "Ulysses Generation" with the sensibilities of a philosopher, the eye of a naturalist, and the revelations of a mystic. He had an essential need to go to sea, to be at sea, and that was enough. He anticipated the critical need to preserve the oceans and was an early environmental advocate. Yet he couldn't find his place in modern society. He was a terrible husband and an even worse father. He dealt with thorny personal issues by sailing away from them. He was a better man at sea than ashore. At sea he was a prophet and his voice carried in the wind, and I was listening in a faraway hospital waiting room in Detroit.

My father was dying and I was trying to understand why. His life had been hard from the start and when at last he found a bit of financial security he was rewarded with a revolt of wayward cells spreading cancerous mayhem through his lungs and bones. I was 16 when my father died; he was 53. Neither number made any sense. Dad died on a brutally cold January day that seemed to last forever. Time refused to ease my pain and slowed to a desperate crawl—those were the longest hours, minutes, seconds I have ever endured. Time is a cold-blooded thief and can't be trusted. Time will look you in the eye, smile reassuringly but demand obedience and sacrifice, insisting you prepare for a future that is at best the hope for an empty chamber in a game of Russian roulette. But we are stuck coping with it. Time is the currency of our life—how we spend it defines our existence.

I reread *The Long Way* that winter, recording passages in my journal and letting my imagination wander. As he soared across the Southern Ocean a second time, Moitessier wrote, "The questions that used to bother me at times do not weigh anything before a wake so close to the sky and filled with the wind of the sea." Back in Detroit I was angry at the world, at whatever gods and gravitational forces had conspired to take my father from me. I felt stranded in the material madness of the suburbs. I longed to find that place Moitessier described, those very coordinates where the moment was unleashed, where the sea and sky could wash my mind clean. My father's death profoundly shaped the course of my life. Planning for a future that was at the mercy of time was too risky, I would not venture down that path. Borrowing a line from *Zorba the Greek*, I resolved to "live every day as though I'll die tomorrow."

My brother-in-law Craig deserves credit for introducing me to sailing. He was the young manager of a Woolworth's department store and won a contest selling more Lavoris mouthwash than any other store. The prize was a 12-foot Styrofoam sailboat that he gave to my older brothers, Tom and Ed. They never minded that I tagged along, each taking me out for a sail, and usually a capsize, on the tiny lake near our house. We went on to sail a sturdier Sunfish, and then, shortly before he died, my father surprised the family and bought a real boat, a Sabre 28 sloop that we moored on Lake St. Clair. Sandwiched between Lake Erie and Lake Huron, shallow St. Clair is where Detroiters dream of the ocean. Great Lakes sailors are zealous, they seize every chance to shove off no matter the weather, in a desperate attempt to maximize their short season. An impressive armada of sailboats call St. Clair home, and we sailed the Sabre, named *Our Way*, every chance we could before my mother had to sell it after my father's death.

My brother Ed, five years older than me, and fighting his own war with time (which focused primarily on finding ways to extend his college experience), was my mentor in all the important things in my life: boats, books, and pole-vaulting. He was the one who taught me to sail and we spent many days in *Our Way*, plying the shallows of Lake St. Clair and dreaming of distant voyages. He shared his sailing narratives with me and later introduced me to Hesse, Camus, Sartre, de Beauvoir, and the other existential writers. Existentialism was strangely comforting in the wake of my father's death. I found the notion of the absurd quite appealing and particularly liked the idea that nothing was preordained, and that no deity was tracking me on radar.

Camus opens the *Myth of Sisyphus* with this powerful line: "I draw from the absurd three consequences, which are my revolt, my freedom, and my passion." I was ready and willing to rebel and accept all the consequences of such an act, I just wasn't exactly sure what rebellion looked like. I was immature and confused but not afraid. What could happen, I might die? The awareness of death at an early age was, in a harsh way, liberating. Camus uses Sisyphus as a symbol both of the meaninglessness of life, but also of the small momentary joys that accompany the struggle, the dualism that befuddles many about existentialism. The obsession to spend my time wisely, or at least in the way I wanted to spend it, corrupted my youthful view of existentialism. One thing I was certain of, I would not be Sisyphus and spend my precious time pushing the rock up the hill, only to watch it roll down again. The very idea that my time could be owned by someone else, monitored by a clock, and traded not for freedom but for money struck me as lunacy. Where did happiness factor in, and what about the desire for a meaningful life defined not by your possessions but by your experiences?

I embraced Sartre's version of freedom. "Man is condemned to be free," he wrote, "because once thrown into the world, he is responsible for everything he does." The notion of spending your days chained to a desk, plodding along at a task you hated in exchange for weekend reprieves and two-week vacations, seemed crazy to a 16-year-old kid, and still does to a 59-year-old man. There was no despair in my existentialism, only a raw-edged freedom and the opportunity to be responsible for my actions. "Happiness," de Beauvoir wrote, "is not only possible but it's our moral obligation." Forty-three years later I couldn't agree more.

Before I accepted a track scholarship and reluctantly went off to college, I clandestinely wrote away to every sailboat charter company in the Caribbean, and several private charter yachts, offering my services. All I wanted was an opportunity to learn more about sailboats and was up for any task, willing to work for food and a berth. I knew that ocean sailing represented the mix of adventure, responsibility, and freedom I craved, but I just didn't know how to get there. I received zero replies.

I felt imprisoned on campus. I was a terrible student and an indifferent pole-vaulter. I dropped out, transferred, dropped out again. My mother was a sage, she knew that setting me adrift at age 21 was the hard dose of reality I needed, to test my youthful notions beyond the suburban and college cocoons where I was safely pontificating on the evils of society. I was saved by a boat—a slow, sturdy, and, most importantly, cheap Bristol 27 sloop that I named after my mother. Living aboard *Jeanne* I learned to sail, to navigate, and to find a way to support myself as I bungled my way around the Florida Keys. I even learned how to use my sextant, which accompanied me everywhere. Most importantly, I learned how to channel my resentment of my father's death into a philosophy that flourished, albeit slowly, in salt water. I was lucky to find an environment where I thrived. The ocean stripped away false pretenses and bristled with beauty and dispassion, my existential ideal mixed with a cup of stoicism and a dash of romance. My father's death ultimately inspired and unshackled me, opening my eyes to the potential of every day.

Gigi's 1983 launch was delayed several times as the British yard scrambled to finish the boat. By the time Ty and I shoved off to cross the Atlantic from England to the Caribbean it was already mid-November. Although we would find our sea legs and sail around Cape Horn together a year later (a voyage described in my book *Cape Horn to Starboard*), that first crossing was a watershed and was almost scuttled early on. We were in Falmouth, just 150 miles west of where we'd begun in Lymington, and I was faltering. A week of storms, headwinds, and homesickness were taking their toll. I knew we had started late in the season, but I was shocked by just how nasty the weather was in the English Channel. I also knew that the Bay of Biscay would likely be worse.

I had asked Ty to buy an expensive Motorola shortwave radio before the passage so that we could receive weather reports offshore. It was a huge contraption with bulky dials and a window across the front showing different time zones. Marconi would have recognized it. Each morning I would take it on deck and tune in to the Met Office shipping forecast. It was always the same: gales and strong winds, rain and sleet, warnings and advisories. After a couple days in Falmouth, Ty ran out of patience. He had time frames and schedules and hated the idea of being "storm stayed," an apt phrase coined in the eighteenth century by a notorious landlubber and wit, Dr. Johnson. It was a rare sunny morning, but dire conditions were forecast for the waters beyond the harbor. "Let me see that radio," Ty said, and I handed him the hefty black box. "I am tired of this damn thing telling us what to do. It looks like a nice day to me." He then tossed the radio into the harbor. It made a feeble splash and sank like the rock-hard English crumpets we'd pitched over the side after breakfast. "It's your call," he told me, "you're the captain, but I suggest we get going." We did, and never looked back.

Ty found his storms in the English Channel and Bay of Biscay. I found what I was looking for too, a sacred place where time mattered and measured you unsparingly. During the excruciatingly long hours of a midnight watch in a Force 10 Biscay gale I thought, "So this is what Moitessier was writing about, this beautiful, terrifying misery." Once again time was up to its old tricks, but I was ready when it slowed to the pace of a loping jog. I embraced life in the unsentimental present. Of course I made plenty of half-hearted efforts to conjure memories, but the past couldn't find me. And yes, I schemed upcoming adventures, too, but the future was blurred by an endless horizon. My discovery was that I was supremely happy as *Gigi* skidded on and on, riding the Atlantic wave train toward the tropics. This short poem in my journal of the crossing summed up my mood.

The Atlantic gives no quarter, so spare your sympathy.
And skip your precious sunsets, and all your poetry.
It's not an eco-destination, and there's no false gratitude.
You gotta just keep sailing, and run down your latitude.

From the perspective of a million, or maybe a billion, waves later, what I remember most clearly about that first big ocean crossing are fleeting moments and flashes, not lofty accomplishments or big storms. I remember when we set the spinnaker for the first time, and I pretended to know what I was doing as I hoisted it sideways and inside out, revealing a lopsided, red nylon square sail with the letters *Gigi* looking Japanese, read from top to bottom as they expanded and collapsed in the wind, and both of us laughing until our guts ached. I remember Ty preparing cornmeal mush and how I smothered it with canned New Zealand butter and thought it was the best thing I'd ever eaten. I remember how we invented Captain's Hour and savored our ice-free gin, or if Ty was pouring, vodka and Tang—"tangos"—and never let a late afternoon slip away without a toast. Those toasts occasionally devolved into infuriating discussions as Ty insisted that without a time frame my life would amount to nothing. I told him that time was an impostor. My lack of concrete, material goals infuriated him. We also quarreled over ridiculous arm-wrestling bouts when

I could only use three fingers to compensate for my larger hands. During one Captain's Hour in the middle of the Atlantic I learned that Ty had also lost his father at a young age. He found him hanging in the basement. A brutal memory he had been running from for 30 years—and probably still is.

I remember a perfect twilight, the dreamy confluence of light and dark pouring across a gentle horizon, a celestial navigator's fantasy. I took three sights on seven stars that morning, creating 21 lines of position, and plotted them all. It was the mother of all fixes and my hubris as a navigator knew no limits. Santa would have been proud of me, and Alain Gerbault and Vito Dumas too. I remember poring over the *Nautical Almanac* and *Bowditch*, which is officially called *The American Practical Navigator*, a massive tome with a daunting subtitle, *An Epitome of Navigation*. I was trying to calculate the exact time when Aldebaran, the eye of the bull, the burnt-orange star in the constellation of Taurus with a declination nearly equal to the latitude of Antigua, would be directly over the island. At that precise moment it provided a celestial compass bearing, the great circle route no less, guiding us toward our destination still more than a thousand miles away beyond the western horizon. Mostly I remember when the fisherman with the booming voice informed me that I'd missed my landfall by 30 miles.

After weeks of perfect trade-wind conditions, the skies turned gloomy and the wind increased to near-gale force as we approached Antigua. I would later learn that these amped-up trade winds are known as the "Christmas winds," but my gift back then was a well-deserved dose of humility. I searched the gray-painted sky for a glimpse of the sun—star sights were out of the question. After all of my navigational wizardry earlier in the passage, nearing landfall, when I really needed to know where we were, I was unsure of our position and relying on dead reckoning, a fancy phrase for slightly educated guesswork based on time, speed, and distance, and a foreign concept that bewilders today's digital navigators but that Columbus understood perfectly.

On New Year's Eve I calculated that we should have been right on top of Antigua, but no land was in sight. All through the stormy night we listened for breaking surf and peered into the gloomy abyss ahead. I imagined *Gigi* being dashed on the rocks and feared not for my life, but for sullying the proud reputation of the Contessa 32 on my first crossing. (That was also one of my chief concerns during the capsize described in the Prologue.) At daybreak I was beginning to worry that the great navigator had managed to miss the entire Caribbean chain of islands, not a small a feat, when Ty mercifully spied land to starboard. Verdant mountains were visible above the clouds. We were just a few miles offshore and soon in the lee, a blessed relief from weeks of relentless northeast winds. We were exultant, high-fiving and hugging. We had crossed the Atlantic.

Ty dropped below to make coffee and I studied the Antigua chart. We were heading to English Harbour and already tasting a hearty breakfast and cold beer. I tried to pinpoint our position for landfall with compass bearings but I couldn't match the island's topography with the chart. Something was wrong. Desperate, I steered toward a small fishing skiff and sheepishly cried out, "Where's English Harbour?" Just as Ty popped back into the cockpit the fisherman replied, "English Harbour? That's Antigua mon, dis is Montserrat. Antigua is thirty miles over there."

Back in Scotland, aboard the same *Gigi* many years later, conditions had moderated. The sun and clouds contorted themselves to cast the long shadows of a late-afternoon northern summer. The island of Barra, near the southern bookend of the Outer Hebrides, came into sharp focus. We followed the Caledonian ferry into the port of Castlebay, creeping before a diminishing wind, resisting the temptation to motor, and finally picked up a mooring just before dark. The next morning Alan hopped in the dinghy and took pictures of *Gigi* gracefully tacking about the bay with the fourteenth-century Kiessimul Castle forming a splendid backdrop. Looking at the photos later, I was struck by how old François and I seemed, two geezers hauling the sheets aboard an ageless, timeless beauty of a boat. But *Gigi*'s story was not all glory, she'd been down and nearly out before a most improbable refit restored her youthful luster.

We rounded Cape Horn in February 1984, a little over a year after that first crossing. It was a challenging voyage, to put it gently, that included months of hard windward sailing, a few terrifying storms that we were lucky to survive, and weeks of mind-numbing calms. I had a different crew for each leg. Molly left in Rio de Janeiro (my being washed overboard as described in the Prologue had sealed that fate) and Ty joined me for the Horn rounding. Bill, a friend from Houston, sailed north with me from Valparaíso, Chile, to San Francisco. When we stumbled under the Golden Gate Bridge we were 162 sailing days outbound from New York. Despite the slow passage we managed to arrive on a slow news day and had our 15 minutes of fame. While I was basking in the glory of the voyage, making the rounds of TV shows and trying to line up a book deal, Ty's life was quietly falling apart. In the summer of 1984 the other Gigi, the flesh-and-bones version, had had enough of his inattentions and far-flung wanderings, and filed for divorce. His business partnership with his father-in-law imploded. Sensing he had to act quickly, Ty had *Gigi* trucked across the country from San Francisco to Newport, Rhode Island. He used a sizable portion of his rapidly dwindling resources for a hasty refit. Then he escaped to sea.

Sailing alone, he headed south until the Southern Cross was almost overhead. He later told me that he felt truly free for the first time because he didn't care if he lived or died. His sense of urgency had been shattered and he realized that living in the moment was all that mattered. He told me about staying up all night just to count shooting stars and how that was more meaningful than counting the dividends of a new business deal. He tarried in the Falkland Islands before rounding Cape Horn again, an incredible feat of guts and seamanship. After a brief stop in Chile he carried on across the Pacific and finally fetched up in Tasmania, a two-month, 5,000-mile nonstop odyssey.

Somewhere in the vastness of the Pacific Ty sailed beyond his demons. He left the boat in Hobart and eventually had *Gigi* shipped to Fort Lauderdale. He had no desire to sail her again, and I didn't have the money to buy her (the book deal amounted a $500 advance), though I desperately wanted to. He ended up donating *Gigi* to the Chapman School of Seamanship in central Florida. He hoped they would use her for sail training, especially for disadvantaged children, but they used her for fundraising instead. They flogged the boat as soon as the tax laws permitted. She changed hands a couple of times and eventually ended up on the muddy shallows of Galveston Bay in Texas. She distinguished herself during a few offshore races in the Gulf of Mexico before falling into disrepair.

When the founder of Contessa Yachts, Jeremy Rogers, heard that *Gigi* was stranded on a cradle in a Galveston boatyard, and had been for years, he bought her sight unseen and arranged for her to be shipped to England. Despite having the lowest of expectations, Jeremy was shocked at *Gigi*'s deplorable condition when she turned up in the port of Southampton. It took him a year to find the will to launch the restoration project. The organizers of the revived Earl's Court Boat Show gave him the incentive, promising to display the revamped *Gigi* next to Sir Francis Chichester's famous yawl, *Gypsy Moth*, which had been restored and dramatically sailed around the world again the year before. Jeremy and his crew painstakingly brought *Gigi* back to life. By the time she was rolled on to the cavernous floor of Earl's Court, she was the nicest Contessa 32 in existence.

My wife Tadji and I were in Paris at the time and happily accepted Jeremy and his wife Fiona's invitation to come to London. I confess, I was a bit nervous about seeing *Gigi* again after so many years. I didn't want my memories of her spoiled, like when you meet your first true love later in life and your glossy memories are tarnished by the brutal realities of time and gravity. I spotted her from across the hall. Her rakish hull shape was as sweet as ever and she glistened with fresh paint. My memories were safely intact. Jeremy was beaming, and the queue to board the boat snaked around the concession stand. He had to explain to people that it wasn't a new boat, but the same old *Gigi* that had twice rounded Cape Horn against the wind.

Tadji, who had recently learned to sail aboard *Quetzal* and was just finding her way into the sailing and cruising life, was surprised how tight *Gigi* was below. "How did you stow enough provisions for those long passages?" she wondered. "You can't even stand up down here." Shaking her head, she added, "I can't believe you actually sailed this boat around Cape Horn." While Tadji admired *Gigi*'s pedigree and her brave story, she was definitely not going to be sold on the idea of downsizing from *Quetzal* to a Contessa 32, an idea that I occasionally fantasized about, especially when paying yard bills. Jeremy kept *Gigi* for a couple of years, sailing and racing her often. When it came time to part ways he found a perfect partner, a kindly Frenchman who knew her history intimately and promised to preserve her legacy.

You could sail with your eyes closed and know you were in the Outer Hebrides. The dampness in the air, the ragged sea breeze, and the pot-holed seas are the region's fingerprints. Of course, sipping a wee dram of single malt whisky would seal the deal, but that would be cheating. François, with his eyes wide open, was wary of the capricious storm winds that sweep across the Outer Hebrides with little warning, and he pointed to the sky. Fish-scale clouds spreading rapidly foretold a change in the weather. The old saw "if you don't like the weather in Scotland wait ten minutes" was proving conservative—five minutes was plenty of time for a dramatic shift in conditions. François and I tacked, picked up Alan, and hauled the dinghy aboard. We lashed it securely to the foredeck—there was no doubt it was going to blow.

Then we reduced sail in the gathering breeze. I remembered how easy it was to tie in a reef on a 32′ boat with a mainsail of just 200 square feet. There was no need to steer into the wind and create a racket by madly luffing the mainsail. Sailing a reach with the wind just forward of the beam, we eased the sheet, then the halyard, and the sail started to drop. Tensioning the single line reef outhaul was a snap; we then hauled the halyard back up, and in less than a minute we had a tidy reef. We never hesitated to carry sail on *Gigi* during our many voyages because when the wind piped up we could shorten sail quickly and efficiently with this basic but bulletproof reefing system. Along with robust headsail furling and a hank-on storm jib set on a mobile stay, *Gigi* had a simple and efficient sail plan to cope with Neptune's wild mood swings.

Our plan to sail offshore to the remote island of St. Kilda was tabled by the forecast of a northeast gale that would make the only harbor untenable. Instead, we made our way to Eriskay, the next island north from Barra, a windswept, overgrown rock, fringed with shoals. We carefully navigated up a narrow, perfectly protected finger of refuge between two rocky bluffs and picked up the only mooring off the hamlet of Acariseid. The expected blow was still several hours away, so we doubled our mooring lines and rowed ashore. We hiked over a moor covered in fragile wildflowers and strong-knuckled krummholz, a mixture of beauty and grit that perfectly defines the Outer Hebrides.

We made our way, guided by natural navigational instincts—an internal lodestone that sniffed out single malt whisky—to the only pub on the island, the Am Politician.

Ducking in out of the biting wind we sat up at the bar. Alan noticed a few bottles of whisky prominently displayed. "They're worth about 10,000 pounds each," the bartender informed him, "give or take a few thousand." He carefully placed them on the bar so that we could inspect them. "They're from the ship SS *Politician*, that's where the pub got its name, and no, you can't sample it." Instead, we ordered a wee dram of 12-year-old Jura, which was fast becoming our favorite, and examined the photos and memorabilia on the pub walls, including an intriguing quote from Winston Churchill. "Never before in history have so few people been so drunk for so long." Topping our glasses, the bartender told us the story.

It was a stormy February night back in 1941 when the 8,000-ton cargo ship the SS *Politician* went on the rocks in the treacherous waters between Eriskay and South Uist. She had left Liverpool bound for Jamaica, and then on to New Orleans, when she lost her way in a blinding snowstorm. The next morning local folks managed to rescue the crew before the ship broke up. Miraculously no lives were lost. Once safely ashore, some of the grateful crew let on that the ship was loaded with an usual cargo—264,000 bottles of malt whisky. The booze was bound for the American market to raise funds for the war effort—it was for export, and no duty had been paid. This inconvenient fact didn't stop the locals from conducting midnight raids to "rescue" the whisky and sneak it ashore before officials arrived from England. Boats came from all over the Hebrides to claim this gift from the sea. The islanders considered the bounty as salvage and thus fair game.

The local customs official saw it differently. He was outraged that the whisky was being pillaged without any duties paid, in effect robbing the Crown of its fair share. He insisted that the police look into the matter and would not relent until a few token arrests were made. When the illegal salvagers received insignificant fines, he was incensed and received official permission from London to have the SS *Politician* exploded to avoid the temptation to engage in further illegal activity. As the ship was blown to pieces one bewildered islander commented: "Dynamiting whisky. You wouldn't think there'd be men in the world so crazy as that!"

Stories still abound of buried whisky on Eriskay, with each bottle worth a small fortune. The weather was deteriorating and we hurried back to *Gigi*, keeping a sharp eye on the sky and for any errant bottles. Back aboard, the wind was howling through the rig and we secured the halyards in a mostly futile attempt to stop the chatter. I went forward and checked our lines and chafing gear. *Gigi* was riding effortlessly, like a swan in the water. Her knife-like entry, low freeboard, and deep keel were keeping her bow to wind as steady as a weathercock on a farmhouse. I lingered on deck for a few moments, letting the wind wash over me. I love weather—good, bad, and even ugly. I feel my chest swell with anticipation as nasty weather approaches, a weird thrill that heightens my senses and reminds me that I am alive. When it started to rain I finally retreated below. It was cozy with three adults in the main saloon, but we were content. François attempted to teach Alan and me a bit of French via a sailing song but, despite the increasing volume, our language skills didn't improve much. I poured us each one last wee dram of Jura, which was distilled on a nearby island that almost changed the course of modern literature.

Just after WWII, English author Eric Blair, using the pen name of George Orwell, retreated to a cottage on the north shore of Jura. He was searching for a secluded place to write and he lived on and off in the Hebrides until his death four years later. He completed his masterpiece,

1984, on Jura. Some critics have speculated that his stay on the drafty island hastened his demise. What is undisputed is that Orwell almost died in 1947 when a small motorboat he was piloting was caught in a whirlpool and capsized. He was lucky to survive the ordeal. *1984* was published two years later. Orwell is remembered for his dystopian novels, but he was also an incessant traveler, and a bit of a sailor, and I suspect would have enjoyed our company in *Gigi's* steamy cabin that evening. He may have found it sadly ironic that 32 years after the year of his novel's fictional setting, which also turned out to be the very year that I sailed *Gigi* around Cape Horn, *1984* was once again attaining bestseller status as many concerned people searched for answers in the face of liberal democracies succumbing to cowardly fear-mongering. We concluded that it was a good time to own an ocean-going sailboat, just in case, and called it a night.

I was in the V-berth, snug in my sleeping bag, when the gale finally turned up in full force. Rain pelted the hatch above my head and occasional lightning flashes illuminated the storm-streaked night sky. The view was spectacular as dark-rimmed clouds raced by my blotted kaleidoscope on the heavens. Pleasantly surprised that the hatch didn't leak, I understood why I had come back to sail *Gigi*. I had come full circle as a sailor, only to discover that nothing had changed. *Gigi* was a time machine, a sorceress indeed. Maybe, for one evening at least, I had wrestled time to a draw.

I wondered if I was a dim, distant star whose light was still visible though I had long expired. Lying wide awake, serenaded by the groaning wind and the thump of waves slapping the hull, I was in the perfect place to reflect on the long arc of my sailing life, my own version of "look-back time" as noted in the *Lapham's Quarterly* quote that heads this chapter. It has certainly not been a well-planned voyage, driven more by serendipity and blind luck than by preparation or skill. But it has been a hell of a ride, with equal shares of terrifying, mundane, and momentous experiences along the way. It just turns out that a small boat, under press of sail, surrounded by the steel blue sea, with a good crew poised to take whatever comes their way, is the perfect environment to unleash eudaemonia. No, that's not a disease, or a new drug for seasickness, it is Aristotle's word for "the good life," or, better put, for "human flourishing." When I finally fell asleep I was back aboard *Quetzal* in the Mediterranean, laughing and joking with my shipmates as we raced before a wicked gale, mulling over the irony that we had nearly perished a few miles offshore an island where everybody else lived forever.

TWO

SITUATIONAL AWARENESS

*Risking All for the Blue Lagoon • Engine Failure on a
Lee Shore • Emergency Rigging • Engine Failure Again •
Secrets of Longevity*

"Situational Awareness is the ability to identify, process, and comprehend the critical elements of information about what is happening to the team with regard to the mission. More simply, it's knowing what is going on around you.

"CONSEQUENCES OF LOSS: When we lose the bubble (i.e., Situational Awareness), we increase the potential for human error mishaps. Coast Guard analysis of navigational mishaps for cutters and boats revealed that 40% were due to a loss of situational awareness."

—U.S. Coast Guard Training Manual

"What would you risk dying for—and for whom?—is perhaps the most profound question a person can ask themselves."

—Sebastian Junger, *Tribe*

The Mediterranean, 2012–13

I am always aware of the wind. I can't help myself—call it an occupational hazard. Naturally wind is vital to a sailor, but even when ashore I notice which way the trees lean, a sure sign of the prevailing winds—and monitor obnoxiously flapping auto-dealership flags to get a read on direction and strength. I pay attention to ripples in ponds and puddles, curious about how the wind and water are interacting. And, I confess, I open the wind GRIB files on PassageWeather.com more any other app. I am a bit obsessed with wind, but it's an important messenger. In most places in the world, certainly near the coast, if you know the wind direction you have a pretty good idea of what to expect from the weather. It was an ominous sign when the crisp early-afternoon sea breeze abruptly vanished, as though Aeolus, the truculent Greek god of the wind, had switched off a giant cosmic fan. An eerie calm enveloped the harbor and the western sky looked as if it was about to be seasick. Within minutes a green slough of cloud cover swallowed up the last evidence of what had been a beautiful morning.

Quetzal was tied to a wobbly floating dock in the jam-packed port of Mgarr on the island of Gozo, part of the tiny but fiercely independent Mediterranean nation of Malta. We were making hasty preparations to get underway for a short sail to a supposedly beautiful anchorage in a rocky outcropping between larger Maltese islands called the Blue Lagoon. It was part of Paradise Bay—the area was clearly named by the tourist board. The forecast made no mention of foul weather, but I had a deep sense of foreboding. And for good reason—it was obvious to even the most pious landlubber that we should wait until the mischief in the atmosphere played its hand before shoving off. Also, I knew better than to trust an anchorage with a schmaltzy name like the Blue Lagoon—it would be packed with tripper boats and never live up to the billing. But I ignored all of my internal alarms. We slipped our lines and made our way past the stone breakwalls just as the color of the sky went from mal de mer green to really pissed-off black.

Our trip was winding down. It had begun a week earlier, under the glare of Mount Etna in Riposto, Sicily, and had been a frustrating voyage. Unlike my offshore training passages, where we expect and even relish challenging conditions, this was more of a coastal cruise with as much emphasis on culture and history as on sail handling, seamanship, and navigation. I had promised the crew that we would have plenty of time to explore the quaint harbors and ancient archaeological sites along the south coast of Sicily and in Malta, and if the winds cooperated, make a passage to Tunisia. I assured them that we'd enjoy delicious Sicilian swordfish and crisp white wine and, hopefully, some of the wonderful French-infused Middle Eastern street food in Tunis. It was mid-October, usually good sailing in the Mediterranean with cool westerly breezes and fair skies. I should have known better: the winds didn't cooperate—it was the Mediterranean after all. Aeolus was up to his old tricks, slinging sloppy south and southwest winds our way all week long.

Most of you know, or have deduced, that I make my living conducting training passages aboard *Quetzal*, my Kaufman 47′ cutter. Yes, people pay for the torment that I promise to dispense, which strikes land people as a particularly devilish deal. They will never understand the promise of respite from shoreside madness and the rare turn of freedom that a small sailboat on an unfettered ocean offers—to some of us it's worth any price. Through 14 years of sailing *Quetzal* my business model has changed. Many of my clients have become close friends and sail with me time and again, as I have a 70% repeat rate. Sometimes I am not sure who is doing the training as I learn something new on every passage. In essence we have shared adventures—the cockpit is our lyceum. It's a good gig and I have no intention of slowing down any time soon.

This supposedly easy, cultural cruise was, however, proving to be a challenge. We couldn't catch a break or a fair wind, and were obliged to beat each day, pounding into jarring seas while tacking offshore to gain a footing before angling back toward land, netting 30 or 40 hard-won miles. Cold and wet, we usually arrived in port after dark. After a quick meal and a glass of wine we collapsed into our bunks. The crew, Mike and Sue, George and Deb, and solo traveler, Deb L., were all repeat customers, with Deb L. nearing double digits for trips aboard *Quetzal*. Unlike some of my crews, these were not hardcore adventure seekers. They were middle-aged sailors and travelers, maybe with a lingering idea of launching a voyage of their own one day but also, like Deb and George, content to sail their 30´ sloop on Lake Michigan. They knew that every passage is unpredictable, that's part of the allure, and they kept their spirits up despite the frequent course and itinerary adjustments.

We gave up on Tunisia owing to a combination of contrary winds, meteorological and political. Persistent southerly breezes promised continued tough slugging and, more importantly, the Arab Spring, which had begun with such promise in Tunisia, had turned violent and it was impossible to know what to expect when we made landfall. Overloaded refugee boats were streaming toward the Italian island of Pantelleria, halfway between Tunisia and Sicily, and authorities were warning yachts to stay clear. Having once sailed blindly into a coup d'état in Yemen—which you will read about in Chapter Six—I decided to err on the side of caution this time. By the time we reached Gozo (at the northern end of the Maltese islands) we had just enough time for a detour to the Blue Lagoon before making our way to Valletta, the dramatic medieval harbor on the eastern coast of Malta, the largest of the island group, where our trip concluded.

It was less than two miles across a narrow strait to the Blue Lagoon—on the island of Comino, in the middle of the Maltese archipelago—and we decided not to bother raising sail, opting instead to hurry along under power and snag a choice spot in the anchorage. The cruising guide promised crystalline waters and beach bars ashore, not a profound cultural experience but just what we needed after a week of late-night landfalls and early-morning departures. Even if it rained, which was almost assured, and even if a bit of wind accompanied the rain, which was likely, it wouldn't last long. I've ridden out countless squalls, and a 20-minute motorboat ride across the strait was not a big deal. Besides, we'd beat the other boats still hunkered down in Mgarr waiting for the weather to clear.

I've certainly made a lot of questionable decisions for someone who is supposed to be an expert, someone with vast sailing experience. Lawrence Gonzalez nailed it his book, *Deep Survival*. "The word experienced," he writes, "often refers to someone who's gotten away with doing the wrong thing more frequently than you have." While experience should help avoid dangerous situations in the first place, it sometimes has the opposite effect, breeding overconfidence, a sense of, "this is nothing, I've been in worse situations than this, hell, I can get through anything." Experience is, however, useful for managing a difficult situation after you've screwed up in the first place, and is essential for keeping panic under control in rapidly deteriorating circumstances. Panic is contagious and debilitating—it's a wild card and a wildfire—it has to be stamped out before it spreads. How you respond to a crisis, a real crisis, in the knowledge that the outcome depends on your own quick decisions and physical actions, reveals much about your true nature—sometimes more than you want to know.

The squall struck with the fury of a Donald Trump tweet and I was stunned how quickly the conditions deteriorated. In a span of two minutes or less the wind accelerated from dead calm to full gale and then blasted right off Admiral Beaufort's scale. Our windspeed indicator was pegged at 55 knots. The rain felt as if it would puncture your skin, and it was difficult to keep your eyes open. The daylight sky turned inky dark, the only light generated by frequent lightning strikes that jabbed the horizon all around the boat—an irate Zeus hurling electric javelins with reckless abandon. We were motoring with the wind just forward of the beam, heeled over 20 degrees and taking water over the side decks. The high bluffs and rocky shoreline, less than 100 meters away, were completely obscured. As long as the motor kept running we were not in immediate danger; we would just have to steer vigilantly and manage our position very carefully until the squall passed. It was absurd how our fortunes had changed in a few scant minutes, from lounging on the deck in the marina to being barely able to stand in the cockpit or see the bow in a furious squall.

I was infuriated with myself. "What an idiot," I mumbled into the wind, adding, "what a pathetic fucking excuse of a captain." I knew there was no reason for us to be in this precarious situation. What had I been thinking to leave port with that sky? I had wanted to give the crew a nice afternoon at anchor after a week of disappointments and assumed we could easily handle a brief squall. So much for my keen sense of situational awareness; they were definitely going to have an experience, a direct result of me ignoring my own lifetime of the stuff.

Already thoroughly soaked, we struggled to climb into our foul-weather gear. In different circumstances it would have been a comical scene as the wind whipped our bibs and jackets, nearly blowing them overboard. My hat did take flight but nobody laughed. Beyond the immediate fear that it invoked, the power of the wind was impressive to behold. Despite my impudence for having shoved off when we did, I realized, not for first time, that it was also a privilege to experience nature in a full temper tantrum. It was honking, and I was surprised that the bimini and dodger had not been blown to shreds and wondered if they'd survive this super squall. There was nowhere to escape the stinging rain—the bimini sun shade was all but useless, flapping in the wind. The almost nonstop lightning strikes were getting closer to the boat and I suggested that the crew go below and keep away from the mast that pierced the main saloon and was stepped on the keel. Deb L., a bit miffed at not being part of the action in the cockpit, is clear headed and always looking to be helpful when she's aboard. "Shouldn't we have the running lights on?" she asked. "Yes," I shouted to be heard over the wind, "good thinking," but my words were blown to leeward before they reached her in the companionway. It didn't matter, and I thought to myself, "it's not likely anyone will be able to see them before it's too late to avoid a collision."

It was nearly impossible to read the small chartplotter, and I furiously wiped the screen with my hand and fervently hoped it would keep working. The radar was not useful, as the rain-soaked images denoting land's edge were difficult to make out, and I was reminded why, in the old days, we used to mount radar screens below, out of the weather. Fortunately the old reliable compass was well lit and I faithfully followed a course of 120 degrees. We were motoring hard, pushing the engine at 2500 RPMs but making just 2 knots of headway while crabbing into the wind to prevent leeway. At least I had not abandoned all my good habits and we had made a thorough study of the paper chart before we left the harbor. We had plotted the course and measured the short distance. We noted the shoals south of the Blue Lagoon and the west cardinal marker that we'd need to pick up before making our way into the anchorage.

As part of the navigational drill aboard *Quetzal* I tell the crew, only half-jokingly, that they should memorize the harbor chart before making an approach into a new harbor. Of course you can't memorize a chart, but you should have a clear vision of where the hazards, navigational aids, and natural landmarks are, especially with respect to your heading. You should know what to anticipate so you're not surprised if visibility is suddenly obscured, or a traffic encounter requires an unexpected course change, or a problem with the boat demands your immediate attention—or an impatient captain sails directly into a squall. Your approach needs to make sense, to feel right, and you should always have an escape plan in mind. The chartplotter should confirm what you already know—you should not just be following a preplotted route with no idea of direction and course. Honing a basic sense of direction is still vital in the GPS age, possibly even more so as we tend to follow our gizmos with a blind allegiance that even lemmings would question. In an emergency a backup plan may be the difference between a disaster and a good story.

Then, as if on cue, the motor sputtered, gasped for air, and suddenly quit like an actor dying in a bad movie, with the overheat alarm singing out. I tried the key once—it turned over, but it was obvious that the motor wasn't going to start without some tinkering. Turning the starter over and over would only make matters worse, and make the engine more difficult to repair later. We had to act quickly as *Quetzal* immediately fell off the wind and drifted toward the southeast corner of Gozo, a dangerous lee shore.

"You need tools," Mike immediately shouted from below.

"No, Mike, forget the motor, we need sail, we have to unfurl the genny, and right now."

George, all 6´4˝ of him, literally flew into the cockpit and began uncoiling the genoa furling line. Mike, trailing close behind, hauled on the jibsheet.

"Keep control on the furling line," I shouted at George, "we need a few feet of sail, no more, whatever you do don't let it all run out."

Mike cranked the winch like a madman and I slowly brought *Quetzal* into the wind. Gathering momentum, we began to claw our way off the rock-rimmed Gozo shoreline. We were less than a quarter mile offshore.

There was no way to tack, or turn the boat, without the mainsail and we could not risk putting the boat in irons, losing the ability to control our direction. If we fell off the wind to gain speed—so we could attempt to tack—we might ground on the hard bottom before we had a chance to bring the boat through the wind. These scenarios were percolating through my mind as I stood at the helm, conning the boat to windward, willing her away from the rocks. My senses were on high alert. I was calm but keenly aware of the situation—it was dicey.

Instinctively leaning to starboard, away from land, I thought, "Come on *Quetzal*, I am sorry for putting you in this mess, just dig in, old girl." It was not the first, and surely won't be the last, desperate talk I have had with my boat—she's bailed out her captain before and probably will again. The powerful blasts of wind made it impossible to hear waves breaking on the near shore. Deb L. made sure the crew had their PFDs and readied the ditch bag. The radio was abuzz with reports of trouble, especially in the Blue Lagoon, where several boats had apparently dragged anchor. "Screw the Blue Lagoon," I thought, "just give me some open water." There was no time to call for help, and in truth I was not sure whom to call—the Maltese Coast Guard? I suspected that—if they existed at all—they'd have their hands full with local boats. As with most crisis situations, we had to contend with the conditions on our own. We created the mess, now we had to clean it up. Diverting our efforts to raise help just might have been a catastrophic distraction.

Time entered the equation. The seconds lingered, they were in no rush to form minutes. The sea always lets you stew in the moment during a crisis—that's why sea stories are so enduring, they marinate slowly and you feel them deeply whether you want to or not. "Mind time" is when an emotional state affects your sense of time, and it is most pronounced during moments of shame, disgust, and fear—you become trapped in your own time warp. You need to push through that debilitating state and think clearly, "There'll be plenty of time to analyze your stupid decisions afterward." I was thankful for *Quetzal*'s deep keel and sweet hull shape. She doesn't make much leeway, meaning that she does not slide sideways from the force of the wind and waves. The course we were steering on the compass directly translated to the course we needed to lay down on the chart to reach safe water. It all depended on the wind—if it shifted the wrong way, heading us, we'd have been in serious trouble. Fortunately the wind shifted the right way, and this corresponded with a slight drop in wind strength. Inch by inch, or so it seemed, we were able to gain sea room. A few long minutes later we sailed clear of Gozo and gained the freedom of open water north of Malta.

We eased out a few more feet of headsail, trimmed it up, gathered a bit of speed, and took a collective sigh of relief as *Quetzal* sped away from danger. We were cold and soaked to the core, but the sense of relief was palpable. Deb and Sue delivered welcome cups of hot coffee, and despite a persistent drizzle, we all gathered in the cockpit. I apologized to the crew for having made a terrible decision to leave port in the first place. I thanked them profusely for remaining calm and responding with vigor when called into action. Coping with the squall was a team effort and everyone had done their part.

While I was feeling like a schmuck, the crew reaction was fascinating to witness. The 30 minutes of sheer terror had completely changed the tenor of the passage. They were animated. Deb, a nurse by training, was cheerily debriefing the incident. George, who has a natural deadpan expression, was beaming and couldn't wipe the smile off his face. He had wanted to encounter some serious weather during the passage and had handled himself very well—now he had a genuine sea story for a souvenir. Mike was a bit shaken—having sailed with me several times before in challenging conditions, he understood the precariousness of the situation. Sue, a new sailor, was amused by everyone's reaction.

Deb L., whose faith in *Quetzal* rivals mine, was quick to remind me that maybe we shouldn't have left port in the first place.

The encounter with the squall was clearly the highpoint of the trip and the frustrations of the past week were forgotten. It was not likely that we would have died had we been washed ashore—we would have stayed with the boat until the squall passed—but it was a possibility. For me, the thought of my beautiful boat and faithful companion being battered on the rocks sent chills down my spine. The close shave with disaster reminded all of us just how quickly events can devolve into a crisis. Unlike a storm building at sea, when the ocean inexorably grinds you down and you are forced to harness your resolve, mentally and physically, and brace for a long fight, the suddenness of the squall left us feeling vulnerable to the capricious whims of nature and one really bad decision.

The thin line between life and death is blurred by modern society. Most of us live gated-off lives, in secure neighborhoods populated with people just like us, isolated from the grave dangers we read about or see on television, going about our daily routines without much thought about being thrust into a life-or-death situation. But that doesn't mean we don't worry about all the terrible things we hear about in the nonstop barrage of news that assaults us around the clock and that is almost impossible to avoid. We express our angst while sprawled out on the couch in the form of a Facebook post or a hasty tweet. As North Americans we stand a better chance of being done in by an errant lightning strike than by a random terrorist act, yet we fret obsessively about events that have virtually no impact on our daily lives. But when the possibility of death becomes very real, everything changes. Death is the hard edge, the frame that defines life and gives it meaning. When actual physical conditions place your life, and the lives of those close to you, in peril, irrational anxieties tend to disappear and you become intensely focused on the present. Past and future worries vanish in the wind. Confronted with a serious crisis, I am always impressed by how the will to survive, when properly directed, can bring out the best in people. I am convinced that all of us have had, or will have, a crisis moment; how we respond is an indelible part of our existence.

We never found out if the Blue Lagoon lived up to its name, and instead made our way south and east to Valletta. We managed to start the engine and George, crammed into the engine compartment like a dolphin in a fishbowl, kept feeding it with water as we eased into the dock. A day later it was over. The crew exchanged email addresses, hugged, and promised to stay in touch as they hefted their duffel bags down the dock, hurrying back to their land lives. It's always a bit jarring how quickly my passages end, as the crew is at the mercy of prearranged airline schedules and the commitments of life.

Quetzal spent the winter in the nearby and nearly impossible to pronounce Maltese port of Birzebbuga (on the southern coast), propped on the hard in a small boatyard operated by a father-and-son team, Anthony and Joseph Baldacchino. The haulout was a bit unsettling as the boat was plucked from the bouncy waters of the commercial harbor by a huge commercial crane. She was then lowered onto a motorized cradle and Joseph used remote controls to direct her to the yard, a kilometer from the port. Despite their unorthodox facility, I took an immediate liking to the Baldacchino family, who trace their Maltese roots back to the Knights of St. John, the fearless soldiers who defended the island against Suleiman the Great and his entire Turkish fleet. I knew *Quetzal* would be in good hands and commissioned several winter projects, including a rebuild of the steering system and rooting out the sudden overheating problem that had caused the engine to unexpectedly stall on the way over to the Blue Lagoon.

I wanted *Quetzal* to be in good condition. Her next sail, scheduled for early the next year, was a 700-mile "heavy-weather" passage from Malta to Kuşadası, Turkey. Every year I single out one or two of my offshore training passages as "heavy weather," and they fill up quickly and usually live up to the hype. What made this passage challenging was not the route but the timing. A mid-March departure promised some excitement. The old refrain in the Med, there's either "too much" or "too little" wind, tilts toward "too much" during the transitional period between winter and spring when pressure gradients are inconsistent and the weather is driven by fast-moving depressions. By the time we finally lifted a glass of Turkish raki, nobody could accuse me of false advertising.

I returned to Malta in early March to prepare *Quetzal* for launching. I was joined by my friend Alan, of course, and also by Steve, another great friend and frequent shipmate from Cincinnati. They had agreed to help prepare *Quetzal* for the upcoming passage and were also part of the crew. Anthony Baldacchino insisted that we stay in his apartment near the yard, and his English-born wife doted on us as if we were her long-lost children. She would stray into our room at any hour delivering clean towels and a few "fingers" of whisky.

Malta is a densely packed, bustling island with a storied past and promising, if crowded, future. It's a retirement haven for EU citizens who flock to the island for sun, sand, and low taxes. The capital, Valletta, built as a stronghold by the Knights of St. John after they fled Rhodes in the sixteenth century, is an enchanting walled city with an array of sandstone-colored domes and arched windows. The warren-like city center is dissected by dark, narrow alleys and is, supposedly, carved with secret underground passageways that were key to the Maltese surviving almost nonstop Nazi bombing during WWII. Valletta was rocked with more bombs than London. We also explored Mdina, the capital in ancient times, perched atop the central plateau, and had a memorable meal. We ordered fenek, or rabbit stew, the national dish, and a nice red wine from Syria. We drank in the dramatic views of the windswept Mediterranean stretching out in every direction. The confused seas and churning whitecaps washing ashore certainly did not look very inviting and we all had the same thought: soon we'd be out there bobbing around in that mayhem. We ordered a second bottle of wine and embraced the moment.

Back at the yard, *Quetzal* was ready for launching. Joseph piloted the remotely controled cradle, edging it toward the commercial port. Walking next to him, I could tell he was concerned. "I don't like the look of that sky," he confided. "First a sirocco is coming, then a big storm, a really big storm." I was more worried about getting the boat safely in the water in the breezy conditions and then hurrying around to Valletta to be ready for the imminent arrival of the rest of the crew. "I can just smell the sirocco," Joseph added. "You should delay your departure."

"We'll be OK," I assured him. "And I'll keep an eye on the weather."

Nikos Kazantzakis, the best writer to never win the Nobel Prize in Literature, opens his classic novel, *Zorba the Greek*, in Piraeus, the port of Athens. "A strong sirocco was blowing the spray from the waves as far as the little café whose glass doors were shut," Kazantzakis writes. He does not feel the need to explain that a sirocco is a dirty south wind that originates as a low-pressure system over North Africa and picks up moisture as it moves north and out to sea. Everyone in the Mediterranean region knows the sirocco—it implies wind direction and weather. Derived from a cross between Arabic and Italian, it's a noun and adjective rolled into one evocative word.

After stopping traffic and surviving a barrage of honking vehicles swerving around the slow-moving cradle, *Quetzal* finally arrived at the port. The stevedores quickly rigged up crossbars to support two well-used lifting straps. Then the massive harbor crane yanked *Quetzal* from the cradle and she immediately swayed in the wind. There wasn't a lot of discussion or planning before she was suddenly airborne, and I was terrified that the crossbars would smash the mast. We wrestled with lines on the bow and stern, trying to corral the bucking boat floating 10 feet above us. The wind was picking up; we had to act quickly. The crane operator leaned *Quetzal* over the rough-edged seawall and hastily lowered her toward the water. We leapt aboard as she slid perilously near the wall and fired up the engine as the straps were released. Alan and Steve manned the fenders, and after several tense minutes when it looked as if we might not gain an offing and would scrape the topsides along the seawall, we managed to pull away. I was relieved to motor out of the harbor and let the lumpy gray seas of the Mediterranean break over the bow and wash a winter of grime off the decks. Boats belong in water, not on land, and most definitely not floating above land.

We moored in the fancy Camper & Nicholsons marina in the heart of Valletta just as David and Sean arrived. David, from New York, was another dear friend who had made many passages on *Quetzal*, including the 2011 Atlantic crossing. He had just turned 74 but had the energy of a 10-year-old, a lovable, insatiably curious, and at-times annoying shipmate who cherished his time aboard and treated me like a son. Sean was a *Quetzal* newbie. He was a classical historian and English language teacher based in Moscow, and his introduction to *Quetzal*-style passagemaking would remind him of Odysseus' misfortunes as he tried to sail home to Ithaca after the Trojan War. At least our ordeal lasted just a few days, although at times Sean felt as if it was a 20-year sentence from Zeus without the benefit of a nice break coupling with Circe. Our final crewmember, Brian, from Syracuse, New York, another *Quetzal* veteran, was delayed by a massive snowstorm in Europe, part of the same weather system that would make our life interesting in a few days. We made arrangements to pick him up, appropriately in Siracusa, the namesake of his hometown, on the southeast corner of Sicily, and our first waypoint.

Steve and Alan hastily provisioned for the short hop north and had to laugh as they left the supermarket. They wondered why some elderly women were having trouble controlling their shopping bags before realizing that they were carrying live rabbits. The critters were not happy at the prospect of being served up for stew and were bouncing around like mad, trying to get away. Alan, who owns two restaurants in Nova Scotia, was impressed with the Maltese notion of fresh meat but I was relieved my shipmates hadn't returned to the boat with a live rabbit.

The sirocco announced its impending arrival with a series of dusty squalls and then heavy rain. Despite the unpleasant weather I viewed the strong south wind as a blessing. It would escort us north to Siracusa and we'd wait there for favorable winds before heading across the Ionian Sea to Greece and then on to Turkey. The sirocco was just the warm-up act, however—the main event was poised to sweep across the central Mediterranean a few days later. The GRIB files were confident that a Force 10 full storm from the northwest would follow on the heels of the sirocco.

Sailing 80 miles north made sense for several reasons. First, Siracusa, sister city to Athens during the height of the Greek classical period, has a terrific natural harbor and would be well sheltered from the storm. Second, I wanted to ride the backside of the depression across the Ionian Sea, and the wind was forecast to clock from northwest to northeast over the next several days. Our route to Turkey was nearly due east—by starting a tad farther north we'd have a better slant as the wind shifted. Third, I hate to delay voyages, and this would give the crew a short overnight passage to find their sea legs and get their adrenaline flowing. And finally, it allowed us to pick up Brian, stock up on cheap but delicious Sicilian wine, and tarry in one of my all-time favorite harbors as the worst of the storm blew through.

We sped north, making landfall in Siracusa a day before the storm struck. It turned out to be a wise decision as Malta was blasted with hurricane-force winds. The south shore of Sicily was also battered and recorded winds of 60 knots. *Quetzal* was in the small marina in the northeast corner of the harbor, secured by two laid mooring lines. I chose to have the bow toward the dock, as opposed to the typical stern-to Med mooring, to take brunt of the blow head on. Powerful gusts of frigid wind ricocheted across the harbor and *Quetzal* heeled 20° one way and then the other. At first I hoped that the two laid mooring lines keeping us off the dock would hold; later, as the storm intensified, I hoped that the entire marina would stay put. I love Italians with all my heart—it is undoubtedly my favorite country—but their engineering can be suspect, and I tried to ignore the rusty chains and shackles holding the marina pontoons to the quay. I couldn't help but picture the entire marina being blown out to sea. Twelve hours later, conditions moderated.

Brian had arrived just before the storm struck, and with our full crew in place we sped past the faded, graffiti-decorated facade of Castello Maniace lighthouse on the south end of Ortigia island under sail. We were not showing off, tacking about the harbor—the engine had overheated again, forcing us to sail. Frustrated and despite 30-knot tailwinds, I tore into the engine once we were safely at sea. I found the faulty part: a short hose that connected the freshwater pump to the cooling manifold had a small crack. Naturally it was accessible only after the removal of what seemed like half the engine. I jury-rigged a heavy-duty replacement, but we didn't need the engine for the next three days anyway. Replacing the heat exchanger in Malta had been expensive and unnecessary, a lesson that I keep relearning about the futility of commissioning boat repairs from afar.

A few hours into the passage, the biting westerly winds piped up to gale force, a steady 35 knots with gusts to 40, and were blowing from dead astern. We wrestled the double-reefed mainsail down and lashed it to the boom. We then raised the whisker pole, a strut that sets perpendicular to the mast and supports the headsail when the wind is primarily astern. With about half of the genoa unfurled we charged toward the Peloponnese peninsula at a steady 8 knots. Occasional surfing runs saw the GPS speed-over-ground reading flirt with 15 knots. It was exhilarating sailing and yet the motion was easy and our rig was not unduly loaded. We rolled a bit, but that's the nature of deep reaching under headsail alone. The fact that we didn't have a boom and the prospect of a dangerous jibe to contend with was worth a bit of rolling. Alan, explaining to Sean the merits of not flying the mainsail, quoted one of my favorite lines: "Sometimes you just have to get the boom out of your life." He then added his own addendum: "It's simple that way, good things in life, and sailing, are always simple." The wind held through the night and we settled into two-person watches with an easy three-hours-on, six-hours-off routine with the autopilot doing most of the helming.

The following day our eastbound express train continued and we couldn't help but congratulate ourselves as we played the clocking winds to near perfection. By steering north of the rhumb line to begin the passage we were able to arc a bit south later, keeping the winds aft of the beam and making life aboard *Quetzal* quite tolerable, especially after we reset the main with three reefs, thus dampening the roll. (For more on downwind sailing strategies, see the Appendix: Wrinkles.) I hoped Poseidon (I decided to call Neptune by his original name since we were in Greek waters) didn't detect our creeping hubris, but we were feeling pretty damn smug as we sped south of Kythira and then raced past Cape Meleas, the so-called Cape Horn of the Med, and into the Aegean, north of Crete. The autopilot stopped working abruptly, but with six aboard and the sailing thrilling, hand steering was anything but a burden. We made a wager: whoever attained the highest speed would get free drinks when we made landfall. Sean, the least experienced sailor aboard, carried the day with a top speed of 14 knots.

As the winds clocked to the northeast we raised the staysail and shed the reefs as the wind eased. We made landfall on the island of Milos under full sail, completing a 500-mile passage in 70 hours. In the fickle Mediterranean, that had to be one of the longest and fastest passages made entirely under sail since the invention of oars. We sailed into Milos Bay, a dramatic natural harbor and one of the largest in the Med, and tied up to the quay in Adamas. We were the only cruising boat in the harbor. There was some talk of launching an expedition to search for the lost arms of Venus de Milo. The tragic beauty was reportedly sculpted on the island in antiquity before she was spirited away to France, and today lives limblessly in the Louvre. In the end we decided instead on a hot shower followed by a visit to a nearby tavern to sample the fresh octopothi and to buy Sean his drinks.

Our unusually swift run across the Ionian Sea, which we had thought would be the challenging part of the passage, gave us time to make a few unexpected stops in the Cyclades Islands of the central Aegean. The winds had clocked to the southeast, affording a pleasant reach to Naxos. We made our way past the giant but unfinished marble arch, the Portara, a temple that was to be dedicated to Apollo, and moored in the congested fishing harbor in the old town. Once again, we were the only cruising boat in the harbor. We rented a van and explored the island that is the most fertile in the Aegean and well known for producing the tastiest potatoes in Greece. Naxos enchanted a young Byron, who claimed it was the most beautiful island in the world. After a delicious family-style meal in a tiny restaurant overlooking the harbor we retreated to the boat and toyed with the idea of spending another day ashore.

Once again our overlords, the weather zookeepers who feed the raw meat of meteorological data into the computers that then somehow spit out GRIB files—those freakishly accurate satellite weather models that forecast wind direction and strength, sea state, cloud cover, temperature, blood pressure, and fluctuations in the stock market (not really, at least not yet), and nonchalantly deliver it back to your smartphone—suggested that we had better not tarry. Another gale was forecast, this time from the south, with winds expecting to reach Force 9 in a few days. We decided to head straight for Samos, 100 miles to the east. I know Samos well, and begging to differ with Lord Byron, consider it more beautiful than Naxos. I was confident that the port of Pythagoreio, or the nearby marina, would be a decent spot to ride out a gale. The protection was adequate and the tavernas excellent.

Before returning the van, we topped *Quetzal's* fuel tanks with cheap Greek diesel fuel from a filling station, making multiple runs with jerry cans. We also picked up some fresh lemons, dried figs, and a hefty bag of potatoes that made Alan, our cook, quite happy. I wasn't overly concerned about the weather. After clearing Naxos it was just 40 miles of sailing before we'd encounter the lee of Ikaria. We would be passing to the north of the long, rugged, sheer-sided slab of an island, and surely it would provide a natural wind and wave break all through the night. It seems I should have been concerned, however, as Poseidon was out for revenge.

Backing away from the quay, we snagged a mooring line in the prop. The risk with bow-to moorings, which I occasionally prefer to the traditional stern-to Med moor, is that you have to be patient and allow the mooring line to sink before putting the engine astern. I climbed down the swim ladder in a half-hearted attempt to clear the line but the water temperature was in the low 50s and I quickly decided $200 to hire a diver was money well spent. We eventually cleared the harbor, tipping our hats to Apollo, and proceeded to encounter strong winds from the east. So much for the southerly gale. We tucked two reefs in the main and pressed on with the staysail. It was cold and occasionally wet as short, blocky seas broke on deck, but we were making good progress and would soon be in the lee of Ikaria.

Ikaria, possibly named after that high flyer Icarus, son of Daedalus, who flew too close to the sun on a pair of wax wings, had been in the news recently. It is one of the five original longevity hotspots identified by author Dan Buettner in his bestselling book, *The Blue Zones*. Along with the inhabitants of Okinawa, the Nicoya Peninsula of Costa Rica, and the remote valleys of Sardinia, as well as the Seventh-Day Adventists of Lomo Linda, California, the people of Ikaria are famous for living long, healthy lives. Many residents live more than 100 years. Buettner has created a "Blue Zones" phenomenon with follow-up books, recipes, and longevity workshops. Suddenly people all over the world wanted to know why the residents of Ikaria lived so long—what was their secret? Was it their diet, the lack of stress, their daily exercise, or the good red wine?

As darkness fell all we wanted from the island was a simple lee, a break from the wind and seas. We were living very much in the present— the cold, miserable present—and not interested in the secrets of long life. But there was no lee on the north shore of Ikaria—in fact, the winds accelerated as we neared the island. Fierce katabatic downdrafts exploded off Ikaria and raked *Quetzal* with storm-force gusts. Katabatic winds, also called downslope winds, are formed when air hitting the windward side of an island climbs over the top and then accelerates down the lee side, gathering density and strength before charging out to sea. They're a well-known phenomenon in the Aegean, and on Ikaria in particular; unfortunately, *Quetzal*'s skipper had forgotten all about them.

Once again we tied the third reef in the main, a struggle in the suddenly severe conditions, but even that was too much sail. We soon dropped the main completely, lashed it securely to the boom, and slugged along under the tiny staysail alone. We had the boom out of our life again, but this time out of utter necessity. It was blowing hard enough to consider reefing the staysail, reducing the total sail area to around

50 square feet, a virtual beach towel, and something we've done only a couple of times during the fiercest of storms. Finally, we found a sliver of a lee, not a calm, mind you, but a small spot of sea where the winds dropped to 30 knots. We understood how Icarus careened off course. He wasn't reckless, just caught in a katabatic wind.

Steve and Alan manned the watch as I dropped below to study the chart with Brian. David, without a care, was asleep in the pilot berth. Sean was feeling terrible and, I learned later, terrified, which made perfect sense as he had done very little sailing. Although we were not in immediate danger because we were being blown away from the island, the intensity of the wind was staggering and he had never experienced conditions anything like that before. Then, suddenly, we all had reason to be terrified as there was a loud clanging noise above our heads.

Dashing on deck, I found that the aft lower shroud had gone slack and was smacking the coachroof. I was stunned. *Quetzal* has a massive rig, and at that time it was relatively new, but somehow the ½" 1x19 wire had unraveled and was spiraling about in the wind. This was serious— the aft lowers are the most important stays on the boat—we might lose the mast. Having lost the mast a few years before, in a tornado in Italy, I found the thought of losing the new spar horrifying. If it went over the side I vowed to give up sailing, move to Ikaria, and live a ridiculously long life herding sheep and drinking wine.

We quickly dropped the staysail to take all load off the rig and fired up the diesel. I managed to toss the pole topping lift over the first spreader, assisted by a lucky gust of wind, and led it to a block on the chainplate and then back to a deck winch to give it tension. It would serve as a temporary aft lower stay, and did, in fact, stabilize the mast better than I thought possible. Then, before we had time to digest our new circumstances, the lee vanished. The winds and seas that washed over *Quetzal* were truly astonishing, significantly stronger than the squall we had encountered between Gozo and Malta the previous fall. It was crazy. Motoring at full throttle, all we could do was maintain our position two miles north of the island to try and keep the bow into the wind.

Then the engine quit—yes, once again, although this time, as we would soon learn, it was a self-inflicted problem. Within seconds we were blown away from the island. Fortunately we had a lot of sea room to the north: the nearest island, Chios, was 40 miles away. In a span of a few hours we'd gone from being incredibly smug sailors who had outfoxed the weather gods, to running before a full storm unable to sail or motor. Poseidon was chuckling. As we sped away from Ikaria under bare poles, at times reaching 10 knots, I joked to Steve that it seemed cruelly ironic that we might meet our demise just offshore of the island where everybody else lived forever.

Alan, Steve, and I took turns manning the helm. It was tricky steering and imperative to keep the stern directly into the seas to keep them from breaking aboard. At first light we took stock of our situation. We were not in any immediate danger. We still had plenty of sea room and even mused that we could run all the way to Istanbul if we had to. *Quetzal* was seaworthy and the crew was actually rested and for the most part cheerful. We just had to decide where to spend our energy: on the rig or on the engine? Sean suggested we call the Greek Coast Guard but I told him that the last thing I wanted was to be "rescued," which might entail abandoning the boat or a brutal tow that would be sure to cause a lot of damage. I explained that if our lives were in danger I would do everything possible to call for help, but our lives were not in danger. I went on to explain that self-reliance is a fundamental aspect of ocean sailing and that this was an opportunity to learn how to respond to a crisis. I am not sure he agreed with me, but to his credit he did all he was asked despite feeling sick from a nagging head cold and having to contend with genuine fear.

We decided to fix the engine. I didn't want to chance setting a sail that might result in a dismasting—my feelings about that subject are on the record and unambiguous. After fixing the overheating problem earlier in the passage, the engine had run very well and I suspected it was something simple. We made a plan. Alan, our steadiest helmsman, steered for hours and was then spelled by Brian. David, who has an amazing ability to sleep at sea, actually missed the drama off Ikaria. When he finally emerged in the cockpit he wondered if he'd missed breakfast, before noticing that we were in a rather precarious state and breakfast was delayed. Disappointed that he'd missed so much excitement, he was determined to do everything possible to help. He was up and down the companionway many times, fetching tools and parts. More importantly he kept everybody buoyed with his natural good cheer. Peering into the storm-tossed seas he saw beauty and history, marveling aloud that Odysseus had seen the same conditions. Sean, the historian, was living fully in the moment and trying to blot out the past. He produced a very welcome fresh pot of coffee. Steve and I tackled the engine.

David was right of course. There is hardly anything more spectacular than a front-row seat from which to observe the unleashed power of the sea, especially from the vantage point of a seaworthy boat's cockpit, even a temporarily disabled one. At the age of 74, he knew that he was witnessing something special and his enthusiasm rubbed off on all of us, save Sean, unfortunately. He was looking solely for a port of refuge—he was ready to be off the boat. It was a serious situation to be sure, and we were fully engaged. If you embrace that feeling, whether it's adrenaline coursing through your veins or something more mystical, there's no denying that you are very much alive—nothing else mattered but our moment-to-moment decisions and actions.

The look in Alan's eyes as he steered for hours on end left no doubt that he was paying attention. Guided by instinct and reaction alone, as

Quetzal, without sail or motor, was at the mercy of the following seas, he was, as athletes say, in the zone. We were counting on him and he was not about to let us down, conning *Quetzal* one way and the other, keeping her stern to the breaking seas. Brian, who had been battling seasickness off and on during the voyage, had no trace of the malady when he relieved Alan. He was completely focused on his task. The two of them took turns calling out when a wave was about to overrun us, hooting and hollering in the process.

One reason that sailing endures and thrives in the face of much better and more efficient ways to travel—and the reason that nautical literature is transcendent—is the visceral connection you feel to mariners of every epoch. David spoke of Odysseus, Homer's fictional hero, and I thought off all the human sailors who had plied these very same ancient seas, in calms and storms. They had felt the same thrills and terrors, been drenched by the same waves, chilled by the same breezes, and in many cases their remains littered the bottom 3,000 feet below us. Our voyages are interconnected—as sailors, we'd understand each other. There's a blessed eternity to the sea, and time loses its greedy grip on our experiences.

Quetzal's engine is best accessed through the cockpit sole, and while this provides natural light and plenty of space to work, it also leaves the engine prone to soaking from spray and breaking waves. David and Brian manned a makeshift canvas cover as Steve and I assessed the situation. Steve was in his element. He'd made many trips with me over the years, and his sailing and seamanship skills had evolved steadily, but at times he lacked confidence. In a way he craved this storm, and he rose to the occasion. Throughout the ordeal his judgment was sound and he was seeing things with clarity—the opposite of what happens when you're seized by panic. In a weird and wonderful way, something that I understood deep in my soul was something he now seemed to be enjoying himself. He has a natural acumen for dealing with people and I counted on his advice. I later learned that Steve had reassured Sean throughout the night—Sean had been terrified and thought we should be putting out a VHF MAYDAY.

Working knee to knee in the tiny engine compartment, it didn't take Steve and me long to learn that it was a fuel problem—specifically, a bad fuel problem: the diesel fuel was laced with water. No wonder it had been so cheap back in Naxos—it had been sitting in tanks all winter, leaky tanks no doubt, and the stuff we filled our tanks with was at least 30% water. We worked for hours, pumping and spilling fuel as we coped with wicked rolls. We eventually rigged a bypass tank from a milk container and filtered enough clean fuel to start the engine and limp into the harbor at Chios. As we secured the boat along the quay, our humility was fully restored and we had new respect for crossing the Mediterranean in March. Once again, the heavy-weather passage had lived up to the billing. That night, at a well-earned feast ashore, I told the crew that I was feeling charitable and was going to throw in the extra-credit experiences—steering under bare poles, emergency rigging, and diesel repairs—for free.

Postscript

Quetzal made it to Pythagoreio (on Samos), and then on to Turkey, on schedule, and moved into a berth at the huge marina in the heart of bustling Kuşadası. A dear friend, another Steve, from Iowa of all places, flew over to oversee a refit project that included fitting new aft lower shrouds. Labor is good value in Turkey and the work is high quality. Still, I wasn't going to commission unsupervised work from afar again, and Steve, who is a skilled craftsman, as his impeccable Baba 40 cutter attests, was happy to spend some time in Turkey and be my point man.

I completed a couple of training passages later that spring before Tadji turned up for her summer break. She was still teaching then, but we were kid free for the most part and spent the bulk of the summer exploring the Turkish coast. However, before she arrived, one of our passages took us back to Ikaria, and this time the weather was settled. *Quetzal* was one of two cruising boats sandwiched into the tiny basin at Ayios Kirikos and we spent a day exploring the island.

Naturally we wanted to uncover the secrets of its inhabitants' longevity. An old sea captain, who was still spry at 80, shrugged his shoulders when asked about why people lived so long. Clearly, like everyone else on the island, he was sick of the question and not pleased with the many Blue Zone pilgrims making their way to his formerly remote home island. He indulged us.

"So you see," he began, with a twinkle in his almond eyes, "we have the best air in the Mediterranean, it blows straight from Macedonia and is clean and fresh. We have the best soil and our vegetables are delicious. Our vines have to cling to the hillside like goats, and they make the best wine in Greece. And we still walk up and down the steep slopes every day to visit our children. But," he paused, "do you want to know the real secret?" Of course we did. We all leaned in close as he lowered his voice. "We have sex four times a day! It's just one big orgy on the island." Then he burst out laughing, "Nobody knows, we just forget to die, that's it."

THREE

BYEBYEBLUES.COM

"It is not that we have a short time to live, but that we waste a lot
of it. Life is long enough, and a sufficiently generous amount has
been given to us for the highest achievements if it were all well
invested. But when it is wasted in heedless luxury and spent on
no good activity, we are forced at last by death's final constraint to
realize that it has passed away before we knew it was passing. So
it is: we are not given a short life but we make it short, and we are
not ill supplied but wasteful of it… Life is long if you know how
to use it."

—Seneca, *On the Shortness of Life*

"Dwell on the beauty of life. Watch the stars, and see yourself
running with them."

—Marcus Aurelius, *Meditations*

"I twisted in the wind, back in the day, back in the day.

    It's later than you think, it might be time to say, what you need to say."

—Chris DiCroce, "The Fray"

"Talk about choices does not apply to me. While intelligence considers options, I am somewhere lost in the wind."

—Rumi, Persian Poet, *What Is Not Here*

The Aegean, Summer 2013

We were sailing off an ancient shore, the Lycian coast of southern Turkey. Scarred hills, sporadically dappled with gnarled olive trees like the last tenacious hairs on an old man's head, loomed in and out of the haze. Tadji was at the helm, searching for zephyrs as *Quetzal* ghosted over a shimmering sea. The limp headsail was poled to port and the floppy mainsail paid well out and lashed with a preventer to starboard, a futile wing-on-wing attempt to catch the last gasps of the late-afternoon Mediterranean breath. We'd already given up on the asymmetrical spinnaker and it lay in a collapsed heap of red, white, and blue nylon on the foredeck. I was below, rummaging through the navigation desk looking for a detailed chart for the approach to Kekova Roads.

Call me a Luddite but I still use paper charts, especially, as I explained in the last chapter, when making harbor approaches. I also believe in picking up a pencil and dividers and putting the position on a chart at least once a day, even when we are 1,000 miles from land—it just is the right thing to do. I knew the chart was in there somewhere. Thumbing through my well-used and much-loved Imray Mediterranean charts, I couldn't find it. Then I stumbled upon a few neatly folded old Turkish charts. In the upper-left-hand corner I saw my mother Jeanne's unmistakable script, "KAS–CAVUS BURNU–TURKEY." She always wrote in caps, a masculine style that belied her completely feminine nature. I had forgotten that I had tossed some charts from her around-the-world voyage aboard before my last Atlantic crossing.

Scaled at 1:100,000—meaning that an inch, for example, on the chart represents 100,000 inches on earth—the chart did not provide the detail I was hoping for. A harbor chart is typically scaled at 1:25,000 or larger—yes, larger—chart scales are like pieces of pie, or fractions: the smaller the numbers, the bigger the pieces. But details like cardinal marks and wayward rocks no longer mattered. I had lost interest in our approach. Tadji would have to use the chartplotter to con her way into the harbor as I retreated several decades into the past.

"We're becalmed, I am going to start the engine," she called out. It wasn't a question. Without me to protest, to keep sailing despite a complete lack of breeze, she turned the key and the engine rumbled to life. Then she furled the headsail and sheeted the main in tight. She was right of course, it was time to make landfall—still, the motor was an intrusion, a much too common intrusion sailing in the eastern Aegean in the summer.

I was secretly pleased that Tadji had taken the initiative to get moving—not waiting for me to validate her decision—and that she felt confident enough to start the approach to the anchorage on her own. She's not a natural sailor, she'd never set foot aboard a sailboat until I blew into her life. I like to say that we met in elementary school, a line she doesn't see the humor in, and a line I tend to overuse, but technically it's true. She was a teacher making a bit of extra money as my daughter Nikki's reading tutor. Naturally I was interested in Nikki's progress, and after meeting her lovely tutor, became even more interested. I gave Tadji a copy of my book *Flirting with Mermaids*, and to my surprise and delight, she actually read it. The book chronicles my life as a delivery skipper, a time when I was always on the move, sailing all over the world, lurching from one adventure to the next. She had no idea anyone lived like that and I was a bit dismayed when she told me that at first she thought it must be fiction.

I convinced her to let me tell her some sea stories in person, over dinner perhaps, and it was a short path from first date to falling madly in love. We had dissimilar backgrounds and many differences to bridge, but we shared a devotion to our kids and a passion to see the world. Tadji, who is now an accomplished sailor, is the most fervent traveler I've ever known. She's willing to pack a bag on a minute's notice to go anywhere. She has an insatiable curiosity about the world. While I crave close encounters with nature she's intrigued by the culture of a place, the food, art, and beliefs. Glancing up through the companionway, I could see Tadji at the wheel. She was standing on the helm seat (to be able to see over the dodger) and studying the approach intently. Her hair, thick and wavy, hung to her shoulders and her tea-leaf-colored eyes—Persian eyes—focused on the task. It was a nice sight to drink in, a beautiful navigator guiding us into an ancient harbor. So often in the hullabaloo of running the boat I didn't appreciate how much Tadji has invested in making our life together work. She has been thrust into the best and worst of situations when it comes to sailing. As a novice, she appreciated my long experience and was able to find her way into the cruising life without worrying about the competence of her mate, at least concerning nautical matters—ashore was a different kettle of fish entirely. On the other hand, we didn't have a shared learning curve, we didn't have the benefit of having made mistakes together nor of having found solutions together. She was always dealing with "my" boat, a boat that I worshiped in a way she sometimes considered odd, and a boat that was loved by many others too. She was stuck having to endure my know-it-all advice about all things sailing.

Tadji was taking it very slowly and I thought she might give the engine a few more revs—the channel was well marked, after all. For once I kept my mouth shut and returned to the old chart before me. I studied Mom's course line duly noted as 268 degrees true. I was surprised and impressed that they plotted their courses in true, rather than adopting the common practice of using magnetic, a sloppy technique that skips a simple math equation to remove shifting curves of variation. I felt a sense of pride—my mom knew what she was doing: only true courses and bearings should ever be placed on a chart. The position fixes were scribbled in her hand and that of her partner Tim as they shared the navigational duties. They had sailed this coast many years before and I tried to reconstruct their route aboard *Epoch*, their 38′ sloop. They must have left Antalya the night before, as the chart showed morning fixes at 0730, 0845, and the last one, at 1030, in the outer approaches of the same anchorage toward which we were heading. They had taken handheld compass bearings off charted landmarks and furrowed headlands, and advanced those bearings based on speed and course for running fixes. Indeed, a voyage from an earlier era before GPS conquered the world and our minds.

The handsome chart with a dramatic legend and sculpted contour lines was a throwback to a time when charts were not just utilitarian tools, but were inspired works of art and accumulated stores of knowledge. Though printed in 1978, the chart was originally based on a survey from 1886, from the time of the Ottomans, a realization that gave me a chill. There's just something about charts, and for that matter, maps. Ken Jennings, famous as a *Jeopardy* champion, wrote a wonderful book called *Map Head*. Like me, he's been addicted to maps since he was a kid. "There must be something innate about maps," he writes, "about this one specific way of picturing our world and our relation to it, that charms us, calls to us, won't let us look anywhere else in the room if there's a map on the wall." I couldn't agree more. A huge framed chart of the world, Admiralty Chart Number 4000, occupies the port main bulkhead on *Quetzal*.

I pored over the other Turkish charts I had aboard, following *Epoch* as she made her way up the coast, reliving her voyage as she called at

Marmaris, Bodrum, and a host of Greek islands before deciding to winter over in Kuşadası, on Turkey's west coast. *Epoch* was an off-the-shelf Jeanneau production boat with a low-slung deckhouse and a huge cockpit. She was of moderate displacement with a flat-bottomed hull shape and a silly model name, Gin Fizz. She was an unusual cruising boat in those days when you were much more likely to encounter robust double-enders like the Westsail 32, or Robert Perry–designed cutters like the Tayana 37 and Valiant 40. It was also a time of transition as bluewater sailors were beginning to recognize that speed and agility were also important factors in determining the seaworthiness of a boat. Hull shapes aside, all boats of that era would strike today's sailors as simple from a systems perspective, maybe even primitive. Mom and Tim sailed without refrigeration, without reliable electronic navigation, and, for the most part, without weather reports. But they loved their "POCH" and she never let them down.

Departing from Fort Lauderdale, Florida, they made their way south to Panama and transited the canal. They rode the trade winds across the South Pacific, with stops in French Polynesia, Tonga, Samoa, and Fiji, before tarrying for nearly a year in Australia. Resuming their voyage, they followed the prevailing monsoons across the Indian Ocean, up the Red Sea to Suez, and finally spilling into the Mediterranean.

Epoch jumped from an "X" on an old chart into my mind's eye and I could see her clearly: an Aries self-steering windvane perched on the stern, a rakish black spray dodger and bimini top, and an interior crammed with mementos from their travels, including a carved mask from the Solomon Islands and a globe suspended by fishing line and decorated with a red tape line showing their route around the world. Mom and Tim were not experienced sailors, but were kindred souls who met later in life and shared a passion to see the world in their own boat, at their own pace, on their own terms. They had nothing to prove and everything to experience, two 60-year-old adventurers with a life behind them and the world before them. They were sailing in June 1986, the third year of a near circumnavigation. Tadji and I were about to share their anchorage in July 2013. We were both using a chart first commissioned by a sultan. Not for the first time I realized that the world is indeed round and that I have been sailing in circles for almost four decades.

Aboard *Quetzal* we found that the anchorage at Kekova Roads was well protected, and lingered a few days with our friends, Barclay and Oya. Ironically, they were sailing a 37′ Jeanneau sloop, *Mr. Bojangles*, exploring more of the Mediterranean each year from their homeport of Kuşadası. We'd been sailing together for a few weeks, rendezvousing in port, sharing meals and stories. Barclay is Scottish and Oya is Turkish, unique perspectives to provide insights into the clash of civilizations that is modern-day Turkey. Protests in Istanbul that summer foreshadowed the unrest that followed a few years later. Eastern Turkey is traditional and politically conservative while the western half of the country, where Barclay and Oya lived and we were sailing, is as modern and as open-minded as anywhere in the Mediterranean. The current president, Recep Tayyip Erdoğan, is a master at pitting Turks against each other and consolidating his power in the process. He was one of the first to use the phrase "fake news" while he systematically destroyed the country's press. "That's why we have a boat and are learning to sail," Barclay said, shaking his head as we toasted with a glass of raki. "Just in case we need to leave in a hurry. We love Turkey, but nobody knows what's going to happen."

Barclay and Oya had to return home and so headed north. Tadji and I continued down the Turkish coast and left *Quetzal* in a small marina in Finike. We rented a propane-powered car and drove to Konya, the ancient spiritual center in the steppes of central Turkey. Konya was home to the Sufi Mevlevi Order and their famous Whirling Dervishes. It's also where the oft-quoted Persian poet Rumi is buried. Tadji, her Persian pride showing, was a bit miffed that Turkey claimed Rumi, arguing that he spoke and wrote Farsi, the original form of Persian. I teased her that Rumi, who was born in 1207, and who is among the best-selling poets in the world today, would scoff at her nationalism. His wise and somewhat sappy though always beautiful messages of love and peace transcend religion and politics and adorn everything from greeting cards to the chapter heads of serious philosophical writings ... and sailing memoirs. His insights are an ancient lens focusing clearly on the absurdity of the ongoing conflicts that define our time. We carried on to Cappadocia in heart of ancient Anatolia. It's famous for fantastic cone-shaped rock formations and hidden caves that offered refuge for early Christians. Tadji talked me into getting up at 0400 for a hot-air balloon ride over the valley, and it was spectacular, offering a glimpse of a bizarre, beaten-down landscape where past conflicts and differing views of the future are on a collision course.

Once back aboard *Quetzal*, we were in a rush. Tadji had a flight to catch, so we made an overnight passage to Marmaris, the yachting mecca on the southeast coast of Turkey. The Mediterranean bade Tadji farewell in style as we had a perfect reach with 15 knots of warm, steady southwest breeze. Our summer interlude was over and Tadji, at the time a middle-school teacher, had to get back to school. It had been our best summer afloat. Tadji had become confident and capable aboard and realized, on her own terms, that a sailboat was the perfect vehicle for exploring the world. She discovered that she could not only endure my chosen lifestyle, but thrive, albeit in her own, very individual way.

We talked of sailing around the world, and not in an abstract way but with concrete dates and details, including how we'd blend my training-passage business with full-time world cruising. We needed to see all the kids through college, so we had a few years yet, but we decided that as soon as it was practical she'd stop teaching and we'd spend a lot more time together on *Quetzal*. I desperately needed help organizing the details of the passages, so she would take over administration duties, freeing my time for more writing between passages. She also had certain ideas for making *Quetzal* more livable and more comfortable, and although I loved the rough-and-ready nature of *Quetzal* and had to bite my tongue at some of her suggestions, I was delighted that Tadji felt that *Quetzal* was "our" boat now.

That particular season I also had to get back to work. I had a training passage scheduled that would crisscross the Aegean, with six crewmembers due soon. This split life was challenging but we made it work through our profound and enduring love affair, sustained by the knowledge that we would soon sail together a lot more often. (And, by the way, that time is now, as Tadji has officially retired from teaching— but that's getting ahead of the story.)

David, whom you met in the last chapter, and Harry had both crossed the Atlantic aboard *Quetzal*. David sailed eastbound to Ireland and Harry made the trade-wind passage from the Canary Islands to the Caribbean. Both were frequent shipmates, but surprisingly they had not met before tossing their duffel bags aboard on that blistering August day in Marmaris. They were part of a quirky crew, all of whom had sailed with me before, including Harry's lovely wife and constant companion, Velinda. Jerry and Vera, recently married, had chosen to make the passage a part of their honeymoon. My reliable friend and award-winning *Miami Herald* political columnist Fred Grimm, and my daughter Narianna, a college student who detoured to Turkey to spend a week with her dad before starting a semester abroad in Dublin, rounded out the eclectic crew.

After a lively afternoon romp out of the harbor that filled us with hope that the forecast would prove wrong, the wind vanished as predicted and we were left bobbing on glassy seas while the sails slatted annoyingly from side to side. There was no choice but to start the engine, sheet the mainsail and staysail amidships, furl the headsail, and break out the hors d'oeuvres, raki, and red wine. It was 1700, after all. Captain's Hour is a much-loved tradition aboard *Quetzal*, and not just for the drinking, of which there's very little when at sea—more for the camaraderie. This is especially true on challenging offshore passages, when the weather is bleak and forbidding and a gloomy sense of isolation can be pervasive. The crew gathers in the cockpit, lively discussions ensue, and we rediscover our humanity and remind ourselves that we're the lucky ones. It's those unfortunate folks ashore, dealing with the madness of modern life, who should feel gloomy. Some question my decision to allow modest drinking aboard, but I refuse to allow a passage on *Quetzal* to become a rule-driven sailing school with an atmosphere of stress and a list of dos and don'ts posted on a white board that snuff out the essential of joy of being at sea. I also have deep confidence and trust in the people who make their way into my floating world—nobody ever overindulges and many choose not to drink at all. Nobody wants to let their shipmates down.

It was at Captain's Hour during a gale in the Atlantic a few years before when my frequent shipmate Ron came up with a new business model for me. We were joking about how my training-passage clients were getting older and in the future instead of taking live crew I should carry the remains of former shipmates for burials at sea. "It will be a lot more profitable," Ron insisted, "provisioning costs will go way down and you can carry more customers." We even came up with a name, a slight variation of my current website, which is a combination of my daughters' nicknames, yayablues.com. The new enterprise would be called byebyeblues.com, and the trips would be marketed as "the last passage," a joke that would prove to be sadly prophetic all too soon.

In addition to jokes, with a wide range in terms of both subject matter and quality (in their content and their telling), another Captain's Hour standby is the hypothetical question. This is an irritating but always revealing game that asks you to answer "what-if" questions. The questions are usually based on the unlikely scenario that you suddenly find yourself stranded on a desert island. "So, you're stranded on a desert island for one year and you can bring only three books, what would they be?" Variations on the question include three movies (assuming you have a way to watch them, of course), three CDs (again assuming you have a way to listen to them), etc. The answers are always telling. Books range from the Bible, to *War and Peace*, to survival manuals. Movies always seem to include *The Godfather*, while music varies from classical to country. Some try to game the system by choosing compilations—the *Complete Works of Shakespeare*, for example—but these produce boos from the cockpit. For the record, my three books today—they will undoubtedly be different tomorrow—are: *Moby-Dick*, I just can't help myself, I keep rereading it over and over; *Ulysses*, when else are you ever going to read *Ulysses*?; and *Zorba the Greek*—who can resist Zorba when he says, "Life is trouble. Only death is not. To be alive is to undo your belt and look for trouble"? But … instead of *Ulysses* I might substitute *Infinite Jest*, the late David Foster Wallace's magnum opus that I've been meaning to read, or … I told you it was annoying.

Lately, however, I've upped the ante with a new hypothetical question. I've shifted the focus to life itself, or, specifically, how much and what type of life are you willing to wager on? The question is: "If you could, right now, dial in age 78 and know that you will be in perfect mental and physical health right up to that point and then die a swift, pain-free, natural death, would you take it?" The idea being of course that you would avoid a sickly or feeble old age and live life to the fullest right to the very end. The obvious tradeoff is that you might leave many wonderful years on the table if you take the deal.

Bioethicist Ezekiel Emanuel wrote a controversial piece in *The Atlantic*, "Why I Hope to Die at 75." He notes that while Americans are living longer than ever they're also more likely to be incapacitated in old age with a lower quality of life than those just a couple of generations before. He is not talking about taking his own life and he's not a proponent of assisted suicide. His contention is that once he reaches 75 he will have lived a full life and will no longer submit to life-sustaining medical interventions but adds that he'll happily carry on as long as possible. The medical resources that he would consume as an old person would be better spent on those with their prime years still ahead. His article speaks to the idea of making your time count while you're in the full flush of living, and I concur. The notion of being sickly, shuffling from one doctor's appointment to the next—undergoing an endless round of essentially useless treatments, a sad cog in the medical industrial complex—strikes me as a miserable way to end your life. I also agree with philosopher Alan Watts, who merged eastern thought with western sensibilities in his book *The Wisdom of Insecurity*. Popular in the '60s and '70s, Watts' works are having a resurgence today. "Unhappiness comes from the inability to fully occupy the present," he writes, and then further suggests that "anxiety is caused by the desire to live for the future." Ocean sailors know this to be fundamentally true—we're imprisoned in the present and need to embrace those coordinates or be miserable. Incidentally, Watts also suggested that the marriage of wind and sail was a perfect expression of Taoism, one of the purest ways to live in harmony with nature, and he seems right about that too.

Back aboard *Quetzal* during our Mediterranean Captain's Hour, I uncorked the wine and proposed the deal—78 and out in perfect health or take your chances on a longer life? Fred hated the Faustian nature of the question and refused to answer, claiming that the whole notion was absurd. Nari and Vera were young enough that age 78 seemed far in the future, and they took the deal. Velinda and Jerry were wavering, with Velinda leaning toward taking it and Jerry considering a bet on a longer life. I always take the deal, citing my lifelong belief that the future is a bad bet and also noting that longevity does not seem to be a Kretschmer family trait. The most interesting discussion was between Harry and David.

At 6′7″ Harry barely fit on *Quetzal* and he couldn't stand upright below. Unfazed by a lack of headroom, he and Velinda were frequent shipmates and through the course of many shared adventures, including the Atlantic crossing, had become close friends. I always shoehorned them into the starboard aft cabin, where Harry had to snake his way around the bunk to keep his feet from dangling over the edge. A Harvard-trained doctor and a Barack Obama lookalike, though slightly older, Harry was brilliant, humble, and funny. He took the deal. He had little confidence that fate would deal him a vigorous old age, and although he dreaded leaving Velinda, 15 years his junior, 78 seemed like the right age to, as he put it, "call it a life."

As I mentioned in the last chapter, David was the youngest 74-year-old imaginable. He was mentally sharp and physically fit, with a wiry frame and nary a trace of flab. He could occasionally drive other crewmembers crazy with his nonstop curiosity and self-absorption. At times he was in his own world, evidenced by sleeping through the Ikaria ordeal. But he was lovable and a true friend to me, one of my favorite shipmates. David scoffed at the deal, and rightly so—he was already 74 and going strong. His mother was just shy of her 100th birthday and still a beautiful woman. "I am going to live to be 100 like my mother," he said, and then, laughing, added, "I just hope I have enough money to live that long."

What Harry did not tell me that lazy late afternoon in the Aegean was that the leukemia that I thought was non-life threatening had spread into his bones. He had scheduled the sailing passage between treatments, as he was on a heavy-duty regime of chemotherapy and radiation. He did seem tired but always stood his watch, and was at his witty best. "He was just so happy to be aboard," Velinda told me recently, "he treasured his time on *Quetzal*." That was the last time Harry sailed with me, the last time I would see him. Somehow he held out against the flood tide of tumors spreading throughout his lean and once muscular body, but by December

2015, he was clinging to life. I called his hospital room in Houston but he was unable to take the call. A week later I received this email.

John,

I heard you called last week. It was a rough time and I came very close to seeing what was truly beyond the seventh sea. There is a level of pain that you simply can't handle anymore.

Now doing much better. Tumor has shrunk with radical chemotherapy, although talking is still difficult. I am undergoing physical rehab and will go home as soon as strong enough.

Brother, thanks for your friendship and support, and say "hi" to little John, Fred, Mark, James, David, and all of the other "Kretschmernauts" with whom I have sailed.

Harry

I realized that he was he saying goodbye and felt profound sadness. He kept battling but didn't live much longer. Like every death, it seemed brutally unfair. He and Velinda would not go cruising in their own boat after all, and I ached for her too. I understood, or least tried to understand, that our days at sea had really mattered to Harry, and I clung to that, feeling fortunate to have shared many a watch with an extraordinary man who taught me many things.

Our *Quetzal* Med cruise carried on. I have a nice picture of David and me standing on the quay in Kastellorizo, a tiny Greek island less than two miles off the coast of Turkey. It was the last landfall of the passage, a charming port that by all rights should be Turkish. David and I had taken a stroll to admire the mix of ornately fitted-out gullets, doughty cruising boats, and elegant private yachts all sandwiched together, stern-to the quay. David told me how much he enjoyed sailing with my daughter ("She's sassy, so full of fire") and that he admired Fred's wicked humor. But he was really taken with Harry. "He's so smart and a really great guy. I hope we get the chance to do some real sailing together, not this easy summer stuff in the Med." Just at that moment Fred snapped a photo of us, arms on each other's shoulders, smiling, confident that we'd sail together again soon.

That didn't happen. David decided to buy his own boat, an idea I greatly encouraged. We chatted about boats often and he eventually found a handsome fiberglass folkboat, a small but salty vessel in Toronto, and delivered it back to his homeport in East Hampton, Long Island. He dreamed of sailing to Bermuda. He spent the winter fitting her out, commuting often from his apartment in Manhattan. He launched her the next spring but unfortunately didn't get a chance to sail her very much. In July, he was riding his bike, his typical 30-mile dash out to Montauk Point and back, when he veered in front of a car. He was launched from the bike and landed on his head. He was airlifted to a trauma center in the city but didn't survive. He was 76.

David had signed on for a passage from Newfoundland to Nova Scotia scheduled later that summer, writing me that he needed a "*Quetzal* fix." When I emailed to confirm his spot aboard, he wrote back, "You bet I am coming, can't wait." I received news of his passing in St. Pierre, a small French Island off the coast of Newfoundland. I was stunned and it took a few days to find the words I wanted to share with his son Adam and his long-time partner Marcia. David's death wasn't tragic, it just came a few decades before he'd expected, but he had lived like Zorba and died in the flush of things, riding his bike at full speed. I finally wrote this note.

Adam and Marcia,
I am sitting here aboard *Quetzal*, in St. Pierre, a weird wonderful slice of France, not Quebec, but France, just 12 miles off the coast of Newfoundland. It is just the kind of quirky, intriguing place

that David would have loved. He would have thoroughly enjoyed sailing here too, slicing through the fog and bucking a strong wind. I could use his French to help me organize a rigging repair, and he would have loved that too. I close my eyes and see him bounding about the streets, finding a good restaurant for dinner, and chatting with a local shopkeeper.

I am sure the pain of his tragic passing must be brutal for you both. I confess, I had a breakdown yesterday thinking about him as I puttered about the boat. He was a true friend to me, he loved me like a son, and he taught me many things. His zest for life was remarkable and what always amazed me was his genuine sense of awe. He was almost childlike in his appreciation of the moment, somehow he was able to see things for the first time but also with great wisdom. I don't know how he did it, he was a unique and wonderful man and I will miss him so damn much.

I realize that I knew David only later in his life but I contend that sailing together, especially on long passages and across oceans, is one of the best ways to know anybody. You can't hide at sea on a small boat and David relished his time on the ocean. Nobody has ever enjoyed an Atlantic crossing more. He would marvel at a pod of whales and then passionately describe the book he was reading. He and I exchanged many books, and that's a sign of great friendship. He always suggested fascinating books, and we loved talking about them. He was connected to the world, never cynical, and relentlessly curious. He was the youngest 70-something person imaginable.

We sailed the Caribbean from top to bottom, the Mediterranean in the summer and winter, the Atlantic from Florida to Nova Scotia, the Pacific and the Galapagos, so many places, so many adventures, so many good times. He was a great friend of my boat *Quetzal*. When I needed money for a project, he loaned me it without a blink or question. He loved being aboard, and despite his age, was always willing to bunk in the pilot berth. He rejoiced when the engine was switched off and we swished along under sail alone, the sound of the boat cutting through the sea was a beautiful song to David. I am sorry for you both but feel fortunate to have had such a fine friend. David will live on in our memories.

So, dear reader, you must be thinking, what's up with Kretschmer? All this focus on sadness and death, this is the guy who celebrates life, who pays homage to Aristotle's notion of eudaemonia, the so-called good life out there waiting for us once we shove off? Well, none of us gets out of this life sentence alive, and only by framing life with death can we realize the value of our days. Deep ocean sailing takes us to the very edge of time, to a natural place where time matters profoundly and where our own borders are not defined by length and beam, but by our imagination and zest for living. I relish a set of coordinates where I must rely on my own resolve, where my decisions have consequences, and where the sense of community aboard my boat transcends pettiness, politics, and religion. The future is as valuable only as a week-out GRIB file, the past useful only in the lessons learned that serve the moment. Life is another name for the present, and while it's getting harder to find the present these days, I am happy to report that there's still an abundance of it at sea.

Back in Marmaris after a week's jaunt along the Turkish coast and calling at a few Greek isles, I bade farewell to the crew. My daughter Nari and I spent a few days cleaning up the boat, and then took a bus to Izmir and a flight to Dublin. As the plane banked south before heading west, the marina in Kuşadası came into view. Mom and Tim loved Turkey, and Kuşadası, which was much less touristy then, in particular. They spent a happy six months based in the marina, maybe their happiest time together, as they bought a small car and drove throughout the Mideast and Europe over the winter. They continued crossing the Mediterranean the next spring, but sadly their voyage was cut short when Tim died from a sudden aneurysm. Mom regrouped, as she always did, and a year later joined the Peace Corps, at age 66. She was stationed in Fiji and thoroughly enjoyed the experience. Upon returning to the U.S. she was awarded the prestigious Lillian Carter Award in recognition of her volunteer contributions.

Mother of seven, grandmother to a score more, she was brilliant, beautiful, and had a will of steel. She was a wife, world sailor, sage, and my true friend. She died in 1999 at age 76, content with her life. Dying may have been her finest moment as she pulled it off in her own house, in her own bed, and on her own terms. She was able to have her children fly down, alone, without spouses or children, to say goodbye. My sister Terri and I lived nearby and, along with the hospice nurse, were with her around the clock her last few days. She told us again and again that she'd had a wonderful life and was ready to die. Her last words were, "I am ready." We held her hands as she claimed her last breath. Almost as if planned, she died on her first-born child's birthday, passing the matriarchal torch to my sister Kathy.

Back in the plane with my lovely daughter sitting next me, and my mother's favorite marina in view below, I felt suspended in time. I was too old to die young, which, considering the life I've led, was a victory, and realized that if I choked on a Turkish peanut and called it a day right then, I'd have been more than happy with the way things had played out. Sure I had plenty of unfinished business: dreams and schemes were piled up like unread books next to my bunk; our children were just venturing into adulthood and I was curious to see what direction that would take them; and I had a love affair that was blossoming and filled with promise;

but, like my mother before me, I was also content with my life and I am not sure you can, or should, ask for more.

Leaving death aside, I am inspired by stories of survival, which of course have power because they circle close to death but cheat it in the end. Steve Callahan's classic, *Adrift*—the story of his 76 days in a life raft after his boat sinks—is one of the best nautical books ever written and certainly on my all-time-favorites list. I recently read Laura Hillenbrand's remarkable story about WWII airman and Olympian Louis Zamperini, *Unbroken*. I am suspect of bestsellers, maybe it's envy, but I confess Hillenbrand had me from the first sentence. I read the book on one flight. Zamperini's physical and emotional ordeal in a life raft after a plane crash near Midway Island exemplifies the will to survive. The bitter irony of finally making landfall on an island occupied by the Japanese and enduring the raw savagery of a POW camp afterward reveals a wellspring of human spirit that defies simple explanation. I was intrigued by Zamperini's incredible ingenuity as he and his two mates drifted in the Pacific for 36 days in a disintegrating raft. After finishing *Unbroken*, I searched my haphazard collection of 2,000 books and found my treasured copy of Harold Gatty's original *The Raft Book*. Written for aviators and mariners during WWII (unfortunately neither Callahan nor Zamperini had the book aboard their rafts), it's a treasure of natural navigation, complete with tables for measuring latitude from the sunrise, charts of ocean currents, and a navigational guide to seabirds. It's also full of commonsense suggestions as well as encouraging messages to inspire those clinging to life in a raft. Paging through the book, I found that I had highlighted this sentence: "The ability to observe, and the ability to see little things, that seem trivial at first, may become amazingly important and meaningful." Gatty was the greatest navigator of his time, combining in his books and writings what were then state-of-the-art celestial navigation techniques for aviation and marine uses with natural navigational tips and secrets from indigenous wayfinders. I had a copy of *The Raft Book* on *Gigi* during our Cape Horn passage, and Gatty's last book, *Finding Your Way Without Map or Compass*, has always been aboard *Quetzal*.

My current edition of Gatty's book, along with many other books aboard *Quetzal* for that matter, was a present from my friends Dan and Linda who live in a former ship captain's house that leans over Marblehead Harbor, the storied seaport north of Boston. Linda worked for a major publishing company and Dan is a voracious reader of everything nautical. Dan is also a survivor, to put it gently. He's had many life-and-death adventures and jokes that he's currently living his ninth life. One of Dan's close brushes with death, which seems amusing now but was anything but when it happened, points to just how vulnerable we are when stranded on a sailboat during a medical emergency.

Sixteen years ago I chartered a 44´ cutter in Mystic, Connecticut, for the purpose of scattering a dear friend's remains in the waters off Block Island Sound. Don, or "Poppy," as he was known to most of us, was my friend, and then later my mother's companion. Originally from upstate New York, he had retired to Fort Lauderdale but never really fit in to the South Florida scene. He made a half-hearted attempt at being a yacht broker but he wasn't nearly cutthroat enough to survive in that tough racket, and eventually contented himself with doing good works in the community and living off his meager savings and social security. He lived aboard his tired Columbia 45 motorsailer and sailed with me on a few yacht deliveries, including a passage from Fort Lauderdale to Costa Rica via the Panama Canal. He always invited me over to the boat when I was in town for a "home"-cooked meal. Like my father, he had been a B26 bomber pilot in WWII. Unlike my father, he relished his war experience and rehashed his exploits with anyone who would listen. He also had a copy of Gatty's *The Raft Book* sitting on a wobbly tray table in his main saloon where we'd pore over the charts.

Cancer, that insatiable malady that seems to attack every family, eventually found its way into Poppy's lungs, making him gravely ill. I visited him in the hospital a few times but I confess, I find no solace in hospitals, they give me the chills, and I didn't see him as much as I should have. He called me the day before he died and said that he was in terrible pain but that he found temporary relief by picturing himself at sea, sailing before a steady trade wind. There must be something about sailing as a metaphor for a last refuge, a place of peace amid the terror and uncertainty of dying. Writer, transcendentalist, and occasional river sailor Henry David Thoreau's last-known words were "and now the good sailing comes." Poppy had honeymooned, and later vacationed, on Block Island during his younger, happier days before his marriage failed. I solemnly promised that after he died I would find a boat and take his ex-wife and six children sailing and spread his ashes in Block Island Sound.

Poppy donated his body to science, so it was a couple of years before his ashes turned up and I made plans with his family to carry out my promise. I mentioned this unusual mission to Dan, and he immediately volunteered to be my first mate, telling me that he "needed some sailing." I had met Dan and his brother Paul when I delivered Paul's boat, an older but lovely Hinckley Bermuda 40 sloop, from St. Thomas to New England, and we all became great friends. Like his older brother, Paul is literary minded and his former house on Beacon Hill in Boston was so stuffed with books it was hard to open the door. A friend of Irish poet and Nobel laureate Seamus Heaney, Paul was a pallbearer at Heaney's funeral. Both Sullivan brothers are smart, full of life in that charming Irish way, and very successful businessmen. Dan's also an accomplished sailor and has owned a series of interesting boats, including a Rhodes 19 that he raced quite successfully around Marblehead, an Alberg 37 that he lost in Hurricane Bob (a storm I knew intimately), and his then-current boat, a handsome Pacific Seacraft 40 cutter.

Dan picked me up at the airport in Hartford, Connecticut, and we made our way to Mystic. Our plan was to sail out to Block Island, just 20 miles to the east, and rendezvous with Poppy's ex-wife and family the next day. The family was staying on the island, in the same hotel where Poppy and his bride had spent their honeymoon. After the ceremony, we'd drop the family off and Dan and I would sail back to Mystic—but not before detouring around the Sound, enjoying a couple of days of sailing as a reward for our good deed.

As we loaded our gear aboard I noticed that Dan was sluggish and sweating profusely. He confided that he'd actually been to the hospital the previous day with chest pains. After a thorough examination, including a stress test, the doctor concluded that he was healthy, just literally overstressed and suffering from reflux. He suggested that a sailing trip was just what he needed. Dan had recently negotiated the sale of his business, a stressful process indeed, but one that netted him a lot of money.

"Are you sure you're OK?" I asked Dan. "You don't have to come, I can do this by myself, it's not a big deal."

"I'm fine," he insisted, "it will do me good to go sailing. Besides," he added with a laugh, "if I die on the way you can do a two-for-one service and drop me overboard along with old Poppy."

We cast off, cleared the railroad bridge, and started motoring down the long marked channel toward Fishers Island Sound. Just past Ram Island I raised the main, unfurled the jib, and shut down the engine. Dan looked terrible. We both agreed that something was clearly wrong, and that it made no sense for him to sail out to Block Island. I started to tack to return to Mystic when I noticed that Dan seemed pale and had a glazed look in his eyes. Then he clutched his chest and I watched the color drain out of him even more. I dashed for the radio just as he came to.

"I'm OK," he said, obviously in pain. "It's just that damn reflux."

"You're not OK, Dan; something is seriously wrong, we are going back now," I said, my voice shaky. "I am calling the Brewer marina, they're the closest marina, and tell them to have an ambulance standing by."

"You don't need to do that."

"Dan, just try to relax." I forced him to take a slug of water and swallow an aspirin. I rigged a makeshift shade over him, started the engine, and dropped the sails. I wanted to get back to the marina as quickly as possible. Just as I returned to the wheel and pushed the throttle ahead he clutched his chest again. Within seconds his color disappeared—he was completely white, as if someone had opened a petcock and drained the blood from his body. I put out a MAYDAY on the VHF radio and, trying to remain calm, announced my plan to make all speed toward the Brewer marina fuel dock. Although it was less than two miles away, and we were motoring at 7 knots, the distance closed slowly. I soon heard the wail of the ambulance and prayed to whatever gods that might intervene that Dan would still be alive when we reached them.

Waiting until the very last moment, I slammed the boat into reverse and careened alongside the dock. The crew at Brewer had cleared the fuel dock and the EMS team was standing by. I threw the stern line to the dockhand and the second it was secured, two first responders jumped aboard. Checking his pulse, one of them said, "We got nothing, we need juice right now." They immediately set up a defibrillator and zapped him, shocking his heart back to life. His heart was beating, but just barely, as we all lifted him off the boat and into the ambulance.

I rode in the ambulance to the nearest hospital in New London. It was touch-and-go—twice the paramedics had to shock him to keep his heart pumping. They wheeled him directly into the emergency room. I waited outside. Twenty minutes later the young doctor came out to talk to me. He was subdued. "Can I speak frankly?" he asked. I nodded my head. "We really don't know why your friend is still alive, he's suffered a massive heart attack." He was pacing nervously. "We don't have the ability to do invasive heart procedures at this hospital. All we can do is give him a large dose of blood thinners, but the truth is that will almost assure he'll have serious brain damage, and that's on the very unlikely chance that he survives. I don't mean to be so direct but I suggest you contact his family ASAP; this does not look good. And by the way, do I have your authority to administer the drugs?"

"My authority, why me? I am just his friend."

"You're the one who brought him, and we don't know how to contact his family. There's no time to waste."

Shaking my head, I couldn't believe this was happening. A sailing trip to scatter one friend's ashes had turned into another's fight to survive.

"Go ahead, do what you think is best."

The doctor returned a few minutes later.

"We gave him the dose but there's no change, he's just clinging to life."

I had grabbed Dan's PalmPilot—an electronic gizmo that predated smartphones for storing data—from the boat but couldn't open it as every password I tried failed as I desperately tried to reach his family. Then I had an idea. We had to get Dan to a better hospital—no matter what—and I asked the doctor where that was. He said that the hospital at Yale, in New Haven, was the best cardiac hospital around but assured me that Dan would not survive the helicopter flight, adding that it would be an expensive waste of money.

"Screw the money," I blurted out. "Dan can buy the damn helicopter, let's do it, we have to try." The helicopter was arranged and they were soon airborne, whisking Dan toward Yale. After many phone calls—do you know how many Dan Sullivans there are in Boston area codes?—I finally managed to reach Linda back in Marblehead and gave her the sobering news. She was amazingly calm and thanked me, and said in a steady tone, "Don't ever underestimate Dan." I made my way back to the boat, found Dan's car keys, his small bag and his watch, and drove to New Haven. Linda and I arrived about the same time and the doctor grimly informed us that although Dan was alive, his chances of survival were slim. They had done emergency heart surgery and installed a balloon stent in his coronary artery but he was in a coma. I waited through the night with Linda before returning to Mystic. I still had ashes to scatter back at Block Island. I hugged Linda and, placing Dan's watch on my wrist, told her, "I won't take it off until Dan walks out of this hospital." It was reassuring bluster—I was certain that I'd never see my friend again.

I found the boat at the Brewer marina—they had secured it in a slip and refused to charge me for dockage. I then sailed to Block Island and picked up Poppy's family. Despite a blustery day with near-gale-force winds and driving rains, we had a beautiful ceremony, scattering his ashes into the Sound. But all I could think about was Dan back in New Haven. I dropped off the family and sailed through the stormy night back to Mystic. I returned the boat and drove Dan's car back to the hospital. I was a zombie when I arrived and Linda informed me that nothing had changed, but she remained strangely optimistic. I assumed it was just her way of coping with the grief that was imminent. I stayed another night and then flew home.

I called Linda every day for a week—there was no change in Dan's condition, he was still in a coma. I had to get back to work. I was a yacht delivery skipper in those days, and I had to deliver a new Hylas 49 from Fort Lauderdale to the Virgin Islands. I was away for a week, completing the 1,000-mile slog to windward in six days, just another working passage for a working sailor, and then flew back to Fort Lauderdale. The next day the phone rang. Picking it up, I was shocked to hear Dan's voice. "Hey," he said, "how's it going?" I couldn't respond. Finally I muttered, "Dan?"

"Ya, it's me, sorry for the trouble I caused. By the way, I heard you stole my watch."

Sixteen years later Dan is still going strong. He just turned 80. He's had several heart incidents, leukemia, and a range of other maladies but he battles through them all with a combination of physical and mental strength, guts—and willingness to try different options—and an unquenchable human spirit. When I think of Dan, and the happy years he's enjoyed with his now-adult children and lovely wife Linda, I realize that my "78 and out" hypothetical question is a nonstarter. Life, every damn second of it, is to be lived—it's the spirit and the content that matters, not the years or page count.

Postscript

Dan later told me that after he emerged from the coma he was known in the Yale cardiac ward as the "miracle man." For several weeks he had around-the-clock care and, as is his wont, became great friends with the nurses. One night, one of the nurses asked, "Do you remember anything at all from the time when you were, technically, dead?" Dan told him that he did. The nurse was amazed. "Can you tell me about it?" he asked in a hushed tone. Dan replied cheerily, "Sure."

"I remember being in this long white tunnel, I wasn't sure where it was leading." The nurse hung on his every word. "Did you see anything else?" he asked.

"I did, actually," Dan continued. "I saw flames, that's when I turned around and came back." It took a few seconds for the nurse to realize that Dan was joking.

FOUR

STORIES IN THE STREAM

Gulf Stream Strategies • Autumn Atlantic Storms •
Heaving-To • Central American Cruising • Aground in the
Bay Islands, Honduras • Timeless Cruising in Ranguana Cay

"There is a river in the ocean. In the severest droughts it never fails, and in the mightiest floods it never overflows. Its banks and its bottom are of cold water, while its current is of warm. The Gulf of Mexico is its fountain, and its mouth is in the Arctic Seas. It is the Gulf Stream. There is in the world no other such majestic flow of waters."

—Matthew Fontaine Maury, *The Physical Geography*
of the Sea (1855)

"He sighed in astonishment and worry. He had been a seaman all his life. Like his people a thousand years before him, he had plied the deep blue waters and treacherous shallows in great canoes, laden with honey, salt, slaves, chocolate. He had fought enemies upon its rolling surface, had ridden out great storms, he knew every port and people that graced its shores. The sea was his world, world *of his ancestors, great and dangerous and rich in precious, holy things. Now it had vomited up this monstrosity—a canoe that was a house."*

—Linda Schele and David Freidel, *A Forest of Kings*
(a fictionalized account of Mayan mariners first
encountering Columbus's fleet in 1502)

The Atlantic, South of Lunenburg, Nova Scotia, October 2014

Quetzal is a workhorse, no kelp grows under her keel—she earns her keep logging bluewater miles year after year. After her Mediterranean interlude where mortality talk ruled the cockpit she made way her back across the Atlantic in January. She then sailed up the East Coast in April and spent the summer exploring northern latitudes in Newfoundland and Labrador. By late October she was poised in Lunenburg, Nova Scotia, and we were making final preparations for our annual rite of passage—the voyage to the Caribbean. The 1,600-mile run south to St. Martin is always interesting and invariably lives up to its billing as a heavy-weather passage. While the weather conditions can range from appalling to "not that bad," the X-factor is the Gulf Stream. First mapped by Benjamin Franklin, this "river in the sea," as pioneering oceanographer Matthew Fontaine Maury later called it, needs to be negotiated with great care. Getting across it is always the first waypoint on a passage south.

Sitting at the bar in the Grand Banker, a cozy restaurant overlooking the almost-empty harbor (most sensible sailors had already departed for warmer climes), I pored over the latest Gulf Stream downloads with the freshly arrived crew, who were brimming with nervous excitement about the upcoming passage. According to infrared satellite data, the northern reach of the Gulf Stream was confused, zigzagging in every direction like a punch-drunk boxer trying to stay off the ropes. Conventional wisdom suggests that the world's most potent current, and one of the planet's major climate drivers, follows a well-worn path as it rumbles unperturbed most of the way across the Atlantic. A vast corridor of warm, ultramarine water that intrigues scientists, inspires artists, and unsettles the stomachs of unsuspecting sailors, the Gulf Stream is a western boundary current that traces the edge of the continental shelf off the coast of the United States. The Stream, as sailors often call it, closes with land as it approaches the Carolinas and nearly kisses the sandy but treacherous headland of Cape Hatteras before arcing east toward open sea.

Historians have never given Maury his due—he should be better known for his climatic accomplishments. I am a bit obsessed with nautical history, I'll admit it, but there are worse faults. Not long ago—last year, in fact—I was explaining this vital nugget of history to my daughter Annika. She'd flown up to Maryland, where *Quetzal* was being refit, to give me the rather shocking news that she was engaged. I was having trouble digesting this new state of affairs and decided to take a day off from boat work and visit the Civil War battlefield of Chancellorsville. Annika's also a history buff and, more importantly, it was a two-hour drive, which gave us time to talk. As we were driving, I noticed a small, nondescript historical marker off Virginia Route 218. Annika soon found herself schlepping up an overgrown forest trail to visit the birthplace of Matthew Fontaine Maury.

"I had no idea he was born here," I said, huffing but excited, and relieved to divert our conversation away from her upcoming marriage. "His pilot charts and sailing directions are among the most important navigational developments of all time," I assured her, "right up there with the compass, Mercator's projection, and Harrison's chronometers." She rolled her eyes. "They helped make climate a science and U.S. shipping dominant in the sailing age. Our ships were leaving the British in their wakes because we knew where the favorable winds and currents were."

It was hard to say if Annika was less impressed with Maury's great accomplishment or with the sad pile of rocks that marked his birthplace, but she's a good kid and cheerfully bounded along the trail with her old man. I never seem to catch up with history but I do make discoveries along the way and they're always rooted in the present—like my coming to terms with the astonishing fact that my baby girl was now a lovely young woman soon to be married. Kids are the tree rings of our life, navigational aids in what can seem like an empty sea. While we may not spot the gray hairs or wrinkles in our own reflections, our kids' milestones are confirmation that we are indeed getting older.

The Gulf Stream forks rear the Azores archipelago, with one branch, the North Atlantic Current, shooting off to the northeast. Although this current is mysteriously losing steam of late, and its climatic role has been questioned by some scientists, most agree that it's still the primary source of the moderating temperatures that keep England and Ireland mild in the winter and that it's why the English have the hutzpah to call the Scillies, off Cornwall, their tropical isles. The other branch, the Canary Current, turns south off the coast of Portugal before tracking back west across the tropical North Atlantic, fueled by the steady northeast trade winds. This gyre, the clockwise rotation of winds and currents around a dominant high-pressure system (in the Northern Hemisphere, that is—it's the opposite in the Southern Hemisphere) is caused by the winds being stiff-armed to the right by the earth's rotation. This effect, named for the French mathematician who first described it, Gustave Coriolis, creates the prevailing winds that have escorted sailors back and forth across the Atlantic for five centuries.

Back in Lunenburg a powerful blast of wind shook the Grand Banker, and the old building seemed to sway like a ship at anchor. It was a little kiss from Neptune, a not-so-gentle reminder of what loomed ahead once we cleared the harbor breakwalls the next day. Collecting ourselves, we returned to the printed current diagrams on the table. While the main body of the Stream was behaving itself, churning eastward approximately 300 miles south of Lunenburg, there was mayhem to the north. Two significant meanders—wave-like deviations from the main current—as well as a host of small eddies spinning off the meanders, promised to make the passage more challenging. We would be picking our way through a minefield.

"This one is trouble," Bruce noted, pointing to a sliver of red jutting north. Studying the color legend, with brighter shades representing stronger drifts, or current speeds, he added, "It's flying, it looks like it's moving at 4 knots. That will stop us dead in our tracks, and it's due south of Lunenburg."

"This is definitely the place to be," Mike B. chimed in, "but it's way east of the rhumb line."

He was noting another slash of bright red. The current arrows showed it flowing south, which would translate into a nice boost as we headed toward Bermuda, but reaching this favorable meander required a significant detour from the straight-line course. Complicating both meanders was the wind model, which I had also downloaded and printed out earlier that morning. It showed a moderate westerly breeze, ideal for our departure the following day, gradually fading away. A near gale nor'easter was predicted to rake the waters 36 hours later, followed by a massive cold front producing strong but favorable northwest winds. How this dynamic weather window would play out amid the caprices of the Gulf Stream was a hell of a good question.

Despite the meteorological uncertainty, I was excited about the passage. I'm always excited about passages, about getting offshore where days unfold with a natural rhythm, and where wind, waves, and clouds regain their status in the hierarchy of what you pay attention to. *Quetzal* was ready too. She was in top condition. She had a new heavy-weather staysail made by a local Lunenburg sail loft and a beefy upgraded traveler for better mainsail control. The canvas dodger had been repaired and new cockpit weather cloths were lashed along the lifelines. Alan—who hailed from Lunenburg and whom you've met in earlier chapters—and I had also installed a new satellite communication system that supposedly would allow us to consistently download GRIB files underway, but I had my doubts. "I am tired of being responsible for you," he joked. "I think you actually like stressing me out with these heavy-weather passages." Like most mariners in Nova Scotia, Alan has an intuitive understanding of how fronts interact, nurtured from years of enduring the region's bipolar weather conditions. He was *Quetzal's* volunteer weather router, and he took the job seriously. He's a busy guy, and it was not only time-consuming, as he analyzed GRIB files every morning, suggesting strategies and insights that he then sent to me via satellite text, but, as he said, stressful. "Now you can blame the experts when the weather goes to shit and I won't have to feel guilty." He was trying to be earnest but I knew he'd continue to pay close attention to our route—sometimes I think he worried more about the passages than I did.

I had a great crew assembled for what was sure to be an intense learning experience, which of course is JK code for cold, wet, and miserable—priceless, in other words. Most were former shipmates and good friends as well. Bruce, from British Columbia, sailed on *Quetzal's* very first training passage and he's accompanied me many times since, including on challenging northern voyages. He's a friend, a fine sailor, and a terrific shipmate—strong and steady under duress—it's just a shame that his jokes are not always as sound as his judgment. It's always a relief knowing he's aboard and I know his judgment is seasoned from years in the remote bush of British Columbia, where mistakes are not long tolerated. Mike B. and Mike F., both from Minneapolis, had sailed with me previously, including on heavy-weather passages. Mike B., who took the cover shot for my book *Sailing a Serious Ocean*, is hopelessly addicted to offshore sailing. He has been known to steer for hours on end, deriving endless pleasure from that near-mystical relationship between sail, keel, rudder, and wheel. No matter the conditions, he's perched behind the helm, swaying to the boat's natural rhythm, and the silly grin on his face says he wouldn't want to be anyplace else. Mike F. is a bear of a man. A former college football player, he is renowned for his good cheer in spite of hatches leaking over his bunk, and for telling hilarious stories. They both have Robert Perry–designed cruising boats built by Passport Yachts and are making plans for serious voyaging. They both also have talented and lovely wives who share their cruising dreams.

John and Cindy have sailed with me time and again, on voyages all over the world, from the Mediterranean to the Caribbean, from the Galapagos to Nova Scotia. They are signed aboard for an upcoming transatlantic passage, which they see as their graduation. They have a handsome Valiant 42 that they've been diligently preparing for extensive cruising as they methodically accumulate sea time and patiently see their kids through college. The only line lacking on their *Quetzal* résumé was the heavy-weather passage, and they were about to check that box with a vengeance. Judy, from Texas, rounded out the crew. A fresh *Quetzal* victim, she was justifiably nervous but always armed with a smile. She had just bought a 32′ Island Packet cutter and harbored dreams of singlehanding to distant islands. That they all survived the passage is a testament to the power of dreams.

We planned a two-part voyage. Leg One, 700 miles from Lunenburg to Bermuda, included two main variables: coping with potentially bitter temperatures and, as noted earlier, crossing the Gulf Stream, which could be especially tough if it was in a foul mood. The second leg, 900 miles to St. Martin, is decidedly warmer and usually less demanding, though often a slog if the prevailing easterlies have a southern slant. I have made this passage many times and have determined that leaving earlier, in late October, is a better bet than leaving in November. The weather is less volatile and the chance of encountering gales is reduced. Indeed, there should not even be a question about this strategy. However, most boats, including the armada of sailboats that leave New England and the Chesapeake Bay every year bound south, usually wait until November to shove off. Why? Because their insurance policies dictate when and where they can sail and still be covered.

It's all about hurricanes, or more specifically, named tropical storms. Most insurance companies have deemed November 1 as the magical day when the threat of encountering named storms has reduced enough that sailboats can safely venture offshore. It's crazy. The potential risk from late-season hurricanes pales when compared with deep low-pressure systems spawning gale-force northeast winds that collide with the Gulf Stream. These "nor'easters" intensify in November and some years roll out to sea every three or four days. They're the root source of many legendary storms, including the so-called Perfect Storm described in Sebastian Junger's bestseller of the same name.

Late-season hurricanes are almost always extratropical by the time they reach the Gulf Stream, between 35 and 40 degrees north latitude. The temperature difference between the cool air above and the warm waters below tends to suck tropical energy out of the tightly wound eye wall. Extratropical storms move fast, propelled by upper-level troughs typically associated with west winds, their potential to inflict damage limited because they don't linger in the same location for long. They become less cyclonic and actually expand in size, but lose intensity in the process. I am not suggesting that late-season hurricanes are not incredibly dangerous, and it's always a dicey proposition riding out a tropical storm of any kind in a small boat.

Late-season extratropical storms typically do not spawn the huge, confused seas that make a prolonged nor'easter deadly. It's almost always the seas that cause catastrophic damage to small boats, not the wind. Also, you'd have to be oblivious to all forms of news and weather to miss hurricane warnings. They're tracked relentlessly from the moment they form. Like football games, they're ideal for media coverage, including plenty of time for expert analysis and commercials. Nor'easters, on the other hand, are more unpredictable, certainly in terms of intensity, and because they tend to impact only mariners, not land interests, they are not nearly as well publicized.

We shoved off October 25. It was overcast and a bit clammy, but the southwest wind was favorable and steady at 15 knots, perfect sailing conditions. *Quetzal* sliced through gray lumpy seas with a sense of urgency—she was ready for warmer climes and seemed to know the way. We had made the decision to head east-southeast, a course well to the left, or east, of the rhumb line. We hoped to hitch a ride on the edge of the south-setting meander that, according the latest satellite models, had intensified.

The long-term outlook showed that the strong northwest winds we were counting on were likely to be short lived. Hopefully they'd blow just long enough to escort us across the main body of the Stream. Looking further out, three or four days—which in the North Atlantic is about as valid as choosing a mate based on her astrological sign—the forecast showed nothing but moderate winds, primarily from the east. We knew the Gulf Stream would kick us east, even as we made our way across as quickly as possible by sailing at a right angle to the current, but we were not overly concerned. Buoyed by a Panglossian belief in the forecast, we were convinced that once we reached the other side of the Stream it would be a pleasant reach all the way to Bermuda. It was an elaborate plan and a far cry from the pre-GRIB-file days when you shoved off, aimed for Bermuda and endured whatever weather came your way. It looked beautiful on the computer screen, pure navigational poetry. In the back of my mind I heard Neptune snickering.

The first night of a passage is always telling. The excitement of pushing off the dock has worn off, the cameras and phones have been put away, wool caps, sea boots, foul-weather bibs, and jackets are de rigueur. You feel weighed down with gear, expectations, and doubts. The sobering safety talk is complete and every person aboard knows that falling off the boat in the 50-degree waters would be a likely death sentence. Bermuda—which seemed so close staring at the chart the night before in the Grand Banker, just an outstretched hand away—is suddenly a long way off, sequestered beyond an ugly horizon. Time calculated at 7 knots, or maybe 6 knots, or maybe less—and not always heading toward your destination—is a calculation that requires a sanguine nature to not let it drag you down. But there's just no rushing an ocean passage, and questions percolate in your mind: "Why am I out here, and did I actually pay for this?" The prewatch meal has either settled, or, in many cases, not settled, and sleep is hard to come by for even seasoned sailors. Sailing in the North, in the fall, when ominous cloud layers circle the horizon and undermine confidence in an already uncertain forecast, requires confidence in your boat, in your crew, and in yourself. It's not a casual enterprise. It's serious sailing.

The winds held steady through the night but picked up in the morning. The motion became noticeably rougher as we plowed into building seas. Nobody was interested in breakfast. Unfortunately Cindy was not feeling well. She's a remarkable woman who has overcome physical ailments that would have defeated a less determined person. She's a pharmacist by training and an adventurer by spirit. She and John have backcountry camped, hiked to the bottom of the Grand Canyon, and ridden motorcycles across country. They viewed sailing as the ultimate way to combine their passions for travel and adventure. Cindy's desire at that moment, however, was to make it through the next hour. With each breaking wave she was feeling worse.

Luckily we reached the intersection of the 42nd parallel and the 62nd meridian—the proverbial X on the chart, the waypoint where we hoped to join the parade of water flowing south—just as the weather started to deteriorate. The winds continued to back to the southeast as the low-pressure system deepened. The original forecast calling for gale-force winds proved accurate. So much for our elaborate plan—it was already falling apart and we had to cope with it. Scanning the horizon through 360 degrees offered little hope that things were going to get better soon. On nasty days hope springs from within, from experience, from knowing that offshore sailing unfolds minute by minute, and you need to embrace that notion because the alternative is a one-way passage to despair.

We shortened sail in degrees. We had tied a single reef in the mainsail the first night, and then tucked in the second reef early the next morning. Each time we reefed the main we rolled in a bit of the headsail—it's vital to keep your sails balanced. If you are sailing upwind you can't take the easy way out and reef just one sail, typically the headsail, which is almost always less of a project to shorten than the mainsail. Your sails need to be proportional and analogous to the conditions. The ability to make your sails small and still efficient is critical to successful upwind sailing in breezy conditions. It's another flaw—unequal sail plans—of many modern boats, but we'll talk more about that later. (See the Appendix: Wrinkles.)

As we headed into our second night, *Quetzal* was trimmed for a slugfest. We had taken the third reef in the main, set the staysail, and rolled in the headsail altogether. With just two small sails we had the boat under control, the autopilot was coping, and we were making great speed with a nice assist from the current—but the ride was brutal. It was wet on deck, wet in the cockpit, and wet below. Breaking seas were sweeping over the boat, not an unusual occurrence given *Quetzal's* low freeboard—and it's inevitable that some of that curious water finds its way below. Much of it plunged through the leaking hatch above Mike F.'s bunk. The crew was looking at the prospect of a second sleepless night.

Balancing in the galley and trying to cook in those conditions was a challenge. Bruce, lending a hand, braced himself along the low side and propped his foot against mine to prevent me from literally falling out of the galley. Despite being flung about and frantically clutching seven bowls that were launched across the counter with every lurch, I was determined to produce a hot meal, even if was just a bowl of spaghetti. I cook in all but the worst conditions as I know that both a hot meal and a sense of normalcy are helpful to the crew. "Hey, it can't be that bad, he's down below cooking." Then I had a really good idea.

"Let's heave-to," I announced, popping up through the companionway. "We'll have to tack twice though, to make sure we heave-to on port tack." It had dawned on me that we didn't need to pound into the wind, essentially forereaching, to make way. We could simply park the boat, or heave-to, and let the south-setting meander carry us along. Heaving-to is a technique that essentially stalls the boat by backing the sails and locking the wheel. I wanted to make sure that when we came to rest, with the wind approximately 50–60 degrees off the port bow, we were aiming south—hence the need to tack twice.

Sailboats don't change directions, or tack, very often on ocean passages. Even if you're beating against the wind, in essence laying angles of 45 to 50 degrees against your course line, you might typically tack every 6 hours at the most. On many long passages, when the winds are right, we've gone days, even weeks, without tacking a single time.

Mike B. was at the wheel and he brought the boat into the wind. After trimming the sheets we were heading about 100 degrees off course. On the second tack we brought the boat into the wind again but did not release the staysail sheet. The mainsail flopped a bit until we found the right balance with the wheel. The staysail was trying to pull *Quetzal* through the wind while the mainsail and rudder were trying to steer her back into the wind. We were stalled. It was a thing of beauty, as if Aeolus had abruptly called in sick—suddenly the same 35 knots of wind that had made our life miserable a few minutes before were now quite manageable. *Quetzal* was happily hove-to, crabbing slowly to leeward, but thanks to the current making 5 knots, right on course. Not only does heaving-to ease the motion, but also the natural slick that forms to windward of the hull tends to prevent seas from breaking aboard. In short, life aboard took a dramatic turn for the better.

"Not too shabby," Bruce chimed as we tweaked the sheet leads and wheel position to find the right balance. "Let's just drift to Bermuda. I love it."

"Well, this is another thing I was hoping to learn," John announced. "I'd read about heaving-to in a storm but didn't really think it would work."

"This almost feels like cheating," Mike F. added with a laugh.

Feeling a bit smug, and hungry, as always, I announced, "It's dinner time, who wants some spaghetti?"

"Not Mayan spaghetti?" Mike B. asked in a mocking tone. "It's too early in the passage for that!"

"No, Mike, not Mayan spaghetti, you're right, we're not that desperate, not yet anyway."

"What's Mayan spaghetti?" Judy wondered, concerned, and for the first time in two days, Cindy laughed. "Well, Judy, it's a better story than dish, that's for damn sure, and I think the captain needs to tell it over dinner. Just hearing a story about the tropics will make me feel warmer." Cindy was feeling better.

Lying hove-to in the Gulf Stream must be what it's like being in orbit, inexorably pulled along by an invisible force that you have no control over, literally going with the flow. Moving without the effort of sailing felt as though time was suspended, that somehow these miles made good toward Bermuda were free, or at least that they should be deducted from the total at the end of the voyage. After two days of holding on tight, whether moving about, sitting, or even lying down, the easy motion was a welcome reprieve. Cindy was right, with our core muscles relaxed it was a perfect time for storytelling. I love stories, telling them and listening to them, and have found that they do more for crew morale than stern-faced lectures. Bruce and I served up the spaghetti in deep-sided bowls and the crew huddled in the cockpit like cowboys around a campfire. I took a bite, swallowed, and began. "It was back in my Mayan Period...."

I had spent several off-and-on years in the '90s exploring the shallows behind the Belize Reef and sojourning on the nearby islands of Honduras and Mexico. Through conducting research for a film about Mayan mariners, building and launching a replica Mayan sailing canoe with university students, and cruising the area extensively in my own steel ketch, I had come to know the pristine waters and intriguing characters that make this far corner of the western Caribbean alluring.

While stone pyramids rising from dark jungles conjure images of mysterious and lost civilizations, silent canoes leave no footprints, no record of passing along the protean sea. Despite this lack of evidence, scholars now realize that the ancient Maya were not just inland temple builders but accomplished seafarers as well. They bridged their vast empire with waterborne commerce. Pre-eminent Mayanist Sir Eric Thompson dubbed the Maya "the Phoenicians of Middle America." Our voyages and researches lent credence to Thompson's theory.

Sadly, as intriguing and noble as those projects were, they were not wildly profitable and I had to figure out a way to make enough money to sustain my fascination with the Maya. I made my living back then as a delivery skipper and sailing journalist. I was based in Fort Lauderdale, and though I sailed all over the world to pay my bills, I often returned to Central America between ocean passages. I wrote several magazine articles about sailing in the region and even delivered a talk about ancient Mayan mariners to the Institute for Mayan Studies in Miami, an august body of archeologists who seemed a bit miffed that a dropout sailor was giving their keynote address. But it was a chance meeting with an expatriated American, Chet Smith, that provided me with the inspiration for what became another mostly unprofitable sailing business, alas.

Smith, who ran a well-known, if a bit ramshackle, guesthouse in southern Belize, was sick and tired of organizing trips to Mayan ruins for his guests. Sitting on the cool verandah of his place, Nature's Way, he clapped me on the shoulder and said, in a friendly way, "You're crazy."

I was confused.

"What I mean," he continued, stroking his mustache and starting to get worked up, "is that you are always looking for dead people, dead stories, you're searching for ghosts, man, it's insane, let it go. You are stuck in the past, start living in the moment. The Maya are right here, right under your fucking nose. They're alive, man, you know, living, breathing, farting, alive and kicking. The Maya didn't disappear, they just moved out of those drafty, mosquito-ridden pyramids. Why go pick through a pile of old, snake-infested rocks when you can spend time in a real village where the Maya are, well, where the Maya are being fucking Mayans?"

He drove me to Laguna, a small Maya/Ketchi village a few miles inland, and along the way told me about T.E.A., the Toledo (a district in southern Belize) Ecotourism Association. Their idea was to link several small villages in a loose network providing adventuresome travelers with a genuine Mayan experience. Each village had a guesthouse, typically rough-hewn from local hardwoods with bunk beds and a communal dining room. There was no guarantee there would be electricity and running water. Visitors would eat local foods family style, take jungle hikes, learn from a shaman about traditional plants, roast cocoa beans, dye and weave wool, and in some cases wield an adze and work on a dugout canoe. It was a way for the Maya to participate in Belize's booming ecotourism business without selling their souls to a corporate developer.

I became intrigued with the T.E.A. concept and resolved to organize sailing trips that would include visits to coastal villages to support the guesthouses. I managed to convince just enough people to make their way to southern Belize to give T.E.A. a modest assist. I was based in Placencia, a tiny but charming village that wasn't easy to get to in those days. After arriving at the international airport in Belize City, you had to transfer to the hectic local airport and take a small plane, usually a Cessna 182, from there. The landing at Placencia, on a randomly paved strip, was always an adventure and crashes were not all that uncommon.

I would fetch folks at the strip in my friend Sonny's battered pickup truck, and they would spend the first night ashore at his place, a simple motel right on the beach. We would usually go to Brenda's Barbecue for a rustic but delicious dinner, rounding out the local experience. Placencia was essentially a black village, with a handful of Maya and expatriate gringos about, but we were often the only white faces in the crowd at Brenda's. Nobody noticed, or if they did, they didn't care, and we always had great fun. The sailing trips lasted five days, with three days spent picking our way along the coast visiting T.E.A. villages and a couple days anchored out behind the thundering reef.

Fortuna, my 45′ steel ketch, was, in many ways, ideal for these trips. She was a lot like the Mayan guesthouses: rough-hewn, just not finished as nicely. Mayan shipwrights that I knew would have scoffed at her Home Depot interior. She was a homebuilt beauty, tough to be sure, and not particularly "yachty." Designed by Bruce Roberts, the patron saint of backyard metal boatbuilders the world over, she had nice lines if you blotted out the hull wrinkles caused by an inexperienced welder. A center-cockpit model, she was roomy and seaworthy, and I loved her, but staying ahead of the rust and corrosion was a full-time job.

I remember dropping anchor off Placencia for the first time. *Fortuna* was looking smart, fresh from the yard in Fort Lauderdale and brimming with white paint. We had just wrapped up a nonstop passage to Belize. There was an older but handsome steel boat anchored nearby. I felt a sense of kinship, a steel-boat brotherhood if you will, and rowed over for a visit. The skipper was on the foredeck. "Nice boat," I called out, but he ignored me. Wearing a floppy hat, he was bent over, chipping and painting. "She's steel?" I knew this of course but I was just trying to start a conversation. Finally, exasperated, he looked at me. "I'd like to talk to you, buddy, but if I stop now the boat will get ahead of me." And with that he returned to his hammer and chisel. I soon came to know exactly what he meant. Rust never sleeps and steel-boat owners are in a pitched battle, hand-to-hand combat no less, to keep their hulls from corroding out from under them.

It was May, and after a single season in the tropics *Fortuna* was already looking woebegone as I prepared her for the last trip of the season. Her hull was streaked with rust and she seemed to have aged ten years over the winter. I had decided to sail back to Fort Lauderdale after the charter trip and leave her ashore for hurricane season. I had arranged a transatlantic delivery and consoled myself with the knowledge that if she rusted through while I was away, at least she wouldn't sink.

One question that people always seem to ask is, "Do you ever have people aboard that you can't stand?" My answer is, "Almost never." The people who find their way to my floating world are motivated sailors, talented and interesting. But—there was one exception. A couple from the

Midwest had booked *Fortuna* for the last trip. Normally I sold individual berths, as I do on *Quetzal*, but they wanted *Fortuna* to themselves and were willing to pay a premium for the privilege. I was happy to oblige. I assumed they were ardent Mayanists and would be keenly interested in visiting the village guesthouses. I was at the Placencia landing strip when the Cessna banked and started the approach. When the whining single engine sputtered to a stop, the ground crew, consisting of a sleepy guy staying out of the sun under a makeshift tent, reluctantly roused himself. He sauntered to the plane and propped the tail with a weathered 2 x 6. The pilot emerged first and, wiping his brow, said, "These folks are something, they're all yours, skipper. Good luck."

My clients struggled to get out of the plane. The husband was a huge fellow who stood well over 6 foot and must have weighed close to 400lb. The wife was tiny, and very thin, almost dangerously so, and after much effort, and a few curses, they had their feet on the ground. He was wearing a safari suit, including a pith helmet, and was drenched in sweat. She was clad in a simple dress and did not seem very happy to be in Placencia. The pilot and I struggled to lift their enormous suitcases out of the hold and eventually dropped them in the back of the pickup truck.

"So are you John?" the husband asked in a husky voice.

"Yes, John Kretschmer, it's a pleasure to meet you."

"Well, thank God you're white, I mean no offense and all, but this country is darker than a moonless night."

With that the pilot, who was black, glanced my way, giving me a look that said, "I told you," and escaped into the plane.

"Well," I mumbled, "you know Belize is a primarily black country." I was stunned, not sure what to say next. I mumbled, "Um, well, let's get you two to the boat. You must be tired."

Bouncing along a pot-holed hard sand and gravel road, I was driving slow, never sure that Sonny's truck would make it back to the village two miles away in one piece, but thinking fast. It was obvious that staying at Sonny's was a bad idea, and going to Brenda's Barbecue was probably not a smart move either. I was shocked that someone could come to Belize and not know anything about the country's demography—and horrified that anyone still harbored such base racial biases. I decided that I'd move them directly onto the boat, where I could hide them, safe from any encounters with the locals.

Fortuna was moored at the head of a sporadically planked, half-rotten dock in front of the ice plant. That's how things were in Belize in those days, shoddy and utterly unsupervised, and I loved it. I hefted both suitcases and warned them to be careful as we inched down the dock. Stepping over an especially wide gap between planks, the wife lost her balance and, without making a sound, fell into the water 10 feet below. The husband, looking a bit miffed but otherwise unconcerned, said, "Well, look at that, she fell straight through the damn dock." I instantly dropped the bags and leapt into the water. Fortunately she was not seriously injured, just scraped in a few places, and I helped her back to the beach. She insisted on getting on the boat and I took her arm as we tried the dock for a second time. She was remarkably calm. Her husband assured me, "She's fine, just fine, she's tougher than she looks. She'll scab over."

When we reached the boat, it was a major operation to get them both on deck and I considered using the main halyard to heft the husband before he crashed aboard on his own. When they were finally situated in the cockpit, I passed up hydrogen peroxide and bandages for the wife and a chart and article about the Maya that I'd written for the husband. Then I poured them each a stiff rum punch and collected my thoughts. I was worried about the trip scheduled to depart the next morning. How would I ever get these two into the dinghy? The ride up the Monkey River in a dugout canoe was definitely out. The husband interrupted my thoughts.

"You know another thing, John, I don't really give a damn about the Mayans. Mayan schmayan, seen one Indian you've seen 'em all. They're past their prime anyway." He burst out laughing.

Now I was angry. "Why the hell did you come down here anyway? You're obviously not fond of the local Belizians and now you tell me you're not interested in the Maya either, that's what this trip's all about." I would have happily refunded their money if I hadn't already spent it. I was stuck with them. "I've made commitments for us to visit several villages and they're planning meals and events for us."

"Pay 'em off, cash fixes everything, just tell me how much it is."

I seriously considered cracking him in the jaw with a hard right, and he sensed that he had pushed me too far.

"John, here's the deal. I love to sail and I have wanted to sail the waters down here for a long time, and you are about the only game in town. We don't even care if we get off the boat for the next five days. We just want to sail. We're not really culture people, right," he said, looking at his wife, who was bleeding through her bandages, and silent. "We don't want to be difficult."

We shoved off the next morning, riding a warm trade wind toward Ranguana Cay, one of my favorite islands along the reef. The Belize Reef, which extends north to the top of the Yucatan Peninsula, is the second-longest barrier reef in the world, trailing only the Great Barrier Reef off eastern Australia. There are countless small islands and overgrown coral spits that provide protection from the easterly trade winds and that are ideal for tucking behind and dropping anchor. The day went better than expected as we limited our discussions to wind direction and compass courses and let the poetry of near-perfect sailing fill the voids.

We nudged as close as we dared to Ranguana Cay, anchoring in 8 feet of turquoise water, which left a foot below *Fortuna*'s keel. I swam ashore, hoping that the local conch divers had some fresh fish for dinner. No luck, they were off the island. I swam back out to the boat and after priming the crew with more rum dropped below to make dinner. I had very little food aboard because normally we ate at the guesthouses. I did have a few ancient jars of Ragu sauce, a couple of boxes of spaghetti, and several rusty cans of corned beef. "Screw these people," I thought and decided to toy with them. I concocted a fanciful story to go along with the dreadful concoction simmering on the stove. After secretly pouring a jar of Ragu and a couple of cans of corned beef into a simmering pan, I began to tell them about an amazing discovery we made during our research about the Maya.

"Marco Polo got it all wrong," I started. "He thought the Chinese had invented spaghetti and supposedly brought the recipe back to Italy. Actually it was the Maya."

Intrigued, the husband replied, "You don't say."

"There's no doubt about it," I continued, "the Maya were eating spaghetti for thousands of years. They loved the stuff. We even found an old stela, you know, an erect stone monument, with hieroglyphs showing Mayan war lords having a spaghetti fiesta."

"Really? Got any more rum?"

I topped his glass and continued.

"What's more, and this is the really cool part, and you have to swear to keep this a secret—we were able to decipher the glyphs and figure out the original recipe, and you guys are about to taste it right now."

"That's amazing."

"Wait until you taste it."

To my complete amazement they loved the stuff. And it was a good thing too, because they ate it for the next four nights. By the time I saw them off at the landing strip in Placencia they had, at the very least, a new appreciation for ancient Mayan cuisine.

A lifetime later, back aboard a hove-to *Quetzal* in the Gulf Stream in late fall, we had finished dinner and were doing dishes. To save water and to avoid making a bigger mess in an already messy galley we often wash up in the cockpit. It's a two-bucket operation, quick and easy, and the whole crew pitches in. Once the dishes were rinsed, dried, and stowed away below, the off-watch crew made their way to their bunks, trying to maximize sleep time while the ride was relatively smooth. Cindy and I had the first watch.

"You know that's a ridiculous story," she said, "but I laugh every time I hear it. You must have other stories of the time when you did all that sailing in Belize? I mean, it's cold out here, I was feeling warmer just thinking about Mayan spaghetti. The way I see it, we have three hours out here, take me back to Belize, please."

"Well, I do have one good story, or maybe bad story—it's about the night we almost lost the boat on a reef near the Blue Hole. I haven't told you that one?"

"Nope, but I am all ears."

I was between Mayan charters, and had sailed to northern Belize, from where I had scheduled an offshore training passage. *Fortuna* was anchored in just enough water to float, off Ambergris Cay, as I took on provisions, and no, Mayan spaghetti was not on the menu. We were bound for the island of Roatan in the Bay Islands of Honduras, with a planned stop at Lighthouse Reef, home of the Blue Hole. An almost perfectly round, incredibly deep sink hole, the Blue Hole is well known by divers the world over. It was early February and an uncharacteristically cold northwest wind was sweeping across Central America. Cold fronts rarely reach that far south, but this one would later develop into a "norther" for the archives, coined "the storm of the century." There's no denying that it was a serious blow, but we do tend to hyperventilate when describing storms.

I've been alive in only two centuries that I know of but have endured at least five "storms of the centuries"—and counting.

Once the crew was aboard we had to go to sea. The water was literally being blown out of the harbor, which consisted of nothing more than a narrow channel between the beach and the fringing reef. If we didn't clear the harbor soon we might not be able to leave for days, or possibly longer. We hauled up the anchor and steered toward the narrow dogleg pass through the reef but immediately went aground. Backing free, we gained momentum, only to feel the dull thud of the seven-foot keel mating with thin sand and turtle grass. Throwing the engine hard astern, we were free again, but just for a few minutes. We raised sail to heel the boat, with the crew leaning outboard in a desperate attempt to reduce draft. *Fortuna* floated free, gaining a little more precious real estate toward the pass before grounding again. We repeated this drunken scene at least a half dozen times before we finally cleared the pass, reaching the freedom of deep water.

Undaunted by our inauspicious departure, we enjoyed a rollicking 50-mile sail to Lighthouse Reef as the winds and seas built throughout the day. *Fortuna* was no speed demon, but she handled well in heavy going, and we averaged 6 knots under mizzen and staysail. This well-balanced sail plan, called "jib and jigger" by old salts, is one advantage of a ketch rig. Lighthouse Reef is an atoll with a fringing coral necklace stretching 20 miles from north to south protecting a shallow lagoon dotted with a couple of tiny islands that sit atop the reef. It's beautiful, remote, and treacherous. By late afternoon we had the pass at Half Moon Cay on the southeast side of the atoll in view. The sparkling shallows inside promised a respite from the riled-up Caribbean. We carefully navigated through the reef-rimmed pass and found a secure anchorage in 12 feet of water. There were pockets of coral all around us. The setting was both enchanting and eerie. Half Moon Cay is a postcard-perfect tropical island, 100 meters long with a covering of palm and gumbo-limbo trees. A weathered, rarely functional lighthouse marks the eastern end of the island. The wind was shrieking through the rigging, and the seas were exploding majestically along the reef as the storm of the century reached its apex. *Fortuna* was snug, lying to a heavy fisherman's anchor with an all-chain rode paid out to a 10:1 scope. Two heavy-duty nylon snubbers absorbed the load when strong gusts pulled the rode taut. The only other vessel in sight was the rusted wreck of an island freighter stranded on the reef, a silent reminder that help was a long way away and foolish mistakes were not long tolerated in remote atolls.

I had a curious crew. Tim, a dentist from San Francisco, had invested in *Fortuna*, probably much to his regret as he had visions of turning the old rust bucket into a fine yacht but she didn't have it in her to dress for the ball. He had sailed with me on a few deliveries and had been part of the Mayan film team. He was an excellent shipmate and game for any sailing adventure. He had rounded up two paying customers, for which I was most grateful. Robert was a Hollywood writer and producer, best known for work on the television show *Knight Rider,* staring David Hasselhoff and featuring a talking car. Mark was a top executive with Motown Records, which struck me as an odd position for a white guy from the Bay Area. My friend Dave, a doctor from Texas with a lot of sailing experience, rounded out the crew.

I had a sense of foreboding as we dropped below for a quick meal. It's always a balancing act with hunches, whether to pay attention and be spooked, or to use the rational side of your brain and ignore them. The crew moaned when I announced that anchor watches would be necessary. Given the storm-force winds it was the prudent thing to do. Halfway through dinner I suddenly felt a draft blowing through the main companionway. Something was wrong—we were dragging anchor. I flew up to the cockpit just in time to hear the horrible grinding of the boat's keel crashing into a coral head. The darkness was complete and I was further blinded by the glow of our saloon lights. I started the engine and shoved it into gear, but we weren't moving. As my eyes started to adjust to the inky night, I noticed coral heads poking just above the surface along the port side—and along the starboard side. We were in terrible straits.

Small waves were lifting the bow, causing the hull to grind on the reef. Once I had my bearings I was able to determine the direction toward the deeper water where we had been anchored, but I was dismayed at how disoriented I had become. Not surprisingly, the lighthouse wasn't working, and the unlit spire was only just visible. Flirting with panic, I gunned the engine forward and backward, rocking the boat to and fro, but it was no use—she was stuck. Finally, the engine overheated.

"It looks like we better get a kedge out," Dave suggested in his calm Texas drawl. I immediately realized that he was right—I should have set a kedge first thing. What was I thinking? A kedge is simply a word for an anchor that is deployed when you are aground. Kedging is the process of hauling on that anchor in an attempt to float the boat. Before we could set a kedge, we had to launch the dinghy. We lost more valuable time dragging the Zodiac out of the lazarette and inflating it. It soon became obvious that the inflated dinghy was a kite in the wind—impossible to launch or control once in the water. We deflated it.

"What are we going to do now?" asked Tim, the fear obvious in his voice.

"We're going to swim the kedge out, that's all we can do," I said, trying to mask my own fear.

I eased into the water off the bow. I was terrified of slashing my legs on the reef, and knew that Lighthouse Reef atoll was famous for sharks. Dave led the crew on deck as they wrapped the lightweight Danforth anchor in a PFD with a clever quick-release mechanism. Dave lowered it over the side and I swam it out beyond the reef as he paid out rode. Then I released it and dove down to make sure it was set. Underwater it was other-worldly, with weird light reflecting from live coral and bright tropical fish. And terrifying. I tried not to think about a giant bull shark ripping off a chunk of my leg. Once back on the surface, I gave the thumbs-up. Robert and Mark cranked on the manual windlass while Tim kicked the cooled-down engine into gear. The anchor dragged. We tried again. It dragged again. The Danforth was useless. We had to use the traditional fisherman-style anchor, called "da hook" in Belize—it is one of the few anchors that sets reliably in a thin sand-and-limestone seabed. It was the same anchor that had dragged to create this ordeal, but it was our only option.

We managed to retrieve the fisherman anchor from the coral, but it was too heavy for me to swim out. We inflated the dinghy again and struggled to keep it in the water. Once my weight was aboard, however, the Zodiac became somewhat controllable. Time and again I rowed the anchor and all 200 feet of chain out past the reef. Every foot was a struggle. Chopping the water with the stupid plastic oars to hold my position while making sure the rode wasn't wrapped around anything, including my ankle, I mustered my ebbing strength and dropped the anchor overboard. Then the crew hauled in on the manual windlass. We raised the mizzen despite the shrieking wind and sheeted it tight, trying to heel the boat. We pushed the engine as hard as we dared. The anchor chain was taut like a guitar string. Inch by inch we made progress before it would drag, and we'd repeat the process all over again.

We tried to raise other vessels on the VHF radio but were greeted by silence and then, after frantically adjusting the squelch knob, just static. We were alone, stranded on a reef 40 miles from anywhere. Once again, our fate was in our own hands. After at least 10 sets with the fisherman we started to see results. We moved 5 feet one time before the anchor dragged, 10 feet another time. We kept the diesel steady ahead with the mizzen sheeted tight. We were gaining ground—we could hear the chain scratching along the hull. Just when it seemed we might pull the boat free, the bow lurched up and we came to an abrupt halt.

Tim kept checking the bilge, making sure that we were not taking on water. Obviously, the last thing you want to do is haul your boat into deep water if the hull has been holed. The hull was intact, but the grinding and thumping was horrible. My emotions were darting all over. On one hand I felt I had betrayed my boat and crew, yet on the other hand I also felt horrible for destroying precious coral. I was thoroughly exhausted and had to make a conscious effort not to sink into a deep funk; at that moment I needed clear thinking and positive action, not self-pitying introspection. I couldn't know it at the time, but mustering the resolve to stay focused on getting the boat off the reef when logic and physics suggested we should give up would serve me well in crises yet to come in my life. Experience happens when you're too preoccupied to notice.

Sometime after midnight the front passed and the wind eased and stars cast enough light to see just how precarious our situation was. *Fortuna* remained steadfast, impaled on the reef. I told the crew to gather their valuables. I had decided to begin unloading supplies from the boat, ferrying them to Half Moon Cay in the dinghy to lighten the ship—it seemed like our only hope if we were to save *Fortuna*.

"We'll start with our valuables, so get what you can't live without and wrap everything in plastic bags. We'll bury stuff on the island and then come back and keep working. We can't give up. We'll try to run a line from the mast to the far reef and heel the boat that way." I had found my will, I was not going to lose my boat without a fight to the end.

It was interesting to see what the crew considered valuable. Robert, who had been observing the disaster somewhat dispassionately—as though it were a scene from a movie script he might write—gathered up his passport and stash of Cuban cigars. Mark took the new CDs he was choosing from for Motown's latest release. Tim grabbed the ship's documents and insurance papers. Dave collected the medical kit and drinking water. Just as we were about to begin loading the dinghy we noticed an abrupt wind shift. Suddenly the mizzen filled on the other tack. It was a miraculous 90-degree shift. We quickly let out all sail and I found the energy to row out one more kedge. This time it was especially long as we joined the Danforth rode to the fisherman's rode. Once back on the boat, I started the engine and gradually gave it more throttle. The guys hauled on the anchor windlass one more time, one deliberate stroke after another. Everybody was physically exhausted. "Come on, *Fortuna*," I cried out, but we didn't move. Risking overheating again, I gave it full power. Suddenly we lurched forward and then shot ahead. We were floating!

We were stunned but incredibly relieved and let out a muted cheer. Then I immediately throttled back and frantically grabbed the furling lines and reeled in the headsails. Dave and Tim let the halyards fly on the main and mizzen and Mark and Robert hastily put on sail stops. We didn't want to sail right back onto a reef. I longed for daylight to see any other lurking coral heads. In those pre-GPS days we could only guess our exact position. Sensing that we were near to where we had originally anchored, we shortened the anchor scope and the boat came to rest, floating peacefully. We had been delivered from the reef, but we were taking no chances and decided to keep the engine running. I broke out our best rum and we each had a small glass. Nobody went below. It had been a night to remember, or maybe forget, but one thing was certain, we all wanted to greet the light of day.

Back aboard *Quetzal* it was hard to distinguish between driving rain and spray. Cindy was shaking her head. "That's a terrible story," she said.

"I know why you don't tell that one very often, wow. I'm not sure I would have wanted to sail again after that. What did you do afterward—you were still in the middle of nowhere, was the boat OK?"

"The hull was scratched and dented but basically still seaworthy—that's the impressive thing about a metal hull. It kills me to say this, but *Quetzal* would not have survived that night. What did we do? We finished the trip. We even dove in the Blue Hole the next day and then sailed on to the Bay Islands."

"One last question, OK?"

"Sure."

"You never said what *you* were bringing ashore to the island, what *you* considered valuable."

"I wasn't planning on the leaving the boat."

Postscript 2018

Just a few months ago I returned to Placencia, Belize, for a ten-day charter that Tadji and I had organized. It had been 12 years since my last visit and I was stunned. The dock in front of the ice plant is now reinforced with concrete, and several stout finger piers house charter boats. You might be able to fall off if you've had too much to drink, but there's no falling through that dock. The village itself is crowded with middle-aged gringos, and there are several top restaurants and even a gelato shop. Unimaginably, Sotheby's has an office, one of several brokerages—real-estate prices are skyrocketing. All the talk is about buying property. I kept explaining to Tadji about how things were in the old days, how rustic and real the place was, and she told me I was beginning to sound like a grumpy old man.

We provisioned our 44´ charter catamaran in a top-quality supermarket, and Mayan spaghetti was not on the menu but chicken in Roquefort sauce was. I realized that your memories of a place, a place ashore, are indelibly stamped with a date and time. However, once we set sail and again made our way to Ranguana Cay, bounding over translucent waters, I also realized that the sea seemed unchanged. Sailing from one familiar speck on the reef to another, I was transfixed and inspired by the beautiful waters lapping the reef's edge. I know, believe me, how fragile this ecosystem is, but compared with what was happening ashore, the ocean seemed unchanged. Ernest K. Gann, the author of many novels, wrote what remains my favorite nautical book, *Song of the Sirens*. It chronicles his many boats and many adventures, and toward the end of the book he writes, "One of the greatest blessings the oceans bestow on man is a sense of everlasting permanence. The oceans DO change, but they take their time about it and a thousand years is only an interval. Time apparently stands still for the oceans—the light and play of liquid, the sounds and scent of salt air, and the inhabitants are basically the same as they were long ago."

Song of the Sirens was published in 1968; we know today that the oceans are changing—rapidly—and as humans we need to do all we can to change this dynamic, for as the oceans go, so do we. Yet, unlike the change we heap upon the earth's surface, bulldozing our stories and memories into the dumpster of history as fast as we make them, the apparent timelessness of the ocean mercifully allows connections to be made between the stories of past and present—this we must preserve too.

FIVE

JUST ENOUGH TECHNOLOGY

*Chartplotter Strategies • Death by GPS • Waypoint
Navigation • Natural Navigation • Seabird Navigation •
Fort Lauderdale to Japan*

"A good pathfinder can become so proficient that he can amaze the
average person. If he likes to be mysterious he can easily persuade
his friends he has a sixth sense; but if he wants to be honest, he
must admit that he has nothing of the kind."

—Harold Gatty, *Finding Your Way Without
Map or Compass*

"In the Marshall Islands there is a word, wiwijet, that means
both being lost and panic. According to anthropologist Joseph
Gent, a navigator who becomes lost and does not receive help
(from a benevolent spirit) to discern the direction toward
land will lose his mind and continue to sail disoriented until
his death."

—John Huth, *The Lost Art of Finding Our Way*

The Caribbean, Near Isla Aves, 2013

The frigates were on a mission, flying in stacked formations like the B26 bombers my father flew during the D-Day invasions in 1944. Fork-tailed, streamlined with long, pointed wings and painted stealthy black, frigates can be seen up to 300 miles out to sea. But they are day sailors, not voyagers, and by late afternoon they're almost always on their way home, flying at full throttle toward the nearest land, like Friday commuters on the interstate. The sky was also alight with brown boobies—it was clear we were not far from land. We were approaching Isla Aves on the second morning of a trans-Caribbean passage. We were sailing in a chartered 53′ sloop, as *Quetzal* was taking the winter off, marooned on the hard on the other side of the Atlantic in Malta (as you read about in Chapter Two). I had a crew of six aboard and we were all excited to lay our eyes on the tiny spit seemingly in the middle of the Caribbean. Aves had been the object of some intense celestial navigation exercises and sighting it would confirm our good work, but it would not be easy.

Isla Aves is a furtive shoal of sand and limestone lurking just above sea level in an otherwise deep stretch of cobalt blue Caribbean where soundings of more than 1,000 fathoms are common. It's disputed as to whether Isla Aves is actually an island or just a rock, but for navigators it's more cautionary tale than choice real estate. It's claimed by Venezuela, whose military maintains an outpost consisting of a stark cinderblock building covered with antennas precariously perched on stilts. By insisting that it's an island, the Venezuelans extend their exclusive economic territorial claim 200 miles in all directions. I don't blame them—a rock, according the U.N. Convention on the Law of the Sea, is only good for 12 miles of unlimited bounty.

Isla Aves, or Bird Island, lies 100 miles west of its nearest neighbor, the island nation of Dominica, which also stakes a claim to the overgrown reef with its two or three scraggly palm trees bent by the prevailing easterlies. Based on dimensions alone, I think the rock argument has merit. It's just over 300 meters long, never more than 50 meters wide, and, on a rare calm day, about 3 meters above sea level. In a tropical storm, Aves is completely under water. Rock or island, it's a long way from the Venezuelan mainland, 300 miles to the south. The ownership of Aves has been disputed over the years. It was actually annexed by three guys from Boston in 1857 under the terms of the Guano Islands Act, which Congress enacted the year before. The act granted U.S. citizens the right to claim any uninhabited island, anywhere, provided it was covered with guano—literally bird shit. (This law is still on the books.) In 1950 Venezuela sent two patrol boats and one transport vessel to seize the island, or rock, once and for all. According to official reports, the frigates and sea turtles welcomed the liberators.

I've sailed close to Aves many times during the last ten years and have sighted it a few times on one of my favorite and most popular training passages—the "trans Caribbean," which is a nice mix of ocean sailing and island hopping, with many folks signing aboard for their first taste of offshore sailing. That the passage crosses the heart of the Caribbean Sea, is warm and invariably breezy, and includes three days gunkholing in the lovely Grenadines might help explain the appeal. It's the route that makes Aves a focal point of the passage, and challenging for navigators. We depart from Tortola in the British Virgin Islands and sail nonstop to Grenada, a nice 400-mile reach. The course skirts the eastern tip of St. Croix near the end of the first day. After the gently sloping hills of the forgotten Virgin Island fade from view astern, the next sight of land is Grenada, two full days later. When you lay the true course line down on a chart, you can't help but notice that it just about runs over Isla Aves.

The problems occur when you don't bother to lay the course down on a paper chart but instead rely solely on electronic navigation. It is an issue of zooming, or not zooming, not normally a navigational technique, but one that's been in the news recently. Just about every sailor uses some form of GPS with electronic charting these days. For years *Quetzal* was fitted with a small chartplotter that used digital charts, or vector charts, technically called ENCs, or electronic navigational charts, that were produced by C-Map. A few years ago, as I became more farsighted— not intellectually, sadly, just visually—and the islands appeared smaller and blurrier, we upgraded to a larger plotter that uses ENCs produced by Navionics. The 9-inch display is beautiful, a treat for old eyes, and I am already dreaming of a new 11-inch screen on the next *Quetzal* upgrade. Some sailors use smartphones and tablets to access various charts and nautical software, just like ashore—screens are everywhere on cruising boats. All ENCs use cartographic survey databases compiled by hydrographic offices. Most present vector images—map renditions allowing users to zoom in and out seamlessly, in effect providing near-instant access to hundreds of charts of various scales. They're incredibly user-friendly and, for the most part, accurate, and have all but eliminated "raster" charts—those highly useful and accurate scans of actual paper charts requiring a lot more storage, and called RNCs. The Coast Guard still recommends RNCs, but most sailors are using vector, or ENCs. Conning your way through a reef pass or into an unfamiliar harbor with an ENC has never been easier, with a few caveats. As with any chart, you can't follow an ENC blindly, as I explained in Chapter Two—the picture on the screen has to make sense along with what your eyes, ears, and gut are telling you—and ENCs are anything but foolproof. I once watched a beautiful Hinckley Sou'wester 42 motor directly onto a reef while trying to enter a small harbor near Eleuthera in the Bahamas. The skipper's electronic chart was not accurate, but he trusted it more than he trusted his eyes—though the reef was obvious to even the most casual navigator. The other boats in the anchorage managed to pull the vessel off with a harness of dinghies, and fortunately it was the skipper's pride that endured the most damage. Another caveat with ENCs is that you have to remember to zoom in occasionally when sailing far offshore.

Using C-Map, Navionics, or any other vector chart software, if you zoom your plotter out to the point where Tortola and Grenada are both in the frame, Isla Aves disappears. This is typically the zoom level where you do your course planning. You select a waypoint off Grenada and presto!—a line appears connecting your present position to that point. Glancing at the data boxes on the plotter you note the course, in either true or magnetic, and the distance in nautical miles. Looking closely at the course line, you see that there are a few seamounts—literally mountains rising up from the ocean floor—along the way, but none appears dangerous to surface navigation. Aves appears like just another seamount, a point of interest but not necessarily a hazard. We sail right over seamounts all the time. It looks like clear sailing all the way to Grenada. As you zoom in, the words "Isla Aves" appear but no landforms show—it still looks like a seamount. You must keep zooming until the area around Aves is quite detailed before the little splotch of yellow that represents solid land appears on the screen.

I always demonstrate this potentially disastrous hazard to the crew when we're doing prepassage planning. In the past, they've indulged me, pretending to be interested and nodding their heads as I rail about this limitation of ENCs. Lately, however, I've noticed that they've become more attentive, no doubt the result of a terrible mishap in the 2014/15 Volvo Ocean Race. A grueling around-the-world race that pits many of the best sailors on the planet competing in 65′ one-design boats, the Volvo, as it's called, is not only offshore sailing's premier contest, it's arguably the toughest sporting event of all. But even the best sailors make stupid mistakes.

It was during Leg Two, from Cape Town to Abu Dhabi, a circuitous 5,000-mile route across the Indian Ocean, that the Danish entrant, *Team Vestas Wind*, crashed headlong onto the reef at S. Brandon atoll while sailing at 17 knots. The real-time video of the incident went viral, together with aerial photos of the stricken boat lying on its side like a mortally wounded seabird on a fringing reef. The accident occurred just before midnight and miraculously none of the crew was injured. Initial reports claimed that the boat had hit an "uncharted reef," a phrase that ranks right up there with "shark-infested waters" for describing the location of just about every nautical mishap.

The reef in question, part of the Cargados Carajos Shoals north of Mauritius, happens to be very well charted and has been since about 1800. Even Google Maps, notorious for omitting oceanic details, has the shoals in the right place—it just takes a lot of zooming to find them. Google Earth is spot-on and shows details along the reef, with rocky, colored corals standing in stark contrast to the shimmering blue water. It seems that *Team Vestas Wind*'s navigator did not bother to zoom in enough on either of the two chartplotters aboard and assumed the shallows on the digital chart were seamounts and not dangerous to surface navigation. He later claimed that he had zoomed in but miscalculated the depths of the shoals.

In the navigator's defense, the race route was altered one day before departure, allowing the fleet to sail farther west, closer to the shoals, to avoid a developing cyclone, and there wasn't time for a lot of planning. Also, Volvo navigators are often overwhelmed, constantly coping with a variety of data, from performance inputs to ever-changing meteorological updates. They're under intense pressure to choose the fastest-possible route. Still, I know the simple task of putting your position on a paper chart sounds absurdly old-fashioned, but even done just once a day—taking the dividers and measuring the latitude and longitude and putting a pencil mark on a chart—it would dramatically help prevent accidents associated with an over-reliance on electronic navigation. Even the ridiculously small-scale 1:10,000,000 British Admiralty Chart #4701, which covers a huge swath of the Indian Ocean, clearly shows the

Cargados Carajos Shoals. (To their credit, the *Team Vestas Wind* shore command, skipper Chris Nicholson, and Maersk Shipping coordinated an impressive rescue mission. The stricken boat was refloated and hoisted onto a waiting ship. The boat was then repaired, and later rejoined the Volvo for the final two legs.)

Incidentally, after two deadly collisions, it has recently been reported by the *New York Times* that the United States Navy has officially decided to reinstall compasses—imagine that—and paper charts and pencils on every ship. Presumably the navy is going to insist that navigators actually plot their position on paper charts.

A reliance on electronic navigation is not only uninteresting, sucking the essential human element out of wayfinding and dulling our senses in the process, it is also irresponsible. Another accident, and one far more tragic than *Team Vestas Wind*'s navigational error, occurred during the popular Newport to Ensenada race in 2012. Around 0130, just after the sliver of moon set in the western ocean, the yacht *Aegean*, a well-equipped Hunter 37′ sloop with a crew of four, inexplicably ran into the sheer rock wall on North Coronado Island while motoring at 7 knots. The boat shattered on impact and all four men aboard were killed. When their remains were later examined, the authorities concluded that three died from blunt-force injuries and one drowned.

It is just 125 miles from Newport Beach, California to Ensenada on the Baja Peninsula of Mexico. Most boats in the race stay relatively close to the coast as they sail through the night. A key navigational decision is whether to go inside or outside of Los Coronados, four small but prominent rocky islands packed together 15 miles south of San Diego and 7 miles off the Mexico coast. Some navigators place a waypoint on their chartplotters just north of North Coronado with the intention of deciding at that point, based on the local conditions, which route to take. The final report from US Sailing, the sport's governing body, concluded that *Aegean*'s skipper most likely set a waypoint at North Coronado. The boat, on autopilot and motoring at full speed, sped right past the waypoint as the deck watch slept or somehow "lost the bubble," Coast Guard lingo for not paying attention, and crashed into the island.

After some initial confusion, when it seemed more likely that *Aegean* had been run down by a commercial ship, it became painfully obvious what had happened. The crew deployed a GPS SPOT tracker, a satellite transmitter that reports a vessel's position at regular intervals, and it laid bare their course—an unswerving rendezvous with a deadly rock wall. It was still hard for many sailors to accept this dreadful conclusion until the wreckage of the boat was found, in 20 meters of water, directly below the wall. At first glance, this tragedy doesn't appear to have stemmed from a navigational error—it wasn't for lack of zooming on the chartplotter that *Aegean* met her doom. It was a calm, clear night, and they obviously had decided to abandon the race and hurry down to Ensenada under power not to miss the post-race festivities. Whoever was on watch most likely fell asleep.

I sympathize with the families of the lost sailors—it's a horribly sad story, and no one should pay the ultimate price for simply nodding off— that this is a brutally harsh judgment. What I do question is the generally accepted method of navigation that relies exclusively on GPS and the setting of waypoints. Setting a waypoint that is directly in the path of a dangerous rock is simply not prudent, but it's done all the time, and often within a few meters of a marker or other landmark. The assumption is that the ENC is unimpeachably accurate, that the GPS signal will never be lost, and that an alarm will sing out and wake you if you fall asleep. Waypoints should be safe positions from where you then either begin an approach or make a decision to change course; they are not the position where you hope to end up. You should always plot a waypoint with a margin of error, so if for any reason—loss of visibility, sudden gear failure, collision avoidance, a crewmember falling asleep—an escape is needed, you leave yourself with a possible one. If you miss a waypoint it shouldn't result in a crash landing. Another issue that has avoided scrutiny in this tragedy is the construction of the boat. How does a boat shatter from a collision sustained at 7 knots? I have a friend who, blinded by the sun, drove his robust, 1980s-era, Taiwan-built cutter into a bridge rampart at 7 knots. It was a terrible shock, to say the least, and shattered the bowsprit, but there was otherwise very little structural damage to the boat. They didn't take a drop of water into the bilge. I won't go into another rant about the failures of modern boats, but the fate of the *Aegean* seems a travesty to me.

"Death by GPS" is part of the lexicon, and generally refers to unfortunate travelers, usually in automobiles, who have blindly followed GPS instructions over cliffs, off bridges, and into a vast wilderness from which they never return. GPS is not the culprit. The digital maps and charts are the problem, but they're not the culprits either. They're just not always accurate, and navigators must base their decisions on this basic fact. It is easy to assume that just because it appears, or in some cases doesn't appear, on the GPS screen in your car or on the ENC on your boat's chartplotter, it's really there or not there. These charts are only as accurate as the original surveys they were based on and are updated sporadically at best, and usually from voluntary user input. Also, it's vital to understand that vector charts do not contain all the information that is provided on a paper chart—there isn't the storage capacity.

With nautical charts especially, some surveys are very old and governments do not seem enthused about spending money to commission new surveys. A few years ago we explored the Galapagos for several weeks. We had a top-quality state-of-the-art plotter, two iPads, and a dedicated navigation computer. We ran C-Map, Garmin, and Navionics ENCs. Time and again the plotter showed us anchored on shore. When we were anchored in a little pocket of deep water off the south coast of the island of Isabella, the plotter showed us three miles inland—this was a bit unsettling. The charts, based on an old Ecuadorian survey, were wildly inaccurate, probably not much better than when Darwin and Fitzroy sailed there in the *Beagle*. The only safe way to make your way into the harbor at Isabella was by using a paper chart and considering your position in a relative fashion. We took compass bearings and cross-referenced them with soundings, timing our approach in good light with the sun at our back. We were doubtful of the absolute accuracy of the charts but they were still quite helpful. Had we followed the ENC we would have been on the rocks. Should we have sued Navionics? Come on. We are the culprits, as sailors and as humans—we're responsible for our own decisions.

In the summer of 2017 another sad story of a yacht hitting the rocks made news. *Tanda Malaika*, a 46´ catamaran, piled onto the reef at the southern end of Hauhine, a lovely island in French Polynesia. Crewed by a family of five, *Tanda Malaika* was two years into a world cruise. They had left Moorea, near Tahiti, early in the morning and closed with Huahine just after dark. According to the wife's very emotional blog, the husband was at the helm when the depth sounder suddenly went from 180 meters to 0, and before they could do anything to prevent it, the boat struck the reef. They hit hard as they were sailing at 8 knots with both engines on and the jib drawing. Naturally, they claimed the reef was uncharted.

The wife tells a dramatic story of the French Coast Guard evacuating them by helicopter, and her description of watching her children being airlifted off the boat is gut-wrenching. My friend Charlie Doane, who detailed the incident in his great blog "Wave Train," captions a photo of a child on a hi-line rescue rope "not a sight a mother ever wants to see." One by one the family members are lifted to safety. Later they even manage to salvage the boat and have it towed to a nearby island, where hopefully it can be repaired and they can continue their cruise.

Age 13, steering *Our Way*, our Sabre 28 sloop, on Lake St. Clair.

Taking a sight on while crossing the Pacific. I loved that sextant; it was a Plath, the finest one I've ever owned, and I've had four over the years.

Gigi sailing under the Golden Gate Bridge into San Francisco Bay, concluding the Cape Horn voyage. The last leg was 72 days.

Quetzal charging toward Bequia on a trans-Caribbean passage.

Gigi easing along in front of the Kiessimul Castle off the island of Barra in the Outer Hebrides.

Training passage aboard *Caribe* in the Bahamas – great sailing.

Quetzal at anchor in Hare Bay, south coast of Newfoundland.

Quetzal under full sail, showing off along the Lunenburg, Nova Scotia, waterfront.

Tadji on the bow for the approach into an anchorage off the Northumberland Strait, near Prince Edward Island.

Quetzal, with teak, racing along on her way to Bras d'Or Lakes.

Self-portrait with dolphins in the Cabot Strait.

Quetzal under cruising spinnaker in Mahone Bay, Nova Scotia.

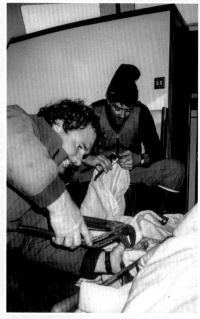

Repairing a sail with Joe Murton. Note the delicate tools!

Alan (foreground), Ron, and Bruce – the teak deck removal crew.

New hard dodger, solar panel arch, and full enclosures, ready for high-latitude sailing.

At the helm in an Atlantic gale.

Getting ready to host the staysail on a long-ago midwinter crossing of the Atlantic.

Self-portrait with dolphins in the Cabot Strait.

With daughters Narianna (left) and Annika, in Newport during our first summer aboard *Quetzal*.

Sailing in the Gulf of St. Lawrence with Tadji.

With daughters Nari and Annika, sailing *Quetzal* in Long Island Sound during their first summer aboard.

The part of the story that upsets me is that they blame Navionics for their misfortune.

Apparently the reef, which circles the island like a glittering diamond necklace, is not perfectly charted along its southern end. I carefully plotted the coordinates provided from *Tanda Malaika*'s blog on a recently downloaded Navionics chart and on Google Earth, and it looks to me that the reef is accurately charted. Even if it is slightly off, 100 meters at most, it is the fault of the survey, not the reproduced chart. Without question Navionics should make every possible effort to make their charts as accurate as possible because they know people depend on them. However, every chart that's ever been printed or digitalized warns you in unambiguous terms not to rely on a single source of information for navigation. Some sailors consider this warning just corporate ass-covering, but it's far more than that—it's the very essence of navigation. We are not just sheep being led by our electronic keepers. While this is a heartrending story indeed, if you want to place blame, place it where it belongs, with the skipper. Why was he anywhere near a reef, motoring as he was at 8 knots in the dark? Why was he planning to make an entry through a reef pass in the dark? Sadly, he cut the reef too close in his haste to get to port, and he was fortunate that his family was rescued.

Sometimes you just have to slow down, even though it's the last thing you want to do. Other times you have to peel away from land and head back out to sea. It is always better to wait for daylight to make an approach, no matter how strong your desire is for a cold beer, a hot shower, and a full night's sleep. This is a foreign concept to many, sailors and land people alike, the idea that just because you arrive after dark you have to essentially pull off the road and wait until daylight before carrying on. It is, however, a time-honored navigational technique. A couple of years ago we were sailing *Quetzal* from Grenada to Fort Lauderdale, a 1,500-mile passage with a couple of landfalls along the way. The trades were in their glory and we were flying. Our next waypoint was Cockburn Harbor, a shallow bank off South Caicos in the Turks and Caicos Islands.

The headsail was poled out and the main deep-reefed to keep the boat from rolling. It was glorious sailing and we were making a steady 9 knots. Unfortunately, despite our speed it was obvious we were going to arrive at the harbor entrance in the dark. I didn't want to chance a night entry into the harbor even though there were approach lights and we had good charts and I had been there a few times before. We made an alternate plan. We would carry sail and make all speed until we were 25 miles from Cockburn. At that point, we would reduce sail and drift slowly, carefully controlling our speed. If we kept moving at 4 knots we'd arrive at the harbor mouth an hour after sunrise.

With the morning light at our back illuminating the brilliant coral reef on both sides of the approach, we entered the well-marked harbor. After several tries, we managed to set the anchor on a mostly hard bottom. Confident that the anchor was holding, we went ashore in search of the usual things sailors go ashore in search of, a cold beer and a good meal. As we made our way to a restaurant on a prominent point, we noticed a sailboat aground just off the beach north of the harbor. Curious, we hiked that way and it became clear the grounding was a very recent event. Wading out to it where it lay stranded on a sandbar, we inspected it carefully. The keel was missing and the transom was cracked and coming adrift from the rest of the hull. It was depressing—the completely flooded boat was damaged beyond repair.

Walking back to the restaurant, we fell in step with an instructor from the School for Field Studies, a marine research center on the island, and he told us the sad story. Just a couple of days before our arrival, the boat hit the reef in the middle of the night. It was a rainy, blustery night, and the two-person crew became disoriented. Instead of steering for the harbor entrance, just a few hundred meters to the south, they steered for East Bay, confused by lights on the shore. They crashed onto the reef and the keel was ripped off before the boat washed over the coral and came to rest in 4 feet of water off the beach. They were making their first passage after buying the boat in the Virgin Islands. Their plan had been to take her to Fort Lauderdale for a refit and then take off cruising. They were exhausted after four days at sea, and desperate to get into port. Apparently they had GPS aboard but became disoriented and lost their way. Not only were their dreams shattered, they were also facing the prospect of a severe fine for creating an environmental hazard. They should have waited until daylight to make their approach.

All of these sad stories have helped reinforce my ever-evolving concept of JET. I must confess, members of my immediate family—basically, Tadji and the kids—hate this theory, but I think it has merit. JET is an acronym for Just Enough Technology. My idea is that everyone has an individual technology threshold, and understanding how much technology you want in your life, at any given time, is one of the keys to personal happiness, not to mention safe navigation. You need just enough technology to make your life work. My JET is low. The hurly-burly pursuit of the latest device, with a bewildering manual undecipherable in seven languages, and its concomitant monthly service plan with the need for vital downloaded updates, completely stresses me out. From a sailing perspective, I contend that an over-reliance on technology can spoil the near-mystical communion sailors share with the ocean environment. It not only clutters the ideas of freedom and self-reliance that speak to the very core of why we go to sea, but in some cases, as we've seen above, it can be dangerous. If you bother to take your head out of the screen and look around, there's a damn good chance your senses will alert you to an impending problem.

This is when my kids start to roll their eyes, and they have a point. Throughout the book I have talked about downloading GRIB files for weather updates and infrared satellite images to locate the Gulf Stream.

I am able to call, text, or email family and friends from the farthest reaches of the ocean. In an emergency I can send an electronic MAYDAY with push of a button. I use electronic charts and am amazed by the vast amount of data available at the tap of a touchscreen. Technology has made sailing imminently safer and more efficient. Just today I have frequently popped online while writing, to check the date when *Team Vestas Wind* grounded and to view the video of the event. I send invoices to the crews that sign up for my training passages and workshops via PayPal and they remit funds directly into my bank account electronically. We post pictures of passages on Facebook, and SPOT messenger sends satellite position updates to social media whenever we remember to deploy it. Technology allows me to run my business, write books and articles, and lead a wonderfully peripatetic life at the same time. But technology is greedy—one development begets another, and if you're not careful, the blind pursuit of the next gadget can snuff out the essential joy of sailing as your precious time is wasted chasing electrical faults, software meltdowns, and all the other technological annoyances that you were trying to escape by going sailing in the first place.

Ocean voyaging offers unfettered access into one of the last truly wild realms on the planet. It's not fenced off and you don't need a park pass to enter. All you need is a seaworthy boat, basic seamanship skills, an open mind, and a willing spirit. You must take the ocean on its own terms, however, and when you do, you can transcend time and space. Pulling your head out of the screens and closely examining your watery environment has the almost magical power to change a dull, two-dimensional screen view of a passage into a three-dimensional masterpiece, resplendent with sounds and smells as well. This is a blend of beauty and freedom, pure and beautifully simple, that ocean voyaging offers, and I strongly suggest you don't spoil it by watching a virtual image of it instead of the real thing.

My minimal JET level affords an easy balance between the rewards of natural observations and the prudent use of technology. I add technology as I need it, but it's not a zero-sum game. I don't discard other skills and techniques that I cherish and rely on. Navigation is surely a science, but there's an art to practicing it well. GPS eliminates much of the anxiety of position finding, and the satellite receiver provides insights into impending weather conditions. This easily obtained information in turn allows you to turn your mind to observing natural phenomena. The sky, clouds, waves, and birds all provide clues about position and weather. More importantly, by incorporating natural signs into the system you use, alongside technological inputs, you will tune into your boat and become a better sailor and a better, more enlightened navigator. A quick glimpse at a star can reassure you that you're on course. The set of waves against the bow confirms the heading. A glance at the GPS gives the speed. The light of the moon allows you to examine the set of a sail. A turn of the winch, maybe an electric winch, to trim the sheet, eliminates the slight sound of a luffing jib. When you listen to the wind, you are, in effect, listening to your boat. Listening is vital to sailing. You just might hear the sound of breaking waves on a reef in time to make a life-saving difference. Natural navigation and electronic navigation work in conjunction.

A few years ago, on a transatlantic passage, we actually turned the GPS off for a week while sailing between Bermuda and the Azores. Two of the crew, Chris and Doug, were avid celestial navigators and anxious to use their new skills to guide *Quetzal* across a swath of sea, and not just compare their sextant-derived results with the GPS, as though the black box was a teacher grading them on a test. They wanted to navigate. Unlike electronic navigation, celestial navigation is a process, and one sight helps confirm and update the one before it. Slowly but steadily your position evolves, as sun lines and the occasional star and planet sights are plotted in combination, and as you advance using dead reckoning. This process of navigation is a hard concept for modern navigators to grasp—we have come to expect instant access to absolute position. Celestial navigation is like going for a walk in the woods. You instinctively pay attention as you go, and though you never know your exact position, you always know where you are, more or less. It was a little unsettling for the rest of the crew as they didn't have GPS inputs to steer by. We are addicted to course and speed over ground, and to minute-by-minute updates on the distance and course to the next waypoint. However, once we were free of this omnipresent data, the passage took on a slower, more natural pace. Log entries became more interesting as it was important to update the dead reckoning before each round of sights. Night watches were more fun as we all wanted to make sure our log entries were as accurate as possible for our celestial navigators. When we rebooted the GPS a week later, the position we had calculated differed from that shown by the GPS by less than five miles.

Ironically, the simplicity and reliability of electronic navigation has helped fuel a resurgence in natural and celestial navigation. As I mentioned earlier, I conduct a workshop that includes the traditional and always-challenging process of learning how to reduce a sextant sight—a process that requires a lot of basic math and memorization of certain steps—along with more intuitive forms of natural navigation. The workshop always sells out well in advance.

Several new books have appeared recently lauding the importance of natural navigation. In *The Lost Art of Finding Our Way*, John Huth contends that if we use technology as a substitute for our innate capacity to find our way we will lose valuable insights into our world. In *Finding North*, George Michelsen Foy writes that the very act of navigating is an essential part of our humanity. The heir apparent to Harold Gatty, the great Australian navigator who first popularized natural navigation and whose work I mentioned in an earlier chapter, is Tristan Gooley.

Tadji and I were in Paris last fall—Paris is Tadji's home away from home—when I tracked down Gooley and made arrangements to pop over to England for a visit. He lives with his family in a quaint village near the south coast. Tall and handsome, with an Aussie-style wide-brim hat, Gooley looks as if he should have a reality TV show about surviving in the wilds with just a multi-tool. His book *The Natural Navigator* is terrific, and, like Gatty's, details natural navigational techniques on land and water. Gooley is a gifted writer and explains, among other things, how you can find direction from the sun, stars, and even spiders using shadows and simple tools. One of his recent books, *How to Read Water: Clues and Patterns from Puddles to the Sea*, intrigued me.

He met me at the train station and we went for a walk. Gooley is the only person to have flown solo and sailed singlehanded across the Atlantic. We had an immediate connection when I learned that he sailed a Contessa 32. We talked about the burgeoning interest in natural navigation.

"It's a combination of things," he explained. "I don't think people are rejecting technology, far from it, but they're feeling a basic need to reconnect with nature. We feel better when we're close to nature, and learning to navigate by nature's signs gives a purpose, a focus for being in the woods, or at sea for that matter."

I concurred and couldn't resist explaining my JET theory. He's a polite chap and indulged me. He was curious to know my opinion on *How to Read Water*, and I said I thoroughly enjoyed the book, especially the chapters on listening to water and reading waves. "I also really liked your voyage in the dhow off Oman," I continued, and we talked about how Arab mariners were navigational pioneers. "I am also fascinated by working sailboats," I added, "and have been lucky to sail in Mayan canoes, Sri Lankan oruas, and Haitian sloops. Haitian fishermen routinely sail 100 miles north to Grand Turk and they don't even carry a compass."

"I'm not surprised," he said. "We have an innate ability to navigate, and we've lost that. Natural navigation is not a survival skill anymore, but just looking about enriches everything we do."

We talked about trying to organize a natural navigational workshop together but concluded we were both too busy to pull it off. After a quick lunch, I was on my way, delighted to have met a kindred soul and certain that we would cross wakes again.

My first attempt at serious natural navigation was a long-ago yacht delivery, a 12,000-mile voyage from Fort Lauderdale to Japan in a 50′ ketch. It actually began a few months before, when I delivered a 45′ ketch, *Here and Now*, across the Atlantic from Miami to Gibraltar. The owner, Roger, was a dear friend, and he and his wife Myrna were among the first students at my navigation school back in Fort Lauderdale. A tall, imposing man with an accent to match his North Carolina mountain roots, Roger had taken up sailing later in life, and he was smitten. He wanted to explore the islands. He bought a Morgan Out Island 41, a tough but sluggish boat, and hired a captain to take him from Fort Lauderdale to Bimini, a distance of 55 miles. The captain started the passage drunk, and then a few miles later became miserably seasick and decamped in the aft cabin and never moved. Roger carried on, steering throughout the day and into the night, but he underestimated the strength of the Gulf Stream. He was unsuspectingly swept north of the Bahamas. He realized that something was wrong a day later, and tacked back toward the coast. The Gulf Stream kicked him north again and he eventually made landfall at Jacksonville, just below the Georgia border. "It was a learning experience," he told me, with typical understatement. He fired the captain, motored down the Intracoastal Waterway, and took every course I offered.

Roger and Myrna spent a few winters in the Bahamas honing their sailing and navigation skills and then decided to sail to Europe. Roger assembled a crew and hired me to be the skipper. During the crossing

I read one of Roger's collection of books, a hefty tome called *Seabirds: An Identification Guide*, by Peter Harrison. Other than Harold Gatty's indispensable handbook, *Finding Your Way Without Map or Compass*, it was the only book that gave navigational insights gleaned from pelagic birds. It wasn't dramatic reading, but I plowed through most chapters and studied the lovely color plates. When I left the boat in Marbella, Spain, I accidentally tossed it in my seabag.

Not long after I returned I set off on my long voyage from Fort Lauderdale to Japan, delivering a 50´ ketch called *Country Girl*. During this 12,000-mile odyssey via the Panama Canal we crossed the Pacific with stops only in Hawaii and Guam. I took the book with me, and on the 3,500-mile leg between Honolulu and Guam dutifully recorded seabird sightings. I was curious to see what the birds might teach me about navigation. The 23-day nonstop passage was perfect for this purpose because it included stretches when we were far offshore and also skirted several islands and atolls, including seabird breeding grounds.

Navigation by seabird identification is at best an imprecise art, and the birds didn't always follow the rules laid out in Harrison's book. However, as the late master Micronesian navigator Teeta Tatua told famous sailor and author David Lewis, "seabirds are a navigator's best friend." I think most navigators would say that high-orbiting GPS satellites have replaced birds when it comes to favorite flying friends, but birds are certainly more fun than satellites. From red-tailed tropic birds, to flocks of black-footed albatross, to curious brown boobies, we had a menagerie of visitors as we reached across the vast Pacific. Seabirds have, for the most part, defined distances that they travel from land, and that's what makes them useful to navigators.

The many islands of the Hawaiian archipelago, stretching 1,000 miles east of Oahu past Midway Island, are seabird breeding grounds. Running before a steady northeast trade wind, with a poled-out 150%

genoa and the mizzen, we quickly left the landlubber birds astern. Seagulls, a misnomer, rarely travel more than 50 miles offshore. At first light, four days outbound from Honolulu, we spotted a pair of brown boobies flying at us from the direction of Johnston Atoll, which was 70 miles south. Boobies have a usual range of about 100 miles from land, and when seen in large numbers are rarely more than 50 miles from land. They usually fly away from land in the morning, then toward land in the afternoon: natural compasses in the sky. Later that day we saw 16 black-footed albatross, a sure sign that we were nearing the breeding colony on Johnston Atoll.

And so it went—the bird sightings became a highlight of each day and connected me to the oceanic environment in a way that a screen never will. I was intimately aware of my surroundings, observing not just birds but clouds, swells, schools of fish, and debris. I spent hours watching the waves and swell interact, and became able to predict wind shifts with great accuracy. But it was the birds that provided navigational insights. Skirting the atolls of the Caroline and Marshall Islands, a solitary tropic bird was always an indicator that we were less than 200 miles from land; a flock meant we were within 100 miles. By the time we approached Guam, after more than three weeks at sea, seabirds were like signposts in the sky. Bonin petrels—not to be confused with their deep-ocean cousins, storm petrels—and tropic birds were the first to appear. Then the boobies showed up, followed by majestic frigates, and finally the gulls, squawking like touts at a cruise-ship dock, as we made our way into Agana harbor.

The passage had a few bits of drama, including a brush with Typhoon Roy as we neared Guam, but there was never any drudgery. Tuning into the natural environment changes the dynamic of a passage. You don't stare at your watch, counting down the time until you can go below. Once you raise the curtain on nature's stage, you don't want to miss anything and time literally flies by. After the passage I wrote an article for *Ocean Navigator* about navigation by observing seabirds. A few weeks after the piece appeared I received a short letter from Roger: "John. So let me get this right. When we crossed the pond you didn't know a robin from an albatross. Then you steal my book and the next thing I know you're the damn John J. Audubon of the sea. Nice article."

Back in the Caribbean many years, many miles, and many seabird sightings later, we were approaching Isla Aves. The sea was also full of clues to help ascertain our position. We were sailing southeast and the wind was just a tickle north of east, a lovely reach. It was breezy but the sea state had moderated significantly in the last hour. As mentioned before, Isla Aves lies nearly 100 miles east of the island of Dominica. But it's Guadeloupe, the island just north of Dominica, that throws a significant wind and wave shadow reaching far out to sea. The prevailing northeast winds that form off the coast of Africa and blow unabated across the Atlantic create a prominent sea swell. Waves that form on top of the swell and change direction more quickly as the wind changes also tend to line up with the swell in the heart of the trade winds, combining to make the general motion of the sea a natural compass in the water. When the waves run differently to the prominent swell, the wind has shifted, or is about to do so. The waves are the wind's messenger.

The swell and waves that eventually crash ashore on the windward side of Guadeloupe have had a nearly 3,000-mile-long fetch, or open ocean run, and have become large and regular. Once they approach the island and encounter shallow water they slow down and get refracted—that is, they bend until they are parallel to the shoreline. That's why breaking waves always seem to approach a coast from directly offshore. It is also why in most cases, excluding Ikaria and other islands raked by katabatic winds (as discussed in Chapter Two), it's calmer on the lee side of the island. The waves reforming from the lee side take time to build again as the wind is light near shore. In fact, there's often a counter swell that forms on the lee side, usually at right angles to the prevailing swell, and this slows the formation of waves that will eventually reach out to sea. By the time they reach Aves, the fetch is just over 100 miles and the swell and waves are noticeably smaller those than that have carried on undisturbed through the wide passes between islands. An astute natural navigator sailing well offshore but on the lee side of the Caribbean islands can almost always tell when she's behind an island by observing the change in sea state.

We spied Aves from a distance of about five miles, which was close enough. Our celestial navigators were beaming with pride as their morning sun lines of position were accurate to a few miles. Soon the radio crackled to life. It was the military base, and they were not happy that we had come by for a visit. In stern Spanish, they asked where we had departed from, where we were headed, and our ETA. In my best "present-tense-centric" Spanish I tried to answer their questions. They wanted to know the boat's registration number and tonnage, and a host of other things that didn't seem to be any of their business. Then the radio operator turned his attention to the crew. How many of us were aboard, what were our nationalities? He also wanted to know how many men and women were aboard. I told him we were six men and one woman. When he asked the age of the woman aboard I turned off the radio and we tacked away from Isla Aves. It was the last time I've seen it.

SIX

MAGNETIC ANOMALIES

Cruising Newfoundland • High-Latitude Cruising •
Lunenburg • Escape from Yemen

"Newfoundland is of the sea. A mighty granite stopper thrust into the bell-mouth of the Gulf of St. Lawrence, it turns its back on the American continent, barricading itself behind the 300-mile long rampart which forms its western coast. Its other coasts that all face the open ocean are so slashed and convoluted with bays, inlets, runs, and fjords they present more than 5,000 miles of shoreline to the sweep of the Atlantic. Everywhere the hidden rocks and reefs wait to rip the bellies of unwary vessels. Nevertheless these coasts are a seaman's world, for the harbors and havens they offer are numberless."

—Farley Mowat, *The New Founde Land*

The Cabot Strait, off the South Coast of Newfoundland, August 1994
The pilothouse of a sturdy sailboat is an ideal place to watch a gale unfurl. Our cozy perch was secured to a concrete wharf built to accommodate ice-breaking supply ships that carry vital rations for the small village

of Rencontre East at the northern end of Fortunate Bay. The wind tried to blow us to sea. Sipping a glass of Louise's homemade wine—surprisingly drinkable—I watched low clouds that looked like blocks of granite scud across a withering sky. Storm clouds in Newfoundland have a permanence—they're not the towering cumulonimbus of the tropics that come and go—these mean business, and the land is scarred from the gale-force winds they generate. Trees are bent like old men and scratchy brush clings to rocky headlands with a hint of desperation. While there's a sense that the land is new, untamed, thrust up by impatient glaciers not that long ago, there's also the feeling that those who live in the sparse clusters of coastal clapboard houses are also desperate, clinging to a way of life the next storm might just blow away. My reverie was interrupted when Louise announced it was time for supper. That fact that I was sailing in Newfoundland at all was a quirk, a result of a random phone call, another serendipitous turn in the life of a man always on the lookout for, well, serendipitous turns.

I almost never answer the phone. No, it has nothing to do with my low JET, I can handle a phone, even an iPhone—but of course in 1994 we were still using primitive landlines. I know myself well, I am a talker, and if I do pick up, a long conversation is likely to ensue. It's not unusual for friends and acquaintances, often with just a hint of desperation in their voices, to track me down. They're looking for an honest, unvarnished opinion about a certain boat or a certain time of year to make a passage, or a certain reassurance that they're not crazy to be thinking about quitting land life to voyage beyond the horizon. That I might be considered a voice of reason is a scary thought, but we all need our dreams supported. Even if it's a complete stranger calling, I am easily suckered into chatting about boats and sailing; it's a disease and there's no cure for me. Pacing around the house, I banter and listen and then banter some more, and before I know it an hour has evaporated and the email, article, or chapter that I was supposed to be writing has gone unwritten. For some reason I decided to pick up the phone on a sultry Fort Lauderdale day in late July.

"Hello."

"Is this John Kretschmer?" The voice was deep and the accent unique.

"It is. What can I do for you?"

"My name is Peter and I am calling from St. John's."

"Did you say St. John or St. John's?" I replied, genuinely curious.

"Now why do you ask, b'y?" The voice was suddenly excited.

"Well, I was just wondering if you were calling from New Brunswick or Newfoundland?" I was showing off—I am something of a specialist when it comes to capitals: world, state, and yes, even provincial.

"THUNDER, B'Y, THUNDER. Say it again, say it one more time, say the name of the Rock, b'y."

I was a bit shaken by the caller's sudden passion but completely under his spell.

"New'-fin-land," I answered, as if on trial.

"By God, that's amazing! You're the first Yank that's ever pronounced the Rock properly. We must get together."

From that odd first encounter, Peter, who passed away just a few months ago, and I went on to become dear friends. Although he was calling to get my opinion of a boat, a terrible boat in my unvarnished opinion, our conversion soon tilted back to the Rock. I was intrigued with Newfoundland, and the prospect of northern sailing had haunted me for years. I made a mistake of mentioning Farley Mowat as one of my favorite writers (not telling him that it was in his book *The Boat Who Wouldn't Float* that I'd learned to pronounce Newfoundland). Like most Newfoundlanders, Peter had no patience for the famous Canadian author who is generally detested on the Rock and whose overall reputation is not aging well. "He's just a CFA, making up stories and telling lies."

"A what?"

"A Come From Away, they never understand Newfoundlanders."

Before I hung up the phone Peter insisted that I had to join him aboard his 34´ motorsailer, *Seaboll*, and explore the dramatic south coast. "It's even more beautiful than you can imagine," he assured me, talking about the coast, not his boat, before adding, "and no matter how much you try, you'll never understand the Rock from reading a book." He and his wife, Louise, had been gradually circumnavigating Newfoundland, voyaging a little farther each painfully short season. I was interested, to be sure, but noncommittal. I had a baby daughter, a pregnant wife, and had just returned from a long yacht delivery. I knew that I should at least discuss the idea with my wife before charging off on another sailing adventure. Peter refused to take no for an answer.

"What's your address?"

"Why?"

"You'll see. How's next month look on your schedule?"

"Well, OK, I guess."

A few days later a plane ticket turned up in the mail and a few weeks after that I was on my way to the Rock, the first of many voyages to and around Newfoundland and Labrador.

I'd been dreaming of the North ever since I did an oral book report on Robert Peary in fifth grade. My mother helped me make a fake animal-hair hood with cotton balls that I taped to my winter jacket, and I strapped rickety tennis rackets to my sneakers for makeshift snowshoes. Looking more like a low-budget clown than a fearless polar explorer, I concluded my less-than-riveting speech with the line, "Robert Peary is the greatest explorer in the history of the world." I never was much for subtlety. I didn't know then that Peary was a controversial explorer at best, and the navigational evidence supporting his claim to have been the first person to reach the North Pole was a bit sketchy. But Peary was tough, and never backed down from a fight. He publicly attacked his English rival Frederick Cook, who fraudulently claimed to have reached the pole the year before, and anyone else who doubted his accomplishments. Peary devoted his life to the quest for the pole. Despite his fame, he was desperately broke all the time and was always begging for sponsorship and support. Unfortunately Peary remained embittered even after supposedly reaching the pole in 1908. He was criticized for his harsh treatment of the native Inuit and also for not sharing more of his glory with his African-American partner, or, as some say, manservant, Matthew Henson, who traveled with him every step of the way. Later claims that Peary and Henson fathered children with Inuit women did little to enhance his suspect reputation.

I didn't know any of this as I devoured the boy's-book version of Peary's biography and longed to make northern expeditions of my own. I also didn't know that Peter's great-uncle was the legendary Captain Bob Bartlett, Peary's dauntless skipper and an esteemed polar explorer in his own right. Bartlett, who was from Brigus, a fishing village on the east coast of Newfoundland, made more than 40 Arctic expeditions and was one of the greatest ice navigators of all time. He managed to con *Roosevelt*, the 184´ ice-reinforced ship that Peary had built expressly for his polar quests, to within 150 miles of the pole. For some inexplicable reason Bartlett was not part of the team chosen to make the dash to the pole. It's widely believed that Peary was wary of Bartlett's growing fame and typically didn't want to share his prize. Peter, who later gave me a book, *The Log of Bob Bartlett*, told me, "Bartlett never said a word against Peary, he was his friend and always a true gentleman, but everyone knew Peary was a bit of an ass."

Ironically, Newfoundland is really not that far north, reaching just above 51 degrees, but its location is a mystery to many. The craggy Avalon Peninsula juts North America's first chin into the brooding Atlantic and lies nearly 1,000 miles east of New York. Despite being the sixteenth-largest island on the planet, bigger than Ireland, Cuba, Sri Lanka, and Hispaniola, Newfoundland is weirdly remote. The problem is the Mercator projection. It makes northern lands seem gigantic. Newfoundland is just too far to the east to make it onto most maps of the United States and Canada, which supersize the middle part of the world and squeeze out the extremities. The maps are crowded with more familiar and populous locations, and if you do find Newfoundland it's usually tucked into an inset or hidden in the margins.

Newfoundland's isolation stems from a combination of attitude and geography. Newfoundlanders trace their roots and allegiances east, to Ireland and England, and only grudgingly joined Canada in 1949. It's more Atlantic than continental. At 52 degrees west longitude, it's nearly as close to Galway, Ireland, as it is to Toronto. If you sailed due south from infamous Cape Race, not far from where the *Titanic* found her iceberg, you'd skip well east of all the Caribbean islands and fetch up in the Amazon Delta. Newfoundland even has its own time zone—30 minutes ahead of Atlantic Standard Time and 3½ hours behind Greenwich Mean Time, giving the concept of "island time" a new dimension.

After a delicate discussion with a now ex-wife, plans were made and I was on my way to Newfoundland. I arrived in St. John's around midnight and Peter greeted me at the airport. "I know it's late, b'y, but I want to take you up Signal Hill so you can get the lay of the land and the sea." Like most people born and raised on islands, and like most sailors, Peter was a geographic man. I understood perfectly, a person should always take time to find their bearings when arriving in a new land. I can't stand stumbling out of an airport, shuttling into a taxi, and then being dropped off in a city with no idea what direction I've just traveled. I am even more amazed by people who sit in an aircraft with their window shades drawn and have no idea of the terrain below, or even what direction they've just flown. When I fly, I monitor our course and speed with my iPad and Navionics charts, always impressed by moving along at more than 400 knots.

I stood atop the dark bluff, and the chill westerly wind seemed to cut right through me as I gazed below at the lights outlining St. John's protected harbor. Peter was explaining the vexing relationship between Newfoundland and the rest of Canada. "You see, b'y, St. John's is the oldest city in North America but we're the youngest province in Canada. My father helped Joey Smallwood lead the fight for confederation but I'll tell you, it's never been a smooth marriage, if you know what I mean." I did. However, I was less concerned about bad marriages, of which I was something of a specialist, and Canadian politics than I was about my clothing. It seemed incredibly cold for late August and I was hoping that my lightweight foul-weather jacket and old sailing sweater that my mother had bought in Brittany years before would keep my tropical bones from turning brittle. It hadn't occurred to me to pack my old Patagonia base layer from the Cape Horn days prior to heading north—I had been spending most of my time in the trade winds or along the steamy Mayan coast of Central America, and both seemed a world of latitude away from the Rock.

Seaboll was moored in the charming harbor of St. Pierre. We arrived by ferry from the nearby Newfoundland port of Fortune, a down-and-out fishing village that was struggling to live up to its name. St. Pierre, along with its sister island, Miquelon, is a tiny archipelago just 15 miles off the Newfoundland coast and is an outpost of France. France, not Quebec— you clear into France, and in those pre-euro days, the French franc was the currency. Boulangeries sell fresh baguettes and the grocery store is stocked with affordable Bordeaux, good cheeses, and Dijon mustard, the staff of life as far as I'm concerned. Despite a windswept landscape and harsh climate, the women are fashionable in heels and short dresses, and the bustling streets have an air of colonial prosperity. It's no secret why

France continues to support St. Pierre and Miquelon—it's all about fishing and mineral rights. "It's the oil and the cod, one will run out and one will come back, those frogs know what they're doing," Peter insisted. St. Pierre and Miquelon is a territorial collective and the islanders are citizens of France. "I could be the President of France," a local customs officer told me a few years ago when I returned aboard *Quetzal*, "but of course I wouldn't take the job even if they elected me. I'd never leave St. Pierre."

Charming is not an adjective anyone would use to describe *Seaboll*. Stout, robust, well-ballasted, doughty, resolute, any of these will do, but charming, no. Peter had considered buying another boat, the reason for his phone call, but he loved *Seaboll* and would later sail her south to Florida and the Bahamas. A Westerly Vulcan model designed by famed naval architect Laurent Giles and built in Hampshire, England, *Seaboll* had to be one of the biggest 34´ sailboats afloat and quite possibly Giles's least handsome design. Length is just one measure of a boat's size. *Quetzal*, with her low freeboard and fine entry, is a smallish 47-footer. *Seaboll* was a pilothouse sloop with a spacious and bright interior that included an inside steering station—a very useful feature for coping with the capricious conditions that plague Newfoundland waters—and amazingly, three private cabins. It was really an impressive and purposeful boat, just not a beauty. From the 400 feet of 3/8" anchor chain to the heavy-duty tanbark sails and oversized rigging, Peter and Louise had equipped *Seaboll* for serious northern voyaging.

Fog enveloped St. Pierre as we arrived on the ferry, and Peter was happy about it. "I am glad you can't see how beautiful this place is," he said, only half joking. "Otherwise you'd write about St. Pierre and leave poor old Newfoundland out of the story." The fog persisted into the next morning and we eased out of the harbor under radar and instinct. Standing next to Peter in the cockpit, I said, "I've never seen fog this thick."

"Oh, the fog's the least of it, b'y," he said casually, "the compass can go out at any minute, you know—magnetic anomalies, we've got them too."

I took the remark in stride, chuckling to myself. Many years later I realized that he wasn't kidding. We sailed east to Grand Bank, Newfoundland to clear back into Canada. Peter and Louise were determined to poke *Seaboll*'s bow into as many harbors on their island as possible and we decided to spend my week leisurely exploring the deep reaches and dramatic fjords of Fortune Bay.

We eventually fetched up in Rencontre East, near the head of the bay and not to be confused with Rencontre West. There are not many settlements along Newfoundland's south coast so you'd think that they'd each have their own name, but then again, Newfoundlanders have their own way of doing things. We nosed alongside the government wharf and laid in every fender aboard as gale-force winds were forecast. Fortunately, as mentioned earlier, the wind shifted just enough to blow us off the dock. Then, despite freezing rain and whipping winds, we went exploring. Nothing fazed Newfoundlanders. I was falling in love with the Rock and her hearty natives.

We scaled a small hill and discovered a magical bay rimmed by a saltbox cottage with a broken-down wharf. A nearby waterfall, a watering spot for old banking schooners, completed the picture. These wind-driven working boats plied the bountiful fishery of the Grand Banks for weeks at time, returning to out-of-the-way harbors like Rencontre to water up and dry their fish. We poked around the abandoned cottage and I told Peter it would be a perfect place to hole up and write a book. "Well, you wouldn't have many distractions," he said, "you can only reach Rencontre East by sea, there's no road in." That made the place even more desirable. On the way back to the boat we tried to buy fish from a few locals and, I confess, I had no idea what they were saying.

"Som s'ays ons t'day," one of them noted. Peter heartily agreed. After more small talk, I tried to pay for the fish and one fellow waved his hand and I made out something that sounded like, "Your money's no good here, b'y," and he insisted on giving us all the cod we could eat.

As Louise prepared supper I asked what the fisherman had said.

"Oh, he mentioned that there were some seas on today, meaning it's blowing a gale," she informed me. The small villages of Newfoundland were for centuries among the most isolated outposts on the continent. The language, almost pure Gaelic, in some cases mixed with a bit of Basque, antique French, and graphic colloquialisms, is something of a time capsule and would probably be better understood by a sixteenth-century mariner than by an American from the suburbs. I had come to accept that every male was called b'y, pronounced like bye, but meaning boy, but beyond that I was often at a loss trying to decipher the dialect. Even now, after many voyages to Newfoundland, I am still left scratching my head trying to understand certain words and phrases. Just this year I sailed with Greg, a writer and naturalist who works for Parks Canada and who is a Newfoundland native. "Newfoundland is the Galapagos of linguistics," he said as we stood watch together on a passage from Maryland to the Caribbean. "You definitely have to develop an ear for it. Townies from St. John's can't understand the country people and vice versa. It's an island to itself."

When the gale eased up we sailed back to Fortune and I made my way home. A couple of months later I received another call from Peter and, in his typical way, he came straight to the point.

"It's Peter, remember that house in Rencontre East?

"Of course. Why?"

"You want to buy it with me?"

"What?"

Peter explained that the village priest, who had been convicted of sexually molesting young boys and was serving time in prison, owned the house and it was for sale.

"It's jinxed, nobody in the village wants the place. We can pick it up for $1,000 Canadian. So with the exchange rate and all, that makes your share $350 US, a pretty good deal I'd say, b'y."

"I'm in," I said enthusiastically. "I'll send a check."

"Hold your money till I close the deal, then I'll let you know. In the meantime start thinking about that book you're meant to be writing."

Peter did end up buying the house, and went on to refurbish it into a lovely retreat. Unfortunately, he sold it again before I made my way back to Newfoundland. It would have been a lovely place to write a book, one of many places I've noted over the years and placed in the file "Places to Write Books" and stored in the cloud of my brain. Unfortunately, once revealed, these treasured places are often spoiled, although in my case there is not much fear that they've been exposed by a book I've written. Just ask my editor, she would love for me to spoil more secret locations, or at least finish the books I'm supposed to be writing. Hardcore voyagers are the same way: jealous of favorite and once-remote hideaways, ready to push on as they become popular.

High-Latitude Attitudes

High-latitude sailing is the new frontier for serious ocean cruisers. As once-dreamy tropical destinations become crowded and, worse, gentrified with charter boats, mooring balls, and kitschy beach bars, adventuresome sailors are finding their way to evermore distant anchorages. Far-flung regions of rock and ice that were formerly left to mariners of questionable sanity, sailing rugged, rust-streaked steel boats, today are being explored by cruising couples and families in sleek, capable, modern boats, some expressly designed for the high-latitude voyaging.

The definition of "high latitude" is a matter of conjecture. For some, any parallel north or south of the tropics of Capricorn and Cancer, or beyond the warm trade winds, is considered too high, but of course that's nonsense. Geography is deceptive. In North America, the craggy, unfriendly Newfoundland and Labrador coasts certainly qualify as high-latitude sailing, although they cover a range of latitudes primarily between 50 and 60 degrees. If you carry on north, past Cape Chidley at the top end of Labrador, to Baffin Island, you are definitely sailing in high, ice-clogged, gale-ravaged latitudes. Indeed, if you turned left, or west, you'd venture into the forbidding waters of Hudson Bay and the maze of passages that make up the fabled Northwest Passage. However, if you followed the same parallel east, across the Atlantic, once you crossed over southern Greenland you'd find yourself well below Iceland, just a tickle north of Scotland, and squarely in the rather pleasant, mostly ice-free zone of the southern Norwegian fjords. If you continued on you'd visit Stockholm and Helsinki on the mostly benign Baltic Sea, neither of which is considered a high-latitude destination, at least in sailing terms. In the southern hemisphere, the rocky shores of Patagonia and Tierra del Fuego, which cover a range of latitudes from the high 40s to Cape Horn, at 56 degrees, certainly qualify as high-latitude sailing.

Like most things in sailing, the phrase "high latitude" defies easy definition. I have to offer an aside here about how we sailors speak in circles, sometimes great circles, of which you will read more in Chapter Eight. I recently completed a rollicking passage from Grenada in the West Indies to Cartagena, the jewel of Colombia. The route, along the Old Spanish Main, was definitely not a high-latitude passage, as we never ventured above the thirteenth parallel. One of the crew, Judge, is a powerboater who succumbs to, as he calls it, "a morbid fascination with sailing," and occasionally leaves his sturdy trawler to join *Quetzal* for a voyage beyond the horizon and the range of his 800-gallon fuel tanks. Despite the fact that the wind was mostly behind us, we steered a course that didn't quite follow the rhumb line, angling instead for a better point of sail and a better motion in jumbled seas. This baffled Judge, who loved plotting waypoints into the chartplotter and building routes for us to follow.

"How are we doing?" he asked one night as he and Murray, his watch partner, settled in the cockpit.

"Fine," I said enthusiastically. "We're not quite on course but we're making good time."

He burst out laughing. "That's it, that sums it up perfectly, you sailors are crazy, you never give anybody a straight answer."

It's the same with high-latitude sailing, we are not really sure what makes a latitude high, but we know it when we're sailing there.

An intriguing breed of new boats are being designed and constructed specifically for high-latitude sailing. They're almost exclusively built in aluminum and feature hull shapes for coping with occasional ice collisions, and, more importantly, shallow drafts that allow entry into safe, ice-free bays and coves. These boats almost always feature shallow hull forms, ample beam, and lifting keels or centerboards. These are not your father's centerboarders. For one thing, they're heavy, with ballast-to-displacement ratios similar to many keel cruising boats, and routinely make long bluewater passages. For another, they're engineered to carry extreme loads and are ruggedly constructed. They've been proven seaworthy on countless high-latitude passages. Aesthetically, either you like the utilitarian, unpainted aluminum look or you don't, but there's no denying that these rugged boats are turning up in decidedly low-latitude anchorages as many trade-wind cruisers have realized the merits of blending shoal draft with deep-ocean capability in a near bulletproof hull.

A few years ago, at the Annapolis Boat Show, ocean-sailing guru Jimmy Cornell proudly showed Tadji and me around his then almost-brand-new Garcia 45 cutter designed for high-latitude sailing. Cornell was melancholy, an unusual mood for a man who has an abundance of self-assurance. He is the author of *World Cruising Routes*, a bible for world voyagers, and he also developed a new set of pilot charts based on satellite data—the first improvement in pilot charts since Matthew Fontaine Maury developed them 150 years before. Cornell is the father of the modern cruising rally and a four-time circumnavigator—he's been around and has earned, as he calls it, his Captain Bligh perspective, his own way of doing things.

He had just returned from a failed attempt to transit the Northwest Passage, the ice-choked route across the top of North America that, in the right year, connects the Bering and Davis straits. The Northwest Passage might be considered the new Cape Horn. It's the current sailing challenge that keeps bluewater schemers awake at night imagining making their way from the Atlantic to the Pacific, the ultimate high-latitude voyage. Cornell had organized the Blue Planet Odyssey, an around-the-world rally designed to raise awareness of global warming. An optional route was to go through the Northwest Passage, but in the summer of 2014 the ice refused to yield and Cornell retreated to Annapolis. (He successfully transited the passage the other way, from west to east, the next summer.)

His boat, *Aventura IV*, is ingeniously designed for sailing at any latitude. Built by Garcia Yachts in France, it has an aluminum hull but a fiberglass deckhouse. Twin rudders are supported by small skegs, and the centerboard, when fully deployed, results in a draft of just over 9 feet. "This boat will sail as close to the wind as any cruising boat in this show," Cornell insisted. When the centerboard is fully retracted, *Aventura IV* can creep into harbors with less than 4 feet of water at low tide. As Jimmy showed us the watertight bulkheads and gravity-feed fuel system, Tadji tried to feign interest in esoteric details. What struck her was the severity of the design, the lack of warmth. "I felt like I was in a navy ship," she said as we finally made our way off the boat.

"Ya, but it's a cool boat, really fresh thinking. And when you look at the ballast-to-displacement ratio and length waterline, it's not a lot different from *Quetzal*, just beamier. I'd like to sail it in big seas, to see how she handles."

"Have at it, I'll be on *Quetzal* when you get back, or maybe that Hylas we looked at earlier."

Naturally I was delighted that Tadji had taken such a liking to our boat, and I'm certain we'll sail *Quetzal* off to Valhalla one day, but … part of me is intrigued by this new breed of high-latitude sailboat. I think they represent an intriguing new direction for cruising sailboats, unhindered by any connection to yachting and its much-too-grand traditions. They're expedition vessels, and there's no denying that today's bold offshore sailors, plying higher and higher latitudes, are explorers.

Circumnavigating Newfoundland, 2010, via Lunenberg

Quetzal is not the ideal boat for northern sailing, not even close, but that hasn't stopped her from making four voyages to Newfoundland. The first, more than ten years ago, was much too short, a brief hop to the spectacular southern fjord coast. The second, a year later, was again too brief, as we sailed up to St. John's and back as I had a quixotic goal to round the infamous Cape Race and visit Peter. In 2010, I finally put together a proper expedition and we spent a month circumnavigating the Rock and visiting rugged Labrador. Five years later we returned, spending a summer making our way around Newfoundland, but not before thoroughly exploring the Gulf of St. Lawrence and picking our way through the rocks and fog of the remote coasts of Quebec and Labrador. All of these voyages have a common denominator beyond *Quetzal* and her skipper—they all began and ended in Lunenburg, Nova Scotia, our gateway to the North and one of my all-time-favorite harbors.

Lunenburg bookends the northeastern edge of NGA Chart 108, a far-ranging swath of ocean framed by the coast of North America, the Bahamas, the Great Antilles, and the sixtieth meridian. By rights, Lunenburg doesn't deserve a place on this chart; it's a city of less than 3,000 holding court with all the big-name seaports. But Lunenburg, which somehow seems to turn up in every chapter, is more than a dot on a chart and a cove along the rocky south coast of Nova Scotia. It is a storied harbor with a maritime heritage hewn by graceful schooners, a once-bountiful fishery, and deadly storms that have carved too many names into the haunting granite columns that make up the fishermen's memorial on the waterfront. If you're a mariner and Lunenburg doesn't stir something deep within you, it's time to take up gardening.

When the prevailing southwest wind fills in, keeping the fog banks respectfully offshore, gliding into Lunenburg under sail is the stuff of dreams. If you're lucky, or maybe unlucky, the legendary *Bluenose* schooner might also be returning to her homeport. The first time I arrived, back in 2004, after a nonstop passage north from Fort Lauderdale, *Bluenose* blew past *Quetzal* under full press canvas doing at least 15 knots. It was impressive and humiliating—we were left gaping in her wake.

As you harden the sheets for a close reach past the Battery and into the harbor, the first thing you notice are the church spires marching up the hill and glaring down at you like dueling chess pieces conjured by Lewis Carroll. (For a small town there are a lot of churches, but even for a non-believer like me that seems natural in a town where virtually all of her sons have gone to sea or will do so. Every family, it seems, has a tragic fishing story in their past.) Then the colorful wood-frame buildings just behind the wharves come into focus. The barn-red warehouses of Adams and Knickle stand out—they've been in the fishing business since 1897.

Kenny Knickle has done plenty of work on *Quetzal*'s engine over the years, giving me a financial stake in this yard's storied history.

There are always a few fishing trawlers alongside the rough-hewn wooden wharves, some scallopers and lobster boats, maybe a tall ship or two, but still a far cry from the early twentieth century, when the harbor was typically filled with more than one hundred schooners. It was called "the woods" for its myriad spars. *Quetzal* usually shares the anchorage and mooring field with several sailboats and the occasional cruising trawler. The community understands that yachts are good business and several floating docks have been installed—still, the place is calling out for a real marina.

I met Alan, whom you first met back in Chapter One, on my first visit to Lunenburg. We had tied up at a precarious wharf that was just below his restaurant and he took our lines. We scrambled up the oily planks and made our way to the Old Fish Factory. Alan joined us for dinner and we've been sailing together ever since. Alan traces his Lunenburg roots to 1753, when the English founded the town as a bastion against further French expansion. Recruiting Protestants from all over Europe, including Lunenburg, Germany, and luring them with free passage, the English were determined to occupy what they called "New Scotland" and what the French called "Acadia." England prevailed, and in a move that seems sadly prescient of today's immigration debate, proceeded to boot out all the Acadians and replace them with loyal Protestants. In 1755, 7,000 French Catholics were expelled from their home of more than 100 years, in what has become known as the Acadian diaspora. Some of the displaced French were dispatched to the swamps of Louisiana, a French territory, and the word "Acadian" was eventually corrupted to "Cajun."

As mentioned, I had made my way to Lunenburg early in the summer of 2010, after a near-perfect six-day passage from Annapolis. *Quetzal* and her crew rode a magic carpet of favorable currents and steady 15-knot southwest winds. Tadji and my daughters Narianna and Annika, again whom you've met in earlier chapters, joined me there and we spent a few weeks in Lunenburg. Narianna and Annika carried on with their old man along the south coast of Nova Scotia as we made our way to the Bras d'Or Lakes, the enchanting chain of inland lakes carved out of Cape Breton Island on the eastern end of Nova Scotia. Baddeck, a tidy tourist town at the top of the lakes, became our staging point for the passage.

Annika, who was 15, made her way home to Fort Lauderdale, and Narianna, 17, signed on as part of the Newfoundland crew. She loves the cool north and was willing to put up with her dad's cronies to escape summer purgatory in Florida. Bruce from British Columbia, who has been a vital crewmember on so many *Quetzal* voyages, and Alan, of course, and his 17-year-old son Graham, joined Nari. Ron, another friend and *Quetzal* veteran who also turns up throughout these pages, and Dallas—a writer from New York, a kindred soul, and the only one among us with any true northern sailing experience—rounded out the crew. Dallas helped me plan the voyage, and we broke the trip into two legs. We chose a counterclockwise route that, in theory, gave us a better sailing angle for exploring the fjords of the south coast, more time to tarry in the broad bays on the east coast, time to sneak up to Labrador, and less beating on the return to Nova Scotia.

The Cabot Strait guards the southern coast of Newfoundland like a chastity belt and ensures that those headed north have honorable intentions—or at least sound boats and warm clothes. The 150-mile crossing from the mouth of the Great Bras d'Or Channel is anything but casual. Environment Canada was calling for strong west winds with, in polite Canadian vernacular, "a mix of sun and clouds," or, in other words, near-perfect sailing conditions. Naturally we had fickle easterlies, rain, fog, and an uninvited hung-over swell from the east.

The fog vanished suddenly, as if late for an appointment down the coast. The timing couldn't have been better. We were wary of our approach to Ramea because the sea buoy was missing, no doubt swept away in a Cabot Strait gale. We all rely on GPS for position these days and use aids to navigation to confirm what we hope we already know. Sadly, it's been my observation that lights and markers the world over are poorly maintained, and Canada, a country I love, is one of the worst offenders. If an alien force, or maybe just a tin-pot dictator armed with the right missiles, decides to blast the GPS satellites out of the sky, or more likely, if they stop transmitting their precious signals from lack of maintenance, we'll be back to the early days of sailing, conning our way into harbors by soundings and our senses. I am not appalled by this notion, and think a little time without GPS might be good for the human condition, but as you know, my JET is pretty damn low.

"Breakers ahead," Bruce called out from the bow. A rock, or "sunker" in Newfoundland speak, was lurking just below the surface. Alan, at the helm, instinctively eased *Quetzal* to port. Dallas zoomed in on the plotter and was relieved to see that the rock was on the chart—once again, we just had to zoom in far enough. The paper chart I had aboard, I confess, didn't have much detail. *Quetzal* was suddenly aglow in the oblique rays that only a northern sun can cast. We were peeling off layers of clothes as we eased along the freshly painted government wharf. Ramea, a collection of bald rocks and nasty shoals just a few miles from Newfoundland, was surprisingly busy. After lunch ashore we carried on, anxious to get to the Rock.

The approach to Grey River, along what has been aptly dubbed "the Fjord Coast," was a perfect introduction to this prodigious glacier-sculpted landscape. The entrance, a fissure just wide enough for *Quetzal* and a couple of seals, was between slabs of sheer granite and was difficult to make out from the sea. Waves throwing themselves against the coast ricocheted off the rock walls and set up a lumpy sea state. Stories abound of Newfoundland fishermen finding their way into port in dense fog in the days before fancy electronics. They understood wave reflection and could accurately judge their distance off the rocks by observing where the onshore and reflected waves met. Micronesian navigators of the western Pacific used the same technique. We used our eyes, our ears, GPS, radar, and the depth sounder, and eventually spotted the breakers off Seal Rocks; as we did, the door into a magical three-pronged fjord swung open.

Grey River was shoehorned onto the only piece of flat land in sight and was serenaded on three sides by waterfalls. Once again we made our way to the government wharf, which often serves as the village center for small outposts. We were greeted by several of the 124 full-time residents. The rickety wharf was bustling with preparations for the upcoming jamboree. Folks were cheery despite the fact that the village faced the prospect of resettlement. Two men joined us in the cockpit for Captain's Hour.

"If the mine doesn't reopen, I give it ten years and this place will be finished."

"Don't believe him, he's lying, I give it five years at the most."

Grey River's only contact with the outside world was the twice-weekly ferry from Burgeo, the "big city" down the coast, and the government helicopter which brought a nurse out once a month. With the tungsten mine closed and the fishing industry reeling, there's simply no work in Grey River, and worse, no hope. When the government in St. John's decides that a community is no longer sustainable it gives the residents two choices—take a stipend and move to a less remote location, or stay on but without any government support or services. The cruel nature of the resettlement policy is that all the residents have to agree to move for any of them to receive payment. Michael Crummy's masterful novel *Sweetland* chronicles the fate of a Newfoundland outpost that could very well have been Grey River. Sorry to miss the jamboree, which, we were assured, would bring over 50 people to town, we shoved off the next morning. (As I write, seven years later, Grey River is hanging on, although the full-time population is down to 101.)

The southwest wind was blowing hard, a steady 25 knots with stronger gusts, as we made our way into Hare Bay. The fjords are subject to katabatic winds—yes, those dreaded downdrafts again, only in Newfoundland they call them "blow me downs." As if on cue, the wind veered 180 degrees and piped up to gale force as we entered the breathtaking wind tunnel. At the head of the fjord, buffeted by bone-chilling blasts, we dropped anchor just off a thundering waterfall that poured into the fjord. We had inched our way onto the only shelf shallow enough to anchor on and made sure our 66lb Bruce was well set. It was a stunning if precarious setting. *Quetzal* was a speck, surrounded by vertical rock faces reaching 1,000 feet above sea level. And yes, we stood anchor watch through the breezy night.

The next morning, content that the anchor was holding, we made our way ashore near the base of the falls. We climbed to the summit of a 1,250-foot peak that stands sentinel over the fjord. It was rough going as we lurched through the bent brush of moose and caribou trails and over moss-covered rocks. The reward was a panoramic view of *Quetzal* below. Gazing at my faithful companion, a mere dot below, my beautiful and capable boat, I was reminded of all the seas we've crossed and all the harbors we've shared. I've written before, and I'll write it again: with a good sailboat anything is possible.

We carried on along the south coast, occasionally beating into gloomy east winds that shrouded the coast in fog and other times soaring before crisp westerlies that cleared the air and revealed the majesty of a vast wilderness that is less than 1,000 miles from New York City. We called at St. Pierre, which was still charming, and at Fortune, which hadn't changed much since I'd been there 16 years before. Just up the Burin Peninsula, the Mayor of Grand Bank greeted us at the wharf and proudly informed us that we were the third yacht to visit that year—it was August. A cold northerly snuffed out plans to visit Rencontre East and see the house I should have bought.

We then sailed 200 miles to St. John's, almost completely enveloped in thick fog. Fortunately it lifted as we closed the Avalon Peninsula. We were treated to an engrossing wildlife show. We chased flocks of clownish puffins into awkward flight, and dozens of humpback and minke whales plied the narrow corridor between *Quetzal* and the coast. Long-winged gannets patrolled leaden skies. Dallas, who has written about the currents and their impact on climate change in his book *To Follow the Water*, explained how the rich inside branch of the Labrador Current provides fodder for all manner of sea life.

Alan and Graham left us in St. John's. The passage had a profound impact on Graham. He decided to enroll at Memorial University, in its master mariner program, and today he goes to sea as a mate on a variety of offshore ships. The rest of us continued north. In Bonavista, we moored next to a replica of early explorer John Cabot's ship, *Matthew*, and met Jerry the dockmaster, who's well known for his photos of icebergs. When I returned five years later, on another voyage to the Rock, Jerry shared a funny story.

"You remember when you were here five years ago?" he asked, while taking a sip from a cold beer and getting comfortable in the cockpit.

I nodded.

"Well, I went home that night and told my wife that an American boat was in the harbor and the captain was a writer."

"OK?"

"Well, my wife says, so what's his name? I said John. She said not his first name, you moron, his last name? I said I don't know, Gretshmer, Gretchism, something like that."

"Grisham!" she blurts out, "John Grisham is at the marina?"

"Ya, that's it I said, what's the big deal? She looked at me as if I was an idiot and started calling all her friends. The next morning, she and her friends, must have been twenty ladies, and all carrying their John Grisham books, turned up at the marina. Lucky for you, I guess, that you had decided to leave early."

Our next waypoint was Fogo Island, one of the four corners of the earth according to the Flat Earth Society. It seems fitting somehow that Newfoundland would anchor one of these critical waypoints. Brimstone Head, a huge lump of earthen mound that looks as though it was randomly dropped from the sky, is the actual location. What seems less fitting is that today Fogo is home to one of the chicest hotels in the world, the Fogo Island Inn. Founded by Canadian businesswoman Zita Cobb, it was just being built when we were there the first time. Naturally we ridiculed the project, thinking, "Who would come to Fogo Island?" Today it's a model of environmental responsibility and sustainability and books months in advance. Cobb, who sailed around the world in a 47′ sailboat after cashing out of her high-tech company, feels a deep connection to Newfoundland, and her Shorefast Foundation is devoted to preserving and fostering the art and culture of the region. We are planning to return to Newfoundland, and I've promised Tadji we'll spend a night or two ashore at Fogo Island Inn.

On our 2010 voyage we couldn't resist sailing to a well-protected harbor on Fogo called Seldom Come By, before winding up Leg One in a rare marina at Lewisporte, a virtual metropolis nestled into the foot of Notre Dame Bay.

The Leg Two crew was a mix of *Quetzal* vets and a couple of CFAs. Dear friend and great sailor Rick Thompson turned up at the dock and tossed his duffel aboard. He introduced himself to Dallas, who was aboard the entire voyage. It's always a pleasure to sail with Rick, who has rock-solid judgment, never a bad word to say about anyone, and a lot of sea miles, including two Atlantic crossings aboard *Quetzal*, under his belt. Deb L., whom you met in Chapter Two, is a glutton for adventure and was back for another voyage. Rob and Denise, both newbies, rounded out the crew. Denise would go on to become a regular, sailing aboard *Quetzal* and other boats I've chartered all over the world. She's the skipper of her own boat, a Catalina 36 called *Girl Crush*.

Sailing north, we crossed the 50th parallel under spinnaker and made our way into Croque Bay before dark. Unfortunately we couldn't find the Croque settlement. Villages are few and far between on Newfoundland's northern arm, but we usually managed to find them. We crept up to a small cluster of branches masquerading as a wharf and motored to the head of a serene inlet, but still no village. Finally we eased into the unchartered western reach of the bay, turned a bend and there it was, Croque, all 20 or so houses.

We rafted alongside *Island Queen*, a not-quite-down-on-its-luck fishing boat owned by brothers Gerald and Ray. They came aboard and joined us for a tot of rum and settled in for a chat.

"We're down to about eighty full-timers," Gerald explained, "and that's dropping."

Ray, who didn't say much, added, "No work, no fish, that's it."

I took a picture of the brothers and offered to email it to them. Gerald scoffed, "No email in Croque, b'y." He gave me his mailing address instead.

"Just send 'em to Gerald Kearney, Croque, Newfoundland."

"That's it? No postal code?"

"That should get here, b'y, my wife handles the mails."

We sped north on a tight reach. *Quetzal* thrives in 10–15 knots of wind just forward of the beam, and we zoomed past Cape

Bauld, an ironbound headland marking the northernmost point of Newfoundland, with the mainsail, the 120% genoa, and the staysail all drawing nicely and our speed touching 9 knots. Jibing onto starboard tack, we sounded our way into a rock-rimmed cove just west of L'Anse aux Meadows and dropped the anchor. I was thrilled. I'd wanted to visit this site for as long as I could remember. L'Anse aux Meadows is the only documented Viking site in North America and may well have been the place where Lief Erikson stumbled ashore around AD 1000. Its designation as Vinland ("Land of Wine") has always been problematic because there's no evidence of grapes anywhere, but archeological remains are assuredly Norse. We spent a day wandering around the site and I was thankful that Parks Canada had not Disneyfied this important historical landmark. Viking knarrs, the vessels they used for trade and exploration, were shaped not unlike many of today's cruising sailboats. A typical knarr was around 50–55´ long and 15–16´ on the beam, a beam-to-length ratio that's about the same as *Quetzal*. They were built to be flexible, to ride with the sea, not to overpower it, and featured a low freeboard and a long keel for stability. It didn't take a huge leap of imagination to spy *Quetzal* at anchor and envision her as a close cousin of the ships that brought Vikings to North America 500 years before Columbus. While I doubt whether Leif Erikson would have much luck piloting the Space Shuttle, I am pretty sure he'd be able to steer *Quetzal* from the moment he stepped aboard, and I think he'd appreciate her speed and sea-kindliness. He'd probably also like the chartplotter, the Hydrovane windvane, the refrigeration system, and most of all, her diesel engine, eliminating the need for those troublesome oarsmen.

Our next destination was Red Bay, a former Basque whaling station across the Strait of Belle Isle on the Labrador shore. The fog finally lifted in the afternoon. Rob, scanning the horizon, was the first to see the unidentified mass in the distance. "Could be an iceberg," he said nonchalantly. We scrambled for the binoculars. It *was* an iceberg! It's hard to explain the thrill of seeing one of nature's giant castaways afloat. The radar showed it was about six miles away. We altered course to give it a close inspection. It looked like a Henry Moore sculpture and shimmered above the cobalt sea in a bold defiance of gravity. As we approached I shot its altitude, or height above the horizon, with my sextant. Using the radar to establish our distance away, I calculated that it was 110 feet high, and a vertical sextant measurement translated into a width of 125 feet. It was obvious that it was hard aground in 150 feet of water—a nicely proportioned iceberg indeed.

Bergy bits, small chunks of floating ice, were littered around the berg. Denise suggested we launch the dinghy and haul some ice aboard for Captain's Hour. I rowed out to a bit and knocked off a chunk of blue ice. Dallas, a veteran of several Arctic oceanographic research voyages, assured us it would sizzle when we poured gin over it. Luckily we had bought some Iceberg brand gin for just this occasion and we wasted no time in seeing if he was right. He was.

We were running out of time and decided to head south from Red Bay. We had hoped to make our way along the Labrador coast, heading north toward Nain, but the island of Newfoundland had greedily consumed our time. We made haste down the coast, visiting the UNESCO World Heritage site of Gros Morne National Park. There, glaciers that recently—geologically speaking—carved up billion-year-old blocks of granite like butter, and that frame a beautiful inland pond, have formed massive cliffs—massive even by Newfoundland standards. We tied up at a small marina and the dock attendant was distressed about charging us $22 for the night.

"It's me job, b'ys, and a bloody awful one. I am sorry to soak ya like this."

Newfoundland saved her best for last as we made our way to the Bay of Islands along the west coast near the town of Corner Brook. A civil west wind escorted us to Woods Island. We followed a hand-drawn sketch chart from an old Cruising Club of America cruising guide into a handsome harbor with 360 degrees of protection. The sandy bottom offered perfect holding and the water was even warm enough for a brief and bracing swim. When Deb and Denise returned from the island with a bucket full of blueberries I decided that Woods Island would be nominated for one the coveted spots on my top ten anchorages list.

At Captain's Hour Dallas was thoughtful, and a bit melancholy. He noted that we needed to cradle this perfect moment. A long-time New Yorker, with a keen intellect—he's probably the smartest guy I've ever met—unsullied by sentimentality, Dallas was surprised by his own reaction. "This place just won't tolerate cynicism," he said with laugh. After many voyages together I have come to know that he's a closet romantic, but I'll never tell. Our cruise was drawing to an end and all aboard sensed that this anchorage was a reward for a voyage carried off without drama but one filled with wonder. We'd found our way to an unlikely paradise and nobody could take it away from us—it was ours for an evening and there wasn't another boat or human in sight. Still, one doesn't mess with the seasons in the North. We were into early September, and Newfoundland was seeing us off gently. Soon this perfect harbor would be swept by fall gales and then racked by winter storms. It was time to keep moving. I'd already been away from Tadji and the kids for too long, and I needed to get back to Lunenburg, to get back to my real job of taking willing souls across broad swaths of ocean. In early November we'd be on our way to the Caribbean once again.

I lingered in the cockpit late into the evening, soaking in the light of the full moon. With a few drams of single malt whisky running around my head I realized that rounding the Rock had been another one of my quixotic quests, a nice little adventure, but not one that fostered a deeper understanding of what makes Newfoundland and northern sailing unique. That would require another, more leisurely voyage. I would have to come back—I knew I'd be back.

Return to Cape Breton and Newfoundland, 2015, via Yemen in 1986

Quetzal took the long way back to the North. A list of her landfalls in the interim includes every island in the eastern Caribbean, Venezuela, Bonaire, Colombia, Panama, Belize, Isla Mujeres, the U.S. East Coast, Bermuda, the Azores, Ireland, England, Spain, Portugal, the Mediterranean from Gibraltar to eastern Turkey, Madeira, and the Canary Islands. Five years and 50,000 miles disappeared beneath her keel, but I don't put much stock in totaling miles—I've never believed that sea time should be measured by the distance between landfalls. The bookends of land should not define our sailing experience. It's the in-between that matters, the voyage, the interlude of being at sea, for a month, a week, a day, an hour, that's where the magic lurks. James Fenimore Cooper's character Long Tom Coffin declares in the classic sea novel *The Pilot*, "Never could see the use of more land than now and then a small island, to raise a few vegetables and to dry your fish—I am sure the sight of it always makes me uncomfortable, unless we have a wind dead offshore." For me, I've always had to find a way to balance the thrill of cruising, of nosing the bow into pristine anchorages, and of backing stern-to into historical quays with the freedom I find sailing offshore. I never want a passage to become a mere countdown to the next landfall, but at the same time I don't want to lose the awe and the sheer joy of making new discoveries where land and sea meet. Northern sailing, which demands steady seamanship and acute situational awareness as conditions change abruptly, also offers a powerful blend of natural beauty, cultural intrigue, and the opportunity for discovery.

Quetzal's most recent northern cruise began, like all of her passages, with an offshore passage. I had only just finished a major project, the removal of the teaks decks (which you will read about in the next chapter), when the crew turned up at Spring Cove Marina in Solomons, Maryland. Undaunted by the need to schlep not only provisions but also sails, lines, cushions, pots and pans back aboard as I had *Quetzal* stripped, they leapt to the task and we shoved off more or less on time. Although we had a windless passage and had to motor most of the way, the crew formed a bond. Tige, Fletch, Peter, Tom, Steve, and Miles got along famously. Miles later bought a 54´ cutter, *Chasseur*, and most of the crew from that first voyage have become regulars, joining Miles for offshore races, including the classic Newport to Bermuda. They've not only sailed together but have become close friends, a connection shaped by the sea. They've all led busy lives and would likely not have met, much less become friends, without a week of isolation—and a lot of time for discussion at Captain's Hour. We had been scheduled to sail direct to St. John's, Newfoundland, but ran out of time because of lack of wind and ended up sailing into the Bras d'Or Lakes. Only Peter had time to sail on to Newfoundland. Later, Alan, Steve, Fred, Doug, and another friend, Gordon, joined me for a cruise back to Baddeck, as *Quetzal* crisscrossed the Cabot Strait.

Henry Fuller has lived in Baddeck since the early '70s. His Cape Breton Shipyard has been a beacon, a friendly home away from home for many voyagers. You wouldn't guess that he is as old as he is—he's tall and handsome, with a shock of unkempt hair and a distracted air. Henry is a trusted friend of nearly every northern sailor of note, and although I am anything but a northern sailor of note, having just barely scratched the surface of northern voyaging, I am also lucky to count him a close friend. He's a throwback, a man you can count on to watch your boat when you are away, and he will give you honest suggestions for repairs, and fair prices. He's a fount of reliable information about the North, and can also discuss the details of seemingly every nautical book ever written.

I left *Quetzal* under his care for a few weeks in the summer of 2015, and then got to know him when Tadji and I returned to make preparations for a voyage into the Gulf of St. Lawrence and north to Quebec, Labrador, and Newfoundland. Henry was facing a difficult prospect; recent legislation passed in Ottawa was threatening to put his small shipyard out of business. The government geniuses had decided that foreigners should not be allowed to leave their boats in Canada for more than a season without paying a stiff import tariff. The Cape Breton Shipyard's main source of income was storing American yachts over the winter. With the swipe of a pen, his business of almost 40 years was undermined.

He was philosophical about the situation. Drinking wine in *Quetzal*'s saloon, he confided that he was ready to be free of the responsibilities of the yard.

"I am more sorry for my guys—they've been with me a long time—than I am for myself. I am OK with shutting things down. It's been a long run."

He was planning a hiking trip to New Zealand with his friends Maurice and Katie. He'd met them years before, when they left their 34´ cutter *Nanook* at the yard for a winter. They were early circumnavigators and high-latitude sailors before the term existed. They sailed for 35 years, from Cape Horn to Siberia, from Alaska to the Mediterranean. Maurice is a highly talented artist, and Henry surprised us when we visited him at his house by presenting us with a haunting and altogether lovely painting Maurice had given him of *Nanook* rounding Cape Horn. A series of six woodblocks, it captures the mood of the Horn brilliantly, right down to gray scud filling the sky. It occupies choice real estate in *Quetzal*—the port forward bulkhead.

In the small world of sailing, we discovered we had a mutual acquaintance, the recent recipient of the Cruising Club of America's prestigious Blue Water Medal, Trevor Robertson. Trevor is a mariner of astonishing experience and is the only person to winter over unassisted in the Arctic and Antarctic, aboard his self-built 34′ steel boat, *Iron Bark*. Trevor later married Annie Hill, another famed ocean sailor, and the ceremony took place at the Cape Breton Shipyard with Henry officiating. I was delighted to hear that Trevor was not only close by in Newfoundland but considering sailing to Cape Breton for a visit. I had last seen him in Djibouti, a tiny desert country on the horn of Africa, 30 years before. A long time ago to be sure, and a long way from Cape Breton Island, but it was one of those experiences that you don't easily forget—one that's worth me taking you on a short detour back to the Arabian Sea here.

Molly and I were aboard *Epoch*, helping my mom and Tim sail from Sri Lanka to Cyprus in the Mediterranean. Our route took us north to India, across the Arabian Sea, via Oman and Yemen, and finally up the Red Sea to the Suez Canal. Mom, the driving a spirit of *Epoch*, reluctantly left her beloved boat in Oman as she was sick with pneumonia and the doctor feared she might become gravely ill if she didn't take an extended rest. The voyage assumed a delivery air after that. We had a job to do—get to the Med and leave the volatile Mideast behind as quickly as possible. We came within an eyelash of losing the boat in the port of Aden when we sailed blindly into the middle of a rapidly escalating coup d'état.

Yemen was a supposedly friendly port for cruisers in 1986, and the moderate Marxist state was known as a good spot for cheap provisions. We planned to make a brief stop and then carry on for the Straits of Bab el Mendab and the Red Sea passage. Seven yachts were anchored in the inner harbor of Aden when *Epoch* began her approach. We never made it, as the sky and nearby waters erupted in a furious volley of explosions. Despite the waters roiling less than a quarter mile from us, incredibly we thought that we had stumbled into a military exercise—not a civil war. Not until a rusty gunboat with a raggedly clothed but heavily armed crew charged toward us and emphatically motioned for us to anchor, immediately, in the deep waters of the outer harbor did we realize the nature of our blunder. We had sailed directly into a full-scale war.

From our vantage point we could see soldiers ashore, dashing from building to building, squaring up and firing with automatic weapons. Fighter planes buzzed low over the harbor and raked the city. Gunboats fired at land targets from just beyond the harbor while shoreside artillery tried to take them out. A game of deadly ping-pong was taking place right over the top of us. Every time a shell hit the water, *Epoch*'s iron keel reverberated. It was terrifying. A BBC World Service broadcast confirmed the conflict. A hardline Marxist insurrection was trying to overthrow the government and the situation was chaotic. Causalities were numerous.

The cruising yachts in the inner harbor were in worse straits than us. When one yacht, ironically named *Innocent Bystander*, was shelled, the other crews decided their only shot at survival was to abandon ship. A Russian freighter in the harbor opened its hull door and they made a perilous dinghy dash, leaving their boats behind. One of those sailors was Trevor Robertson. He later said that leaving his boat, *Salvation Jane*, was the hardest decision he'd ever made.

When the Russian vessel, leading a convoy of ships, steamed out of the harbor, we realized we had to follow them—it was likely our only chance to get out of Aden with *Epoch* intact. A ring of gunboats rimmed the harbor but they let the ships pass unmolested. We followed them but were losing ground—6 knots never seemed slower. Our hopes were dashed when four gunboats broke ranks and came charging toward us. One slowed as it approached and came to stop 50 meters ahead of us. I altered course to pass it on our port beam. One of the crew made his way forward and positioned himself behind the bow gun. He slowly turned it directly at us. Was he going to blow us into oblivion?

I can see that young man's face clearly to this day. He had a head of dark hair, a dark beard, dark eyes, and he was no more than 20, maybe 25. Our eyes locked. I could feel the bodily fluids start to drain out of me as the seconds stopped. I felt I might collapse. I couldn't stop staring at him. He hesitated. Regaining my composure, I was actually relieved that I had those precious seconds to take stock of my life. I was 28 years old, and things had gone pretty damn well. I was thinking with crystal clarity, again experiencing the phenomenon of slow-motion perception. There was no feeling that time was moving—the earth had stopped revolving. If this is it, so be it—I resolved to die as I had tried to live, standing tall, not crying or sniveling. I know this is absurd, death is death, but these were the thoughts filling what I was certain would be my last seconds.

Abruptly he stood up, pushed the gun turret aside, and hurried back to the cockpit as the gunboat steamed away. We made our escape. As I write these words I realize that I should go back to Yemen to try to find this man, and talk to him. If I could find him, which of course is a crazy thought, the longest of long shots, but if I could, I'd like to know why he spared us. I believe that a common humanity joins us, and it takes a truly evil person to look into someone's eyes, someone unarmed and innocent of any crime, and take his life.

We made it out of Aden just in time, as later we would hear firsthand of the terrors that took place. We set a course for Djibouti, a "friendly" country, and as it turned out, where the Russian ship deposited her yachting stowaways. Trevor stayed with us aboard *Epoch* and described his narrow escape. "Things were reaching the break point," he said, "but we were all reluctant to leave because the authorities had our passports and boat papers ashore. Also, the people of Aden were so friendly, it was really hard to wrap our heads around the idea that a war was developing. But when *Innocent Bystander* was hit, we knew it was now or never."

He explained how they made a perilous dinghy ride across the harbor to the nearest merchant vessel, the Russian ship *Smolensk*, with shells exploding all around them. "At that moment all I wanted was to put a wall of steel between us and the shells. Yes, and we watched *Epoch* follow us out of the harbor, we were pulling for you."

That's not the end of the story, as it turns out. Trevor refused to give up the notion that his boat, *Salvation Jane*, was still afloat. As soon as the hostilities ceased, he hired a crew to take him back to Aden. In an unlit dinghy, he made his way back into the harbor under cover of darkness. *Salvation Jane* was floating, oil soaked and filthy, but more or less seaworthy. He slipped out of the harbor, and would later sail the boat across the Atlantic and Pacific. Wintering in the Arctic was a piece of cake after that.

Back in 2015 aboard *Quetzal* in Baddeck, Henry informed Tadji and me that Trevor had decided to skip Cape Breton and sail nonstop from Newfoundland to Western Australia, a mere 100-day journey or so. I was keenly disappointed at not being able to see him again after so many years, but also found myself smiling at the idea of someone deciding that it was time to get home and setting off on a three- or four-month journey without any fuss or fanfare. He's a true sailor and a throwback to a time when voyagers went to sea to, as Moitessier put it, "save their souls," not for notoriety. Trevor and I exchanged a few emails before he shoved off and I left Henry with some of my books to mail to him when he made landfall. Tadji and I then made plans to sail to Prince Edward

Island. PEI is a bucolic island in the Gulf of St. Lawrence and would serve as the base for our latest expedition north. We had decided to spend a few weeks exploring the remote north shore of the Gulf of St. Lawrence, where Quebec and Labrador meet. We'd then circle back to the east coast of Newfoundland before heading south for Nova Scotia.

I assembled a terrific crew of *Quetzal* veterans, Bruce, Ron, Steve from Cincinnati, and Deb L. Dallas was again aboard, and his friend and steady hand Nick, who also was the team photographer. The incongruous Magdalen Islands were our first waypoint. A collection of sandbars in otherwise rocky environs, the Magdalens are temperate and a vacation haven for Quebecois. Dallas was at the helm as the islands loomed into view off the bow. Just as suddenly as they appeared, they evaporated from sight as we sailed into a fog bank. The wind vanished. We fired up the diesel but suddenly Dallas was well off course. He's a superb sailor and always pays attention to course and trim, almost to an annoying degree, but he was floundering at the wheel. In the fog, the compass is your only frame of reference. No sooner had he brought the boat back on course than he was suddenly 90 degrees off again. "This is crazy," he announced and turned the wheel over to Steve. He had the same problem, careening off course. At first I thought both had just had overindulged at Captain's Hour, but then I glanced at the compass. It was dancing, veering 30 degrees one way, then the other. Then it hit me, and I had to laugh as the boat finally began to settle down.

"What is it?" Dallas insisted.

"Oh, nothing unusual, just a magnetic anomaly. They have them up here."

Postscript

I recently gave a talk at a marina open house in Waukegan, Illinois, and told the story of the encounter with the gunboat in Aden Harbor. I made it sound as dramatic as it was, and the audience hung on every word. When I reached the climax, as the man in the gunboat decided not to shoot, a hush fell over the room. I then mentioned that I would like to go back to Yemen to track down that man who spared my life. An older gent in the crowd raised his hand and said, "Maybe he was out of ammunition—that's why he didn't shoot." We all burst out laughing. I have to confess, I had never considered that possibility before.

SEVEN

THE *ALMOST* PERFECT BOAT

Debating Sea Rescues • Seaworthy or Not? • Hull Shapes •
Sail Plans • Deck Matters • Interiors • Teak Deck
Project • Dodgers

"... his being a yachtsman calls for some compassion: yachtsmen are consumed with the notion that their boats must be one hundred percent sound. They are oblivious to the fact that the majority of the world's working vessels are plagued with rot. Yet these are the ships that do the work, year after year, with no-holds-barred when it comes to weather."

—Sterling Hayden, *Wanderer*

"... and though we have but little wind hitherto, we are jolted to death by the motion of the ship in these rough seas. Yet the captain is every moment congratulating us on the smoothness of our vessel, which he declares is so soft in her motion that one may play bowls on her deck."

—Janet Shaw's journal, *Lady of Quality* (written after a voyage in 1776, and first published in 1921)

Spring Cove Marina, Solomons, Maryland, 2015

Motoring into Back Creek, we were just a few minutes away from my sister Liz and brother-in-law Trevor's marina, in Solomons. While the crew flaked the mainsail and positioned fenders, I had a fit of anxiety. We were wrapping up a nice passage, one I call the East Coast Offshore, a nonstop sail from Fort Lauderdale to the Chesapeake Bay that *Quetzal* and I have made many times. Once we reach the Bay, if we've made a swift passage and have time, we make a few landfalls on the way north to Solomons, a charming sailing town 50 miles south of Annapolis. This time I found myself trying to draw out the passage, as we called at Deltaville and Crisfield before arriving just in time for the crew to catch their flights home. What was the reason for my angst? We were about to take *Quetzal*'s beautiful teak decks off, a massive project that would forever change the look and feel of my beloved boat and trusted companion.

This is the kind of talk that makes some people uncomfortable. It's just a boat after all, a material object, and even the thought of naming a boat strikes them as a bit odd. Attributing a boat with anthropomorphic traits is far worse, and more than a little creepy. Did I really believe my boat would know the teak decks had been removed? Hell yes, and I had a flashback to my first glimpse of the boat, when she was called *Madrigal*—coincidentally, that glimpse having happened in a boat yard about 100 meters to starboard from where we were easing along under power.

It was a snowy day and I'd come up from Florida to see if this particular Kaufman 47 was the boat for me. She fit all my parameters: a well-built performance cruiser, capable of crossing oceans, and with an accommodation plan to allow me to carry passengers. Still, you never know until you lay eyes on a boat whether it's the one. I knew it from my first glance, and I was right. Indeed, my relationship with *Quetzal*—a name chosen with advice from, and the consent of, my daughters—has been one of my longest-lasting relationships. She's been the perfect boat for the life I envisioned back then, continuing to sail all over the world—my definition of freedom—and sharing my knowledge and passions along the way.

I am stirring up trouble, I know, as the words "perfect boat" will cause a spirited debate between any two sailors. Google "is there a perfect boat?" and you will find a slew of interesting comments. New sailors—feeling overwhelmed by the myriad choices—are admonished by the old salts who almost always condemn the basic notion of a perfect anything, least of all a boat. They compare it to the fallacy of finding the perfect spouse, or to boasting of making perfect guacamole. The perfect boat, they claim, is utterly subjective and an altogether ridiculous idea. Everybody's idea of the perfect boat is different, we're reminded, and some see it as an unconsecrated thought that should be banished from your brain before it rears up to challenge the first commandment of boating, that being: "all boats are compromises." Pursuing this fiendish notion of the perfect boat will leave you in a state of profound misery as you inspect boat after boat, a sailor-errant on a noble but futile and never-ending search for the Holy Grail afloat.

Of course the naysayers are right, there's no perfection, in boating or in anything else material—it's a stupid word, and all boats are compromises. Yet there's something about a sailboat, a beautiful ocean-going sailboat, that lets you ponder a shakshuka of small- and large-scale fancies that unshackle the human spirit, that lets your imagination soar and your senses hyperventilate. There may be no perfect boat—but a capable sloop, or sleek cutter, or doughty ketch, or graceful schooner, or spidery multihull, trimmed and balanced, harnessing a prevailing wind and surging over a luminous sea—the delicate fusion of mind and matter, if but for a fleeting moment—is as good a definition of perfection as anything dictionaries have conjured up.

I've owned five sailboats over the years, and written about them in great detail in books—especially *Sailing a Serious Ocean*—and many articles. I've sailed countless other boats, primarily as a delivery captain, which, as I have mentioned, was how I made my living for more than 20 years, and also as a sailing journalist, test-sailing and writing reviews of hundreds of new and used boats. Just struggling along to this stage of the book, you have surely ascertained that I am partial to sea boats, boats that can sail across oceans without making a fuss. The perfect-boat naysayers are spot-on when it comes to defining specific design and construction features—there is no magic formula, no secret recipe for Mayan spaghetti. Every boat is a cauldron of ratios and engineering specs mixed with the designer's aesthetics and the builder's identity and economic realities. Still, despite the vast array of incredibly diverse sailboats sprinkled about the watery part of the planet, I do have one criterion that makes a boat perfect for me. She needs to be willing and able to sail anywhere I want to go. I need to know that I can throw off the mooring lines and set sail with full confidence—for a day across the bay, or a month across a sea—from the Caribbean to Cape Horn. I know that anything can happen at any time—the ocean is merciless, untamable, volatile—that's the risk and ultimate reward of deep-ocean sailing, but giving you the ability to launch voyages with confidence and without limitations or festering back-of-the mind anxieties is what makes a boat perfect.

In the last chapter we sailed north, where the conditions often demand steady seamanship and really good, if not quite perfect, boats. One of the best sources of cruising information online is a site called Attainable Adventure Cruising. It has a northern focus, bent toward high-latitude voyaging, but nevertheless features articles on all manner of serious sailing subjects. John and Phyllis Harries run the site, and do the bulk of the writing. The stories are both detailed and compelling, not an easy accomplishment as sailors are demanding and voracious consumers of information. The site has a lot of feedback from readers, many highly experienced voyagers. A few years ago they tried to develop a reader-inspired design of a 40´ world cruiser called the Adventure 40. Their plan was to actually produce the boat and sell it completely outfitted for around $200,000. Sadly the project didn't progress past the design phase. It was fascinating to read the suggestions and feedback from various sailors—an innovative attempt at creating a crowd-sourced version of the "perfect boat" that was actually affordable by folks of ordinary means. Don't get me wrong, $200,000 is a fortune to me, but when compared with other new boats, the Adventure 40 would have been great value. Sailing, like much of the world's economy, reflects the growing chasm between the haves and the have-nots. New boat prices are almost impossible to fathom, with an average 35´ production boat costing around $240,000 according to the latest data from the North American Sailing Industry report. A top-quality, brand-new world cruising boat of around 40´ can easily cost upward of $700,000 and a 47´ brand-new version of *Quetzal* will command close to $1,000,000. This puts the Adventure 40 project in perspective—it was a noble enterprise.

Dedicated ocean voyagers have never insisted on new boats to fulfill their quests and have been willing to build their own boats if necessary, or refurbish down-and-out sea boats, inspired by the knowledge that when they do go to sea they will know their boat intimately. Recently I was sailing in Belize and came across a tired old Hunter 30 sloop at anchor, crewed by four young people from Uruguay. They couldn't afford a chart so I gave them mine and urged them to be wary of the many hazards along the reef. They were appreciative and told me that they hoped to sail to Jamaica next. I sensed they didn't know that it was a tough 400-mile slog into the teeth of the trades and gently asked them if their boat was up for the trip. "Oh yes," the young skipper, who spoke

English with an Australian accent, told me in earnest, "she's really the perfect boat." Perfection is in the eye of the beholder.

I became a regular reader of Attainable Adventure Cruising after coming across John's piece called "Enough of the Northwest Passage Already." He passionately laid out the case that too many inexperienced sailors in boats not designed for high-latitude sailing were attempting to transit the passage, a notoriously risky route across the Canadian Arctic that, to be successfully navigated in a single season, requires consummate seamanship, a stout boat, and favorable ice conditions. (Jimmy Cornell's *Aventura IV*, discussed in the previous chapter, is a perfect example of a boat purposely designed and built for the Northwest Passage.) And if you don't make it through in a season you must be prepared and provisioned to spend the winter iced in, not a small consideration. John's contention was that the Northwest Passage was not a bucket-list item, and if and when these inexperienced sailors failed, requiring rescue from first responders, it would trigger restrictions and limitations from the Canadian Coast Guard, or worse, even outright bans on yachts heading north.

The piece generated a lively online discussion, with many readers agreeing with him and others suggesting that he had no right to undermine anyone's sailing aspirations. I tended to side with the latter, as most sailors contemplating the Northwest Passage are extremely experienced and diligent in their preparations. The risk of reining in a dream is the more severe of the two evils. Trevor, the Australian Blue Water Medal sailor you met last chapter in Yemen and Djibouti, weighed in with advice that should speak to every voyaging sailor, and to every notion of the perfect boat. Writing with typical clarity and humility, he noted that "if you would not attempt the passage without emergency beacons, radios, and sat phones to call for help, stay down south because you should not regard the ability to ask for assistance as an essential part of your plan." He added that "it might also be interesting to ask yourself, 'If you could never tell anyone about it, would you still go?' If the answer is 'no,' then probably you are out to tick the box, and should not be contemplating this."

Trevor's response translates into what I look for in the perfect boat: a boat that affords us the privilege of self-reliance—indeed, a boat that commands us to be self-reliant—and with that, we must accept responsibility for our actions, which is, of course, the ultimate freedom. When Trevor departed from Fogo Island off Newfoundland bound for Perth, about 10,000 miles away, he accepted all the risks of the journey. This makes me wonder about the Uruguayans I met in Belize. Should I have told them they'd never make it to Jamaica without serious work on their boat—was that my responsibility? I don't think so, and who am I to judge whether their dreams are up to my standards? Nobody would have said that I was prepared for Cape Horn, or even to be a skipper at all. The problem, however, comes back to John's fear that other, less prepared sailors will ultimately cost the rest of us the sacred freedom that offshore sailing offers when those with power over us deem that it's not safe for us to go to sea at all. That's a terrifying notion.

I have never embraced the idea that my private adventures should warrant someone else risking their life to save me from myself. This is particularly nettlesome for me because I conduct offshore training passages for a living, and most of the people who sign aboard assume that if things go terribly wrong we will be able to dispatch an emergency plea for help. Indeed, we spend several hours before every passage discussing our emergency plans, including various ways to make distress calls, and we carry all the things Trevor condemned: radios, emergency beacons, sat phones, trackers, etc. I do, however, always warn the crew that rescue is, at best, a risky proposition and that they need to fully grasp the idea that once we set off we're essentially on our own.

I recently sailed with my friend Derek Lundy, author of the worldwide bestseller *Godforsaken Sea* (and of the foreword of this book). One of the finest sailing books ever written, it's a riveting account of the 1996/97 Vendée Globe singlehanded race around the world. The race that year included several dramatic rescues, and the tragic death of one competitor. Sloshing to windward aboard *Quetzal* on a passage from Antigua to Barbados, we discussed the basic notion of self-reliance. While fully acknowledging that the lone sailors competing in this grueling nonstop race are supreme athletes and incredibly brave folks who blast around the world in 60´ wind-powered rocket ships, I ventured that without the prospect of rescue the singlehanders would sail far differently and in more seaworthy boats. Derek respectfully disagreed with my basic premise, or at least he was polite in telling me that he thought I was full of shit. He believes that we all benefit by supporting sailors who display the unadulterated courage, ironman-like endurance, and consummate seamanship required to sail at breakneck speeds across the most remote regions of the planet. And when things go wrong, the risk and cost of rescue operations pale when compared with what we gain by recognizing and vicariously sharing the spirit of their quest, the same human spirit, he contends, that sent us to the moon and that makes humans the strange and amazing beasts that we are.

Another friend and frequent shipmate, Earl, also suggests that supporting bold endeavors like the Vendée Globe, and offshore passagemaking in general, is an essential part of the social contract. "Once we agree that we will rescue anybody, from a fire, flood, or crime scene, then we agree to rescue everybody." He contends that society spends vast amounts trying to rescue and rehabilitate people who repeatedly make bad decisions. "Why would we not do all we can to rescue a sailor in trouble? You can make the case that saving the life of someone who has the wherewithal to launch an offshore passage is good for our society. That's who we want in our society."

I confess, Derek and Earl have led me to re-examine my ideas of rescue at sea. I have no desire to perish anytime soon. I am supremely happy with this life I've created out here on the fringes, launching voyages and sharing adventures with like-minded shipmates, stretching my allotment of minutes to the max, and now, more and more, sailing with the love of my life. I believe that we have a fundamental human-to-human responsibility to do all we can to help those in distress, at sea and ashore. We always monitor the radio and stand ready to assist fellow mariners in any way possible.

I had the privilege of interviewing several Coast Guard rescue swimmers when I wrote *At the Mercy of the Sea*. These brave men and women are the Coast Guard's elite enlisted personnel, highly trained and committed to saving lives, not judging them. Still, I contend that I am ultimately responsible for my decisions and my actions and that it's not my right to endanger rescue swimmers or anyone else unnecessarily. By the same token, it's not their right to tell me whether I am qualified to undertake a voyage, or insist that I abandon my boat. Maybe that's why I passionately believe that you need a good boat if your intent is to go to sea. Having your own version of the perfect boat, based on experience and research—and it need not always be an expensive boat: you can buy a used Contessa 32 for less than $30,000—is the ultimate key to successful bluewater sailing and greatly improves the odds that you will never need to be rescued.

So, is *Quetzal* the perfect boat? Yes, in that she'll take Tadji and me wherever we want to go. Is she flawed? Oh my, yes—she has almost as many flaws as her skipper, that's probably why we get along so well. I am lucky, I have clear ideas of what features I want in a boat, based, in part, on my having logged many thousands of miles in boats I didn't like much. Falling off waves that make the hull shudder and send shock through your joints, or having to arm wrestle the wheel to hold course, or being launched across a dance-floor-wide interior—none of this is my idea of a nice sailing boat. The perfect boat, or at least the *almost* perfect boat, is a synthesis of design and construction, with design being the slightly more important of the two. A moderately built boat with a sweet design will be a much better sea boat than a clunky design built like a battleship. One consistently false notion that new sailors maintain is that their boat has to be strong enough to out-muscle the sea. I am here to tell you that the sea is pretty damn muscular, and any thoughts of bullying it are utterly misguided. You want your boat to make friends with the sea, that's what an ocean-going design is all about, friendship.

This is not a book about boat design and construction. I have written about these topics in other books and articles until the manatees come home, but some topics are too important to completely bypass and simply must be repeated, reinforced, and driven home without the crutch of subtlety. So, with that in mind, here is a brief, non-technical list of some general design and construction features that I look for in a bluewater passagemaker, always being mindful that these are the thoughts of one sailor. The Appendix, called "Wrinkles," is more enlightening for those looking for a few details, for advice on the nuances of good boats, for a few thoughts on prudent seamanship and safety, and for other observations on the "esoterica" gleaned from a lifetime at sea. There's some interesting nitty-gritty there, so be patient, or jump ahead.

The Right Hull Shape

This is the key to every good offshore boat. A good motion in a lumpy sea is probably the most important characteristic in a genuine ocean-going boat and the most overlooked when it comes to choosing one. What's a good motion? In short, a boat that doesn't pound when punching into seas, that can take a breaking wave on the beam without being knocked down, and that can reach and run without rolling from gunwale to gunwale. Stroll around any major boat show and you can count the boats that will have a decent ride in even moderate conditions with both hands, and that's being generous, as you probably won't need your thumbs. A boat with a soft ride in a seaway, or in conditions that are less than ideal, is something to be treasured. I've been sketching this basic hull shape on cocktail napkins for years. It looks like this: A fine entry, a relatively deep forefoot (the area between the stem and the start of the keel), a deep fin keel, and a substantial rudder mounted well aft and tucked behind a protective skeg. Variations of this hull shape have been escorting me across far-flung seas for nearly 40 years. A soft ride dramatically reduces crew fatigue, is the best anti-seasickness medicine there is, and also inspires confidence that offshore passagemaking is an attainable goal.

And while on the topic of hull shapes, a boat that tracks well sailing upwind will prove wickedly more efficient and satisfying than one that doesn't. Tracking is different from pointing—it's the net result of windward sailing over the long term, not the momentary thrill of sheeting the sails tight and sailing close to the wind to lay a mark. One of the vital parameters that we use to navigate, and to steer by, is "course over ground" (COG on your plotter). This function measures the actual track laid down, as though the water was temporarily sucked from the sea and your boat's keel etched the course line along the seabed. A boat that does not give up a lot of seabed to the influence of wind and waves tracks well and does not make "leeway." Remember back in Chapter Two when *Quetzal* had to claw off the lee shore in Malta during a nasty squall? Her ability to track may have saved her. *Quetzal* is not particularly close-winded—she doesn't sail much closer than 40° off the wind—and, like most boats, is definitely happier at 50° off; however, with her low freeboard, fine and deep entry, long fin keel, and powerful skeg-hung rudder (my "perfect" cocktail napkin design), she tracks like a cheetah and makes almost no leeway. By comparison, a beamy, high-freeboard, extreme fin-keel boat with a scant forefoot and very tight sheeting angles may point 35° off the wind. But if the sea is up, she easily gives 15°, or even 20° back in leeway, ice skating across the sea and sacrificing a nice motion in the process.

Although there is a lot more windward sailing in world cruising than some think, especially these days as we voyagers stretch our wings to discover intriguing locations far beyond the trade-wind belt, there is still plenty of deep reaching and running when sailing offshore. Sailing with the wind coming from anywhere near the stern day after day is glorious, except for one thing—the rolling. A boat that rolls from gunwale to gunwale is extremely uncomfortable. It's an unnatural motion that can be hard to get used to because it's less predictable than being steadily heeled in one direction. Cups, books, iPhones and iPads slide from one side of a counter to the other—nothing stays put unless you secure it. Rolling reveals the absurdity of a centerline queen bunk, which is de rigueur on many cruising boats. However, it must be noted that modern, flat-bottomed boats that carry their beam well aft have more initial stability than the narrow, deep-keeled sea boats I love and usually roll less running downwind. Catamarans hardly roll at all. But don't despair, my sea-boat brethren—in the Appendix we'll look at how to dampen roll while reaching in big seas.

In terms of hull material, solid, uncored fiberglass hulls, especially today's hulls that often blend reinforcing fibers like Kevlar and, in some cases, carbon into the laminate, still outrank aluminum hulls in my book, but the gap is narrowing. I recently inspected many damaged or destroyed boats in Tortola after 2017's devastating hurricanes. Looking at the hulls that survived versus those that were destroyed reinforced my belief that solid fiberglass hulls are better for cruising boats. Steel, wood, and ferrocement is the order in which I'd own them, although I am not sure I would want a ferrocement boat in any circumstances—even as a gift.

On Deck

Back to boat shows for a moment. These lively venues, with flapping banners, specialty gin bars, booths with bewildering displays of gear, and entertaining speakers pontificating on esoteric subjects, are great fun to attend and a lousy place to buy a boat. I am always amazed as I watch folks stand in line to get aboard new boats. Once they've been granted permission to leave the dock (without their shoes), they gather patiently in the cockpit and then finally they're allowed to go below, entering the inner sanctum, where they then ooh and ah over the swanky leather cushions and shimmering joiner work. Covers sell books and interiors sell boats. In both cases it's absurd.

The deck, including the cockpit, is where all the action takes place, where all the sailing fun is, and it's crazy to ignore it when choosing a boat. Fortunately, most serious sailors don't buy new boats, and if they do, they are very particular in fitting them out. The deck, first and foremost, must be laid out for safe, efficient sail-handling. Leads need to be fair (so that lines run smoothly without binding), and easily adjusted to allow as many options as possible. An important aspect of successful passagemaking is the ability to make your sails big in light air and small in heavy air. This sounds simplistic but in reality it's complicated and difficult to achieve on many modern boats. Many of today's boats have fractional rigs with small self-tending headsails with very little trim range, and large, full-cut mainsails constrained by swept-back spreaders. These boats are not well suited for crossing oceans. The trend toward making sailboats simple to handle, in some cases ridiculously so, is not what voyagers are looking for. Sailors, even dedicated cruising sailors who claim they're not in a rush, are not power boaters, they like to tweak sails and make their boats perform better. It's almost absurd how rewarding it is when the slight turn of a winch, or the tensioning of a vang, or the shifting of a lead results in a leap from 6 to 6.5 knots of boat speed.

I am not an advocate of leading all, or even most, sail controls aft to the cockpit. I recognize the safety factor of keeping the crew off the deck, but the logistics of routing everything aft leads to friction and inefficiency, and also, more importantly, I like to be on deck. I like to move when I am aboard—to me it's vital to get up off my fanny, leave the cockpit, and do some work on deck. (For more on this philosophy, see the "Walkabout" section of the Appendix.) Of course, offshore boats need excellent nonskid—a slippery deck is not just inconvenient and a toe-breaker when you unsuspectingly slide into a lead block, it can be deadly. Well-placed handholds are important for sure, but aggressive nonskid is even more so. Teak decks, which we're going to discuss very soon, persist on many boats not just because they look great, but also because they provide excellent traction, especially when wet.

Cockpit

The cockpit is command control when sailing and also where you spend the bulk of your time whether you are underway or not. A comfortable seagoing cockpit should be a priority when looking at boats for offshore passagemaking and extended cruising. *Quetzal*'s cockpit is huge, nearly 12 feet, probably too large. The helmsperson is sequestered behind an enormous wheel where she is well supported and able to focus on steering, but isolated from other tasks. It works for us because the cockpit accommodates plenty of crew and is a safe, secure space to work, with easy access to sheet winches, and, until very recently, it had excellent sight lines for sail trim and overall visibility. It's not ideal for a couple, and we'll talk about those sight lines soon. It is, however, a wonderful sunroom/patio to lounge in at anchor. Cockpit protection—especially on a low-slung boat like *Quetzal* that kicks up sheets of spray when sailing upwind—is essential. Spiteful waves that care nothing for the high cost of all things associated with sailboats have destroyed three dodgers and two cockpit enclosures over the years. This has led to drastic measures—something I will also get to later in this chapter.

Sail Plan

To my surprise, I have become an apostle of the cutter rig, flying two smaller headsails instead of a single large headsail, or genoa. When I started sailing I was a proponent of the high-aspect sloop with a single overlapping genoa and a wide-bodied symmetrical spinnaker (after I learned how to set one, that is—recalling my escapade on *Gigi* recounted in Chapter One). I have since realized that the staysail just may be the most important sail aboard *Quetzal*, especially in heavy weather. The ability to roll in the genoa when the wind pipes up and carry on with a proportionally reefed main and staysail eliminates a lot of stress and allows *Quetzal* to stay the course without excessive heeling. We can also maintain control and good speed. *Quetzal*, like many boats of her generation, is not a true cutter by design, she's a sloop with a staysail, sometimes called a "slutter," and to me that's an advantage. In sloop-like fashion we are able to carry large enough headsails to propel us when deep reaching and make speed when beating to weather in light or moderate conditions. The headsail is slightly higher cut than a genoa, which gives away a bit of sail area but also affords better visibility and maneuverability. The staysail doesn't do much in these conditions and is often lounging on deck. It earns its minutes in between these extremes when we are sailing between 50° and 120° off the wind, which is most of the time, and especially in squally conditions. It serves to steady the boat in a beam wind, helps ease weather helm, and is vital in finding the right balance to allow our much-loved Hydrovane self-steering windvane—a magical and completely mechanical contraption—to do its job.

Another critical part of any sail plan is the poled-out headsail. I rank our whisker pole as one of the most critical items aboard *Quetzal*—I can't imagine making a passage without it. It's fashionable to contend that whenever the wind is favorable offshore sailors will pop a spinnaker. It may be fashionable, but it's simply not true. Serious cruisers rely on poled-out headsails, either one or two, far more than spinnakers, even relatively easy-to-handle asymmetrical chutes. There's a thrill every time the spinnaker goes up and extreme relief when it comes down. The ultimate state of passagemaking is when life aboard surpasses life ashore, meaning that you're eating well, sleeping soundly, regular, happy, and most importantly, unstressed. Reaching before a following wind and sea, with a poled-out headsail providing the horsepower and an amp-free windvane doing the steering, is the definition of low stress. (I talk more about the use of twin poles in the Appendix.)

The Interior

Tadji would love an aft cabin with a centerline queen bunk and no amount of selling or cajoling on my part will dissuade her. She is not fond of having literally to climb over me to get into her side in the V-berth. Her contention, citing the stats from my mother's four-year near circumnavigation, her baseline, is that for every day you are underway, you are ten days in port. Therefore, just based on mathematics alone, comfort should trump seaworthiness. Not surprisingly, I respectfully disagree. Maybe I am unique, or more accurately, just strange, but I feel my blood pressure go down the moment the breakwalls recede and the unfettered horizon beckons. As I have said before, all the bad stuff happens on or near land. Tadji rolls her eyes when I quote Goethe, "Those who have never seen themselves surrounded on all sides by the sea can never possess an idea of the world, and of their relation to it." I base just about every decision about what I want and need in a boat's interior on whether or not it will make the boat more seaworthy, more sea friendly. Tadji has grown to love being at sea too but argues that it's not an either/or proposition. She's right of course, and gradually we've been "Tadjifying" the boat, making it more livable when we are at anchor. I must confess, life aboard *Quetzal* has improved dramatically with new cushions, better lighting, brighter headliners, a few more opening hatches, etc. I still draw the line on the centerline queen berth, however, and I know I am on safe ground. We are committed to sailing *Quetzal* until we no longer sail, and although we've made many changes, large and small, there's no physical way to add a centerline queen berth.

Other features of a seagoing interior include sea berths and heads that can actually be used underway. If a boat has two heads, it makes sense to have them on either side of the boat, one for each tack. Settees make good sea berths with the simple addition of a lee cloth, although a dedicated spot—a quarter cabin, for instance—is usually better. Never underestimate the importance of sleep. Nothing short-circuits the enjoyment of an offshore passage more than fatigue. And when fatigue becomes exhaustion, it's a recipe for disaster.

The galley is vital to crew happiness—well, at least to my happiness. I contend that a boat, even an offshore boat days or weeks into a challenging passage, is not an excuse for a bad meal. The cook has to be prepared to make good food, and a well-designed, seagoing galley can make the difference between a meal of slapped-together sandwiches and a delicious chicken stew cooked in the pressure cooker. First, you must be able work in the galley on any point of sail and have both hands free. I am not fond of galley harnesses, which keep the cook strapped in place but also leave you vulnerable, unable to move quickly if a hot pot or open flame comes your way. I prefer a galley arrangement that allows me to plant my hips on a bulkhead or vertical counter wall. Deep fiddles and deep sinks, which by default become the place where you stow everything while you prepare meals, are essential. The stove must gimbal freely, and adjustable metal pot-holders on the stovetop are quite helpful. A pantry that allows you to easily remove provisions while heeled or when rolling is an often-overlooked galley feature.

The layout is something to seriously consider before choosing a boat. Do you need three or four private cabins? That arrangement works on *Quetzal* because we are in the business of taking people to sea, but if I could design a boat expressly for training passages, I would opt for dedicated single bunks with padded leeboards in smallish cabin spaces without doors. The need for extra cabins is often overrated—your family and friends who promise to come visit rarely do—and cabins usually take up what could more usefully be used as storage space. Modern boat interiors are open, bright, and spacious because the interior furnishings have been pushed out to the hull sides with little consideration given on where to stow spare parts, canned food, and the 100 or so bottles of wine essential for voyaging. Another complaint I have about many of today's boats is that the open floor plan is dangerous for moving about while underway. Here's that ten-to-one ratio again, but it takes only one bad fall to make you think differently. Manufacturers claim that they've dealt with this potential problem by adding extra handholds, usually placed overhead along the headliner. This is definitely better than nothing, but really not very helpful. For one, they're tough for short people to reach, and second, they're about as useful as the overhead handrails on the subway. Think about when the subway makes a sharp turn, and it's hard to maintain your position; now imagine the subway bucking up and down as well—you'd be clutching for any vertical post, or better, a wall to support yourself against. It's the same in boats—the advantage of an interior layout with plenty of bulkheads is that you always have a place to plant a hip, and hipholds are always better than handholds.

The irony of the perfect boat is that it evolves over the years. The more you sail, the more you become aware that features that at one time seemed perfect, or at least vital, are no longer held in such esteem.

At the same time, you come to appreciate what upgrades will make your life better. I laugh when I think of all the changes we've made to *Quetzal*, the so called perfect boat, and whimper a bit when I think of the money we've spent. That's just the way it works. I said earlier that you don't own boats, you have relationships with them, and all relationships need work and money. The important thing is knowing that the boat is worthy of the work and money. A bad boat will greedily consume your resources, and worse, your time, and break your heart in the process.

Refits

Quetzal has undergone numerous refits, retrofits, and makeovers during the 14 years we've been sailing together. We lost the mast in a tornado in northern Italy and had to fit a new rig in record time, a traumatic saga told in *Sailing a Serious Ocean*. We replaced the engine in Maryland, a more involved project than I first envisioned, and dropped and rebuilt the rudder and skeg in St. Martin. We cut in new hatches in Turkey and had the hull painted for the first time in Trinidad. More recently we rewired much of the boat, replaced headliners and worn teak veneers with shiny white laminates, and thoroughly tidied up the interior. The wear and tear of a working boat with 120,000 miles under her keel has demanded continual maintenance and upgrading. We've gone through three galley stoves and two saloon tables, filled a complete recycle bin with electronics, ordered five headsails, four mainsails, three staysails, and three spinnakers, and replaced every bit of running rigging twice. The bits and pieces add up, and over the years we've spent at least $1,000 a month keeping *Quetzal* ready to answer the demands of being the perfect boat. However, two huge projects stand out from the rest.

I mentioned earlier the importance of good nonskid on deck, and noted that teak decks provided excellent footing. *Quetzal,* like many Taiwan boats built in the 1980s, was slathered in teak when I bought her.

Side decks, foredeck, cabin trunk, handrails, coamings—a veritable forest afloat. As someone who is capable of rationalizing almost anything, and because I was able to buy the boat for a great price, I not only accepted the abundance of teak, I embraced it. It was the perfect boat, after all.

Of course I knew that practical-minded sailors scorned external wood; indeed, I was one of them before I felt the magic of teak beneath my bare feet, at least on cloudy days when the decks were not scalding. And yes, I knew that teak decks were becoming scarce on new boats and seen as a liability on older boats. But that didn't stop me from bragging about teak's unrivaled nonskid capabilities and excellent insulating properties. And I loved the aesthetic, boasting that a handsome renewable resource like teak softened the cold, oil-derived glare of a utilitarian fiberglass deck. I was more than a teak-deck apologist, I was a teak-deck snob.

To my dismay, the decks started to show signs of wear and tear just a few years after *Quetzal*'s first training passage. Although I tried, I couldn't ignore the screw heads appearing under sprung bungs, the raised and missing caulking on the foredeck, and a couple of weathered planks that had splintered. But it was a mugging in Trinidad that hastened the demise of my teak dreams. I left the boat on the hard for a couple of weeks and hired a highly recommended chap to lightly sand the decks, reseat a few fasteners, replace missing bungs, and caulk the worst sections. I returned to a crime scene. My beautiful teak decks had been attacked by a belt sander armed with 16-grit assault paper and smeared with black caulk. At first I wanted to cry, then I wanted to commit a crime of my own. But the damage was done, the life of the decks shortened. When *Quetzal* slunk out of Chaguaramas like a shorn English sheepdog I vowed to never again commission work from a contractor I didn't know, especially when I was thousands of miles away from the scene of the crime—a lesson I've learned too many times.

I kept sailing and mending as I went but the decks became more and more of an eyesore. When they started to leak I knew something had to be done. My friends and shipmates grew weary of my incessant fretting over the decks. "Stop complaining and do something," they told me, but I could not decide what to do. I considered replacing them with new fastener-free decks manufactured from templates and mounted with adhesives. These modern teak decks are lovely in every respect except price. When I received an "in-the-business" estimate of $60,000, I became less of a teak-deck snob. I looked into synthetic teak, also known as fake teak, and was impressed by its appearance and practicality. I gathered a box of samples and laid them on deck like playing cards. I stepped on them, and even hosed them down to see how they felt when wet, but after boasting about real teak for years, I just couldn't pull the trigger on installing a synthetic deck. I looked seriously at cork and invited myself aboard several aluminum and steel boats to inspect their cork decks. Cork is a natural, sustainable product but it's also expensive, the installation seemed beyond my talents, and Tadji really didn't like the look. "Cork," she assured me, "is for wine bottles."

With the realization that every option required the same process to prepare the subdeck, I finally decided to remove the teak, fill the thousands of holes with epoxy, fair, and then spray the decks with nonskid mixed in the paint. My teak deck days were behind me—alas, it was on to whiter pastures. The decision was liberating but I underestimated what a massive job it was to create a utilitarian, low-maintenance, oil-derived fiberglass deck.

Solomons, Maryland, has become *Quetzal*'s home when she's stateside—Fort Lauderdale is the hailing port on her transom, but it should say Solomons—and we tackled the project there at Spring Cove Marina. That's the reason I was anxious as we neared the marina. The talented boatyard crew had already made many valuable upgrades and repairs over the years and knew *Quetzal* the way a family doctor knows a long-time patient. The yard is owned and operated by my sister and brother-in-law—Liz and Trevor—my dearest friends and vastly experienced sailors who have been cruising intermittently aboard their Endurance 37 *Wandering Star* (including a circumnavigation) for many years. The cost-controlling plan called for a mix of DIY and professional work. My friends and I were responsible for the demolition phase of the project, removing the old decks, as I am much better suited for destruction than for construction. Time was of the essence—the gap in *Quetzal's* busy schedule gave us one month to complete the entire project. The doubters were plenty.

The first step was to pull the mast, haul the boat, and block her up in the paint shed. Working under cover freed us from weather concerns. Next, we removed every deck fitting—every cleat, clutch, track, anything mounted directly on teak. Fortunately, the designer Mike Kaufman and the builder Kha Shing had used several solid fiberglass islands to mount high-load winches and the traveler base. Still, this was a time-consuming process, requiring one person on deck and one below, and the removal of just about every headliner to gain access to the stubborn nuts anchoring through-bolts.

The next task, removing the teak, filled me with emotion. With heavy heart and cold chisel in hand, I surveyed the once-beautiful teak deck and sighed, remembering times I'd gone forward to reef the main or set the staysail always with secure footing, and the thousands of times I had cast admiring glances at my lovely teak-draped boat. Tadji, an undeniably beautiful woman, used to tease me, claiming, "You don't look at me the way you look at your boat." Of course I told her that was crazy, but there was some truth in it. These days I notice Tadji lingering in the dinghy, staging it so that she can frame the perfect picture of the perfect boat lying to her anchor (and shooing me out of the way so

I won't ruin the picture). Her phone is loaded with pictures of *Quetzal*. Yes, the perfect boat will seduce you.

I imagined a process for teak removal that combined controlled physical effort with a sense of quality and renewal, something Robert Pirsig, author of *Zen and the Art of Motorcycle Maintenance*, would understand. "A person who sees quality and feels it as he works is a person who cares," he wrote in his 1974 classic. I cared. I was even filled with a sense of tranquility. It was going to be OK. The decks had served *Quetzal* well, it was just time for renewal. I imagined saving teak planks and sending them to former shipmates as keepsakes.

In the most caring of ways I slipped the chisel under the teak on the coachroof and pried. Nothing happened. I pushed harder, still not much movement. I pushed even harder—I am not a gentle man and have been accused of having the touch of a Russian midwife—and the chisel popped out and gashed my hand. I cursed, then caught myself. "Come on *Quetzal*, I care," I told her, and reset the chisel and pushed with all my might. An inch, maybe two inches of teak reluctantly broke free and cracked at the fastener. Hmm? This was going to require a lot less caring and better tools or it might take a year to strip the teak off.

We regrouped at Lowes. Bigger chisels propelled by 3lb sledgehammers and a lot less caring started to get results. Then we discovered the rotary hammer and demolition bits. Soon wood was flying and dust filled the air. So much for Zen and deck souvenirs, this was hand-to-hand combat. *The Art of War* by Sun Tzu became our new playbook: "If you know your enemy, and know yourself, victory will not stand in doubt." Stubborn teak planks, tenacious old caulk, and too many stainless fasteners were the enemy.

My fellow soldiers were dear friends and frequent *Quetzal* crewmembers. Of course Alan, from Lunenburg, was there, he's been in the *Quetzal* trenches for years. In fact he was our leader, pushing us through low moments when our knees buckled, backs ached, and spirits drooped. Alan reminded us that the original *Bluenose* schooner, 143 feet of beauty and power, and built in 1921, went from "tree to sea in 99 days," crafted entirely with hand tools—so surely we could knock off the old teak decks in a few days? You met Ron back in Chapter Three. He's an engineer by trade who has crossed the Atlantic twice aboard *Quetzal*, he has round heels when it comes to my pleas for help, he's a pushover. Bruce fell for *Quetzal* in the Caribbean, and came to work by boat. His small trawler was loaded with tools, and by the end of the project we had used them all.

I have, unfairly I must say, been accused of being the Tom Sawyer of the sea, working my friends to the bone and offering them nothing but lunch and a few slaps on the back in return. It's not true. I am in the sail-training business after all, and I could have been charging them for this invaluable experience. Tom Sawyer wouldn't have missed an opportunity like that. All joking aside, I am incredibly fortunate to have many talented friends. There is camaraderie about offshore sailing that breeds genuine friendships. We have had many shared adventures aboard *Quetzal* and those of us who sail her feel a deep connection to her—she's our conduit to blue water, to the good life waiting at sea that I keep mentioning. And when she needs work we all pitch in. It's just not always easy to explain this utopian ideal to spouses. "You paid this guy how much to sail with him and now you're working on his boat for free?"

By the end of day two the teak was in serious retreat. We had most of the cabintop cleared and were making progress on the more challenging side decks. Nothing about the task was easy. We discovered that leaving fasteners in place and zipping them out with a drill afterward was the best tactic. When the head was stripped we used Vise-Grips to remove them; of the 3,000-plus screws that once littered the deck, fewer than 20 remain entombed today. After four days every last bit of teak was in the scrap bin, to hell with souvenirs, I never wanted to see another piece of teak again. We then went after the remnants of the caulk, a tough slurry concocted in Taiwan, but it couldn't hold out against four determined teak warriors armed with air sanders. Six days after we started, *Quetzal's* deck was clean. We didn't rest on the seventh day, we celebrated at the Tiki Bar down the road, a questionable call, as the next morning proved.

Quetzal's deck is a composite construction with Airex foam coring. The top layer of fiberglass is ½"—the Airex is about 1¼"—and the bottom layer of fiberglass is ¼", making for a very stiff deck. A key attribute of Airex is that it resists water, and a close inspection and some heavy-footed stomping about the teakless deck revealed no obvious delamination. This was a huge relief because the process of having to repair or replace some of the coring would have derailed our tight time schedule. The next step was to fill the holes with epoxy—all of them—a tedious job. Don, the yard manager, suggested adding a layer of fiberglass to ensure a watertight deck. Don has also crossed the Atlantic aboard *Quetzal*. "I don't want to be leaked on again on my next crossing," he said, only half-jokingly.

While the yard crew worked on the deck, a new regiment of volunteers arrived to relieve Alan and Bruce, while Ron soldiered on for a second week. Bob, *Quetzal's* patron saint, official consultant, and a veteran of nearly every refit project, didn't want to miss the fun. Dan, who was part of the team that flew to Italy to help with the great mast disaster project, and Earl also turned up to help. With the mast in a rare horizontal plane we seized the opportunity to replace the standing rigging, add a new wind transducer, and pull fresh wires through the spar. We also serviced the winches. In typical *Quetzal* fashion, a full-blown refit was sandwiched into the deck project.

When the fiberglass cured, the decks were primed with epoxy paint. Another friend and Atlantic crossing shipmate, Danny, flew in to lend a hand. The two of us remounted every piece of hardware, including new stanchions and mast rails, using a case of 3M 4200. Danny and I are not small guys, and squeezing into tight corners below to wrestle a wrench onto wayward nuts elicited more than a few expletives and bloody knuckles. Eighteen days after we started, I flew to France to captain a canal boat trip, and returned a week later. I had four days before I was scheduled to set sail on a training passage to Nova Scotia.

To my surprise, Don had not only finished spraying the deck while I was away, he had also sprayed the topsides. "She looked so nice on deck," he said, "I just couldn't deal with those dreary topsides." *Quetzal* looked stunning, at least 20 years younger. Liz and my nephew Will had cleaned the disaster below, vacuuming out bags of dust and grime. In short order the mast was stepped, the rigging tuned, and the cushions, cutlery, tools, books, charts, and everything else carried back aboard and hastily stowed. I was still working when my new crew turned up—you met them last chapter. You couldn't have blamed them for catching the first flight home, but instead they schlepped gear and provisions aboard. They finally tossed their duffel bags aboard just minutes before we threw off the docklines. Thirty days after the project began, we pushed off the dock and headed north. It's amazing what you can do with a lotta help from your friends.

It took me a while to adjust to *Quetzal*'s new "white" look. Alan had insisted that I resist the urge to paint the non-skid deck areas light blue, arguing that "the boat has lousy ventilation and is hot enough down below already, you don't need a dark hull or deck." To prove his point, he led me around the yard, digital thermometer in hand, and we measured the temperature of colored hulls and decks. They were significantly warmer. Just when I had accustomed myself to *Quetzal*'s new, clean aesthetic, we decided to make another major upgrade.

Hard Dodger Decisions, Summer 2017

This perfect-boat stuff is emotionally gut-wrenching. The decision to add a hard dodger, not just a canvas dodger with a rigid top, but a serious structural construction project that would essentially enclose the forward end of the cockpit, was not undertaken lightly. Yes, I had loved the old teak decks, but something had to be done, they were in a terrible state, dying before my eyes, leaking on my customers, and ultimately it had been an easy decision to replace them. To alter *Quetzal*'s sleek profile, her lean and low, fashion-model–like good looks, to concede that avoiding the elements at all cost was now a stated goal, now *this* was a tough call. Tadji and my brother-in-law Trevor, whose opinion on all things nautical I respect more than anyone else's, led the charge calling for a hard dodger. Trevor is annoyingly practical. "How many canvas dodgers have you bought?" he asked—a leading question to be sure.

"This will be my fourth," I answered sheepishly.

"And each one cost how much?"

"Around $5,000."

Shaking his head, he made his closing argument. "The cost of a hard dodger will be around two, maybe three canvas dodgers, and will be a one-time investment. It will be far better in heavy seas, it will make the cockpit a lot friendlier all the time, and," he paused for dramatic effect, "it will make your wife incredibly happy—seems a no-brainer to me."

There was plenty of time for the project. *Quetzal* had a rare free summer as Tadji and I had scheduled four charter trips in the Mediterranean and were away for a few months. Trevor and I scratched out a design and then confirmed our thoughts with Chip, who would be responsible for the final design, its construction, and its installation. I insisted that it had to be built in such a way as to allow it to fail in severe conditions and not structurally impact the rest of the boat. In essence, I wanted a break-away hard dodger, which complicated the process immensely. Marine engineers want to design and build things to last, not to fail, but I have seen too many waves, pushed through too many storms, been flattened more times than I can remember, and knew that if we were in survival conditions the dodger had to go away without ripping a hole in the boat. We decided to go with a welded aluminum framework as the base and then attach lightweight high-density foam panels that were fiberglassed over. The large windows were made of polycarbonate—strong, flexible, and light—the same material that covers the cockpit of jet fighter planes—and the center panel would need to open for ventilation.

Justin, who is a magician with a welding torch, built the frame and then Chip went to work. He's thoughtful, deliberate, and incredibly skilled. I knew Chip was the man for the project and that this was the time to do it because he's just a few years away from retirement. He's the old man of the yard, and all the younger crew, including the yard manager, CJ, come to him for advice, knowing that they're in for a lecture that will include the chemical make-up of certain materials, a history of how those materials were developed, and an unsparing analysis of the way in which they were planning to undertake a certain project.

He's also an authority on the Civil War, and for years participated in reenactments. "I almost died at Gettysburg," he told me as I helped him fit a mocked-up panel in place for yet another measurement. "It was 100 degrees and those wool uniforms didn't breathe. The only way you can really understand history is to relive it as best you can—the heat was nearly as deadly as the artillery." Watching Chip install the finished dodger, I relived a little of my own history. I remembered being knocked down on an Atlantic crossing, not once but twice, and having the canvas dodger rip away in the process, leaving us exposed to howling winds and breaking seas. I remembered another wave, on a rugged passage south from Nova Scotia, that reared up and took out a canvas dodger panel with surgical precision, leaving us naked in the face of a freezing nor'easter. It's a bitter and stark reality to go from being more or less safe and dry huddled beneath the dodger to suddenly feeling exposed to nature's fury as it's blown to shreds before your eyes.

Hopefully, that reality will be part of the past, my own Gettysburg, as *Quetzal* now sports a sturdy, high-tech, hard dodger that has us prepared for coping with the nastiest weather and for voyages to the highest latitudes. We've tested her now on three passages, covering 4,000 miles of blue water, and have worked out most of the kinks. Like the lost teak decks, it takes a bit of getting used to. It's a different look to be sure, and has marred what were once uncluttered sight lines and clean sheet leads. Alas, maybe the perfect-boat naysayers are right after all—every boat is a compromise. I prefer to take a Darwinian approach, and see the perfect boat in evolutionary terms. If that means that *Quetzal* is the "almost perfect" boat, so be it, but I will never tell her that.

EIGHT

GREAT CIRCLE ROUTES

Embracing Calms • Pilot Charts • Route Planning •
Ocean Voyaging

"There are no compasses for journeying in time. As far as our sense
of direction in this unchartable dimension is concerned, we are like
lost travelers in a desert. We believe we are going forward, toward
the oasis of Utopia. But how do we know—only some imaginary
figure looking down from the sky (let's call him God) can know—
that we are not moving in a great circle."

—Graham Swift, *Waterland*

"The shortest line on the surface of a sphere between two points is
part of a great circle... The arc of the great circle between the points
is called the great circle track. If it could be followed exactly, the
destination would be dead ahead throughout the voyage."

—Nathaniel Bowditch, *The American Practical Navigator*

"Now when I was a little chap I had a passion for maps. I would
look for hours at South America, or Africa, or Australia, and lose

*myself in all the glories of exploration. At that time there were
many blank spaces on the earth, and when I saw one that looked
particularly inviting on a map I would put my finger on it and say,
when I grow up I will go there."*

—Joseph Conrad, *Heart of Darkness*

The North Pacific, July 2017

On the ninth day of the passage on *Lady B* we were 1,000 miles from land
in any direction, even from the smallest spit peering above the surface,
and the sea was oil-slick calm. There's something strangely unsettling
about a flat sea in the deep ocean, unruffled by even a zephyr. Bernard
Moitessier wrote, "I hate storms, but calms undermine my spirits."
Voyages seem suspended in calms, as if you've betrayed a cosmic pact
and the punishment is that you'll never feel wind over the deck again.
At the same time, the rational part of your brain knows the wind has
to return and you nervously wonder what will come next. That famous
nautical phrase "the calm before the storm" haunts your subconscious.

When you are making way under sail, whittling away the distance to
landfall, there's a sense of purpose to the voyage. You are not just idling, a
word or state akin to evil in our progress-obsessed society. Being becalmed
is something of a time warp—trapped in the present without the ability to
plan ahead, a very un-human condition. I will never forget the stretch of
calm we encountered aboard *Gigi* on our long-ago passage around Cape
Horn. We were homeward bound, crossing the equator in the Pacific,
when the wind vanished. With no fuel to spare we drifted for 15 days,
making less than 300 miles toward San Francisco, translating into a speed
made good of 0.8 knots. The low point was when the dinner scraps of
the previous night were still in view the next morning. At some point I
accepted our fate, and realized that I needed to embrace the calms instead
of banging my fist against the bulkhead and complaining to the heavens

about how unfairly I was being treated. My mood brightened considerably and the ocean was beautiful again and the winds eventually returned.

Back in the Pacific in 2017, we were trying to extricate ourselves from the time warp of tranquility, rumbling along under power, driven by the need to stay on schedule for prearranged travel plans, which is the bane of too many voyages these days. We were utterly dependent upon the compression power stroke of the diesel engine, that mysterious mix of air and fuel that fires in a cylinder and drives a piston that turns a crankshaft, and finally rotates a prop. We were also dependent on the rapidly dwindling amount of fuel in our tanks, as we still had 1,200 miles to go to the Strait of Juan de Fuca.

I wasn't concerned. I could see the wind coming. I knew we'd look back at the few days of calm as a reprieve, thankful for the opportunity to have had a couple of very close encounters with humpback whales and to marvel at the curious Pacific fur seals who, to our great surprise, had ventured as far offshore as we had. The barometric pressure was dropping and once-lazy whiffs of clouds were straightening their shoulders and lining up along the western horizon like a football team about to kick off. Wind was coming. America's greatest sailor, Joshua Slocum, the first man to sail alone around the world, and a true master mariner, wrote, "to know the laws that govern the winds, and to know you know them, will give you an easy mind." We had all sorts of technology aboard, and had recently downloaded GRIB files that painted a mixed bag of winds for next few days. But I didn't need, or even want, input from the satellites. I didn't want to question my hard-won intuition about the weather. I told the crew to secure their gear below and to get ready for some breeze.

Greedy Ocean Voyager

I did not set out to become a sailing expert. Recalling my early misadventures, and there were plenty as I blundered from one sandbar to another in the Florida Keys, the notion that one day I'd have expertise to share seemed unlikely, and that's putting it liberally. That somehow I've become something of an authority on sailing surprises no one more than me. I wanted to go sea and have adventures, and escape the stranglehold of the suburbs and their false gods. But I didn't plan to become a professional sailor—it just happened. That I have been able to write books and articles that people actually read, and occasionally like, and sometimes hate, is also something of a shock to me, and to a former high school English teacher who signed aboard one of my passages a few years ago. He told the crew that he thought there was a small chance that I might become an Olympic pole-vaulter, but no chance I'd ever write a book.

It's easy to argue that the canvas of my life looks more like an abstract expressionist painting of a man addicted to pressing on at all costs, a collection of rhumb lines hurled Pollock-like across a chart of the world, than a neatly plotted great circle track toward respectability. I agree and disagree. While I never saw the career I stumbled into coming, I have always been a greedy ocean voyager, leaping at opportunities and challenges thrown my way, and those experiences simply piled up under my keel. Sooner or later I had to learn something about going to sea. A close inspection reveals a pattern to my madness, just as Pollock insisted there was method to his splattered works. Sure, I often take the long way from A to B, happy to tarry in the open water between those overwrought letters, but every time I cast off and head for the uncluttered horizon I know that I am sailing a great circle route, the shortest distance between the confines ashore and the good life waiting for me at sea.

I'm not really a Pollock fan, though. The painting that does haunt me, however, is Andrew Wyeth's *Wind from the Sea*. It hangs in the National Gallery, and I have made pilgrimage to DC just to see it. It's spare, delicate, and textured in shades of haunting browns like the rocky

Maine coast it portrays. The thin curtain lifted by a gentle sea breeze is a siren's call, reminding me that I've been ashore too long, that I am lounging on land, and like my friend Ishmael, I know "it's high time to get to sea as soon as I can."

In January 2017 *Quetzal* was in the Virgin Islands. It had been a typical sailing year. Tadji and I uncharacteristically picked a pleasant 30-hour weather window. Escorted by a gentle northeast trade wind, we sailed 200 miles to Guadeloupe without breaking a sweat or tying in a reef. We let our new Hydrovane windvane do all the steering. We spent a month at anchor, occasionally roaming between Deshaies in the north and Îles des Saintes in the south, a vast distance spanning roughly 30 miles. We did make a breezy day sail up to Pointe-à-Pitre for a new battery and provisions, but for the most part we were blissfully lazy. We swam and Tadji paddleboarded. She read and I lumbered along writing this book. In February we sailed up to English Harbour, Antigua, where we conducted our first on-site workshop about how to sail to, through, and around the Caribbean. Then *Quetzal* and I got back to work, our real job, taking folks to sea.

We made a challenging passage to Barbados, the windward-most Caribbean island, and undertook another trans-Caribbean sail from St. Martin to Grenada and back. In April we had a rollicking nonstop sail back to Maryland. Two days out of Norfolk we encountered the Gulf Stream. The sailing was extraordinary, and for a brief moment, with Santiago from Buenos Aires at the helm, we found the perfect confluence of wind, current, and breaking waves. *Quetzal* touched 16.8 knots, skidding along the crest of a steel blue rush of ocean. While some of the crew were terrified, Santiago and I were giddy, calling out the speed over ground from the GPS like commodities traders about to make a fortune. Those mere seconds have turned into fond memories, into a shared experience that can never be taken from us, and they're ours alone.

After her thrilling passage north, *Quetzal* had a lazy summer, as the crew at Spring Cove Marina added the new hard dodger described in Chapter Seven. There had been no summer pampering for her skipper, however, no summer off—he had business to attend to in the Med and the Pacific.

Tadji and I had organized four charter trips for the early summer, one in the Cyclades islands of Greece, one around Majorca, and two along Italy's Amalfi Coast, and although it took place in May and June, we called it the "Med Summer 2017." It was great fun, with crew who were all good friends, and the sailing was decent, and that's all you can hope for in the capricious Mediterranean. It was also interesting traveling as Tadji and I spent each week between charters in a different location. She's brilliant at finding intriguing and affordable places to stay: Kuşadası in Turkey, Venice and Tuscany in Italy, and the stunning village of Deia that clings to the north coast of Majorca, Spain, and that was the long-time home of one of my literary heroes, Robert Graves. As always, the easy living came to an end and in early July I headed back to sea. Friends Chris and Barb had sailed their Hylas 49 *Lady B* from the U.S. West Coast to Honolulu and I arranged a training passage for the return voyage to Anacortes, in the San Juan Islands of Washington. I flew straight from Italy to Honolulu.

A quick glance at a chart of the North Pacific is humbling—it's a big ocean, and it's actually the small half of the Pacific, although just barely. According to NOAA's National Geophysical Data Center, the North Pacific covers 77,010,000 square kilometers, or 21% of the ocean area on the planet. The Pacific south of the equator covers 84,750,000, or 23%. To put that in perspective, each half of the Pacific is about the same size as the entire Atlantic. There is symmetry, as least as far as sailors are concerned, about well-placed waypoints in both oceans. Honolulu is a little more than 2,000 miles away from just about everywhere on the west coast of the U.S.—similar to how Bermuda is about the same distance from everywhere on the East Coast between Norfolk and Nova Scotia, just not as far, about 700 miles. Hawaii is the center of a radius that essentially traces an arc through the West Coast, including Alaska. Anchored between latitudes 19° and 22° north, the main islands lie in the heart of the northeast trades. Sailing to the islands from anywhere east—and most boats head out from the Strait of Juan de Fuca, San Francisco, or Southern California—is lovely reach most of the way. A delivery-skipper friend who has made many return passages from Hawaii says that "a well-provisioned piece of driftwood can make the passage out—getting back is when you earn your money." That's typical delivery-skipper bravado as the trip out can be a challenge to be sure, but the point is well made.

Naturally we were heading back to the West Coast, earning our money and our sea stories along the way. There's a well-worn strategy for this trip, and although it's definitely the long way, it gives you the best chance for sailing instead of just loading the deck with jerry cans of fuel and motoring home. Once you clear Hawaii, the tactic is to sail north, trying to lay down a track that does not give up any longitude to the west, beating against the northeast trades. The hope is that Neptune takes pity on you and gives the trade winds an eastern slant—but Neptune isn't known for compassion. The trade winds ease off as you near the Pacific High, a large area of light wind and, more times than not, the dead calm that we were about to experience. Most sailboats skirt the western side of the high by continuing north and motoring if necessary until the prevailing westerly winds fill in, usually somewhere between latitudes 40° and 45°, although occasionally you have to carry on to near 50°. Once you finally reach the vaunted westerlies, it's usually a vigorous reach all the way to the coast. This was our plan, a 2,800-mile route tentatively sketched out on the computer and one that we hoped would allow us to sail almost the entire way.

Route planning is one of my favorite aspects of ocean voyaging, although I admit there's a Panglossian element to it, a sense that the data you're crunching just has to be right simply because you are crunching it. As climate changes, black swans in the forms of unpredicted storms are becoming more common, as are calms and less predictable winds. Still, for the most part, if you sail at the right time of year, in the right ocean, you are usually able to pick a route with favorable winds and are unlikely to encounter severe weather. Route planning requires a thorough knowledge of climate models, an honest assessment of your boat and crew, and some basic geography and astronomy. Tadji teases me that I have the worldwide wind patterns memorized and, with all humility aside, she's right. To be fair, most ocean voyagers do.

Isak Dinesen, the pen name for Karen Blixen, author of *Out of Africa*, wrote, "God made the world round so we would never be able to see too far down the road." I love the metaphor but I'm willing to up the ante. The earth, which is essentially a perfect sphere for navigational purposes, is also nicely tilted 23.5 degrees, and conveniently rotates on its axis every 24 hours. These two factors are responsible not only for the friendly pattern of day and night and for the change in seasons, as the earth orbits the sun, but also for prevailing winds that are defined by latitude. Best of all, 70% of the earth is covered by ocean. I am not a believer in these things, but if I was, I'd be convinced that whoever created earth had to be a sailor.

Most sailors know the prevailing winds where they sail and plan outings accordingly. Ocean voyagers do the same, on a grand scale, counting on consistent global winds to plan and execute voyages. And we complain bitterly, insisting that we're victims of a great celestial conspiracy, when the prevailing winds misbehave. I've been known to burn a pilot chart after a week of easterlies forcing us to beat when we should have been reaching in the heart of the prevailing westerlies. Petty,

I know, but not quite as severe as King Agamemnon. He sacrificed his beloved daughter in a desperate attempt to conjure up fair winds for his fleet to sail for Troy. Forecasting these days is still a bit suspect, but at least my daughters are safe.

Wind is the metric that drives route planning. To a sailor wind is weather, something Tadji has failed to grasp or, better said, accept. She thinks weather has something to do with temperature, rain, and other unimportant variables like humidity and cloud cover—but to me it's all about wind. Give me a cold, cloudy, rainy day with fair winds and I'm happy. Wind is caused by temperature differences that create pressure variances as warm air rises and cold air takes its place. As we learned from the French mathematician Gustave Coriolis back in Chapter Four, air flows from high pressure to low pressure. Areas of high pressure dominate between latitudes 20° and 40° on both sides of the equator, with low-pressure areas above and below. Winds would be either north or south, flowing from high pressure toward low, except that the earth spins on its axis in an eastward direction, deflecting the winds to the right in the northern hemisphere and to the left in the southern. This is why winds rotate clockwise around a high-pressure system and counterclockwise around a low in the Northern Hemisphere, and the opposite direction south of the equator.

All of this whirling and swerving conspires to create prevailing winds based on latitude. The region around the equator—the doldrums—is officially called the inter-tropical convergence zone (ITZ); it is defined by generally calm winds, gloomy skies, and occasional violent squalls, and is challenging to traverse under sail, as we discovered in *Gigi*. Just north and south of the equator are the wondrous trade winds. These consistent winds are northeast in the Northern Hemisphere and southeast in the Southern. Depending on the season, they blow from 10 to 25 knots. A trade-wind circumnavigation lies predominately in the realm of these friendly tropical winds. This is the route that Tadji has mapped out for our upcoming world voyage; mine strays a bit farther north and south, touching the Arctic and Antarctic regions, those intriguing high latitudes mentioned in previous chapters. It will be interesting to see how these dueling route scenarios play out. Stay tuned.

North and south of the trade winds, the mid-latitudes are better known as the horse latitudes, so named because the early voyagers were reduced to slaughtering their horses for food as they drifted in maddening variable winds. Unlike in the doldrums, conditions are often fair in high pressure, especially in the summer, but there are few pressure gradients to create breeze. Avoiding the frustration of the horse latitudes is one reason many sailors skip Bermuda when sailing from the U.S. East Coast to Europe, and instead sail a great circle route directly to the Azores which puts you squarely in the prevailing westerlies. Above the 40th parallel the winds are generally westerly. In the Northern Hemisphere, between latitudes 40° and 55°, the winds blow from the southwest through the northwest approximately 75% of the time. In the Southern Hemisphere, winds south of 40, the aptly named Roaring Forties and Furious Fifties, blow from the west with the consistency of the trade winds but with a lot more oomph.

Currents are another factor that must be considered on ocean voyages. For the most part currents align with prevailing winds. There are, however, certain currents that must be considered separately when planning voyages. They include, among others, the Gulf Stream off the U.S. East Coast (discussed in Chapter Four), the Humboldt or Peru Current off the northwest coast of South America, the Japan Current in the Pacific, and the powerful Agulhas Current off the southern capes of Africa. Currents are not as neatly charted as we once thought and more than occasionally wander off course, as any seasoned voyager will tell you. Strong currents also throw off meanders that can flow in the opposite direction of the main current. One of the best aspects of real-time satellite data is the ability to pinpoint the set and drift of major ocean currents, allowing logical crossing points to be calculated and enabling contrary meanders to be avoided. (Passageweather.com is ideal for quickly accessing the latest Gulf Stream updates, and a website called oceanmotion.org shows worldwide surface currents.)

There are two indispensable references that every world cruiser needs to have aboard. The first of these I have mentioned in earlier chapters: passage-planning guru Jimmy Cornell's book *World Cruising Routes*. This is the bible of route planning and contains detailed data on every conceivable voyage you might be considering. It is up to its eighth edition. Cornell writes with a lack of subtlety, but that's what you want in a reference book, just the facts please, and that's what he serves. In addition to specific route details, Cornell also provides a concise description of worldwide wind and current patterns. He includes logistics for planning world cruises and a terrific explanation of tropical storms, including where and when they are likely to form and the quickest way out of the mayhem should you be unlucky enough to encounter one at sea. It's about the best $50 you can spend, and I confess I have thumbed through all 600-plus pages. Hardly anything pleases me more than to randomly open the book, usually while visiting the head, and study the best time to sail between Sri Lanka and the Maldives, or Tonga and Fiji, or the Kamchatka Peninsula and the Aleutian Islands. I must admit, I have even chosen *World Cruising Routes* as one of my allotted three books while stranded on a desert island.

To fully understand *World Cruising Routes*, you will need to make a thorough study of pilot charts, the other vital reference you must have aboard. Published by MSI, Marine Safety Information, a division of NOAA, pilot charts are compiled in atlas form for every ocean and displayed by month. While I still much prefer the printed version, they're available free online(https://msi.nga.mil/NGAPortal/

MSI.portal?_nfpb=true&_pageLabel=msi...62...). First conceived and produced by the American naval lieutenant Matthew Fontaine Maury (you may recall that my daughter and I visited his unimpressive birth site back in Chapter Four), pilot charts are climate-prediction charts. They provide location-based data on wind direction, wind speed, wave height, air and water temperature, chances of gales and calms, and much more. It is important to realize that the data is averaged, based on more than 150 years of ship reports. Pilot charts are not weather charts—they're historical indicators used for planning voyages. They're not forecasts, and they can be inaccurate in the short term.

Industrious Jimmy Cornell and his son Ivan have recently published updated pilot charts that are based on satellite data collected over the last 25 years instead of on ship reports, which seems a bit heretical, one more concession to orbiting satellites that keep an eye on us and know what's best for us. The Cornells' *Atlas of Pilot Charts* is adjusted to the needs of small-boat sailors, not commercial ships, and also reflects the impact of climate change. Think what you like, but ocean voyagers are on the front line when it comes to experiencing changing weather patterns. You might say that "change is in the wind," as tropical storms now strike in what were normally safe months, floods reach beyond the rainy season, and even the reliable trade winds take extended holidays. Worldwide route planning will be more challenging for future generations.

According to *World Cruising Routes*, Cornells' *Atlas of Pilot Charts*, and NOAA's pilot charts of the North Pacific, as well as Nostradamus and the Oracle of Delphi (just kidding), July was a good month for sailing from Honolulu to the Strait of Juan de Fuca. Our main obstacle would be to skirt the calms created by the Pacific High, the previously mentioned vast and ever-shifting area of high pressure hovering between the trade winds and the westerlies. As you can tell from how this chapter began, we were not entirely successful in avoiding them.

Lady B was an "almost" perfect boat for the passage. A robust Hylas 49 cutter, she was in excellent condition and had been retrofitted with top-quality gear. As a delivery skipper I have logged thousands of miles in Hylas 49s, and know them to be supremely seaworthy. Chris, her owner, had sailed her to Oahu with a delivery crew, the fulfillment of a lifelong dream. Apart from a wild jibe as they neared the islands, they had a classic outbound passage, fast, breezy, and downwind. My crew and I were waiting for them to arrive, and pounced as soon as they pulled into the slip. They barely had time to celebrate their passage. Thirty-six hours later we were underway.

We were greeted by fresh easterly trade winds as we skirted the shoals off Kaena Point, the western tip of Oahu. It was good going, rough and fast, as we sheeted in the sails and made our way north on a close reach. I served up dinner, chicken stew cooked in the pressure cooker for the meat eaters, rice and broccoli for the vegetarians. Chris and Clare had the first watch. Chris, an Australian but long-time California resident, was making his third passage with me. Although approaching 70, he is strong, steady, and a fine shipmate. As a young man he served with distinction in the Australian military in Vietnam and afterward went to sea to help restore his humanity. He sailed on *Stormvogel*, a famous racing boat, in the Caribbean, and later crossed the Atlantic and Pacific in a couple of rough-and-ready small boats. After a successful business career and a long sailing hiatus, he was delighted to be shoving off on another long sea passage. Clare, sassy and charming, was born in England but raised all over the U.S., and now called Iowa home. Living in the most landlocked of states had only increased her passion for the ocean. New to sailing, she was enchanted by the prospect of world cruising. She had just bought a Hylas 46 and was on a mission to get sea time as quickly as possible. A frightening bout of cancer had profoundly altered her plans. Time, she realized, was not her friend—she was ready to launch her dreams.

Rik and Bruce had the second watch. Rik, a Dutchman from Amsterdam, was also making his third passage with me. He is a dentist, a skilled sailor who plies the North Sea in his beautiful Comfortina 38′ sloop, and a devoted vegetarian. Despite being extremely fit, the former competitive marathon runner was diagnosed with coronary disease ten years ago. His doctor recommended immediate bypass surgery. Rik considered other options and decided instead to adopt a total plant-based diet. Today, his scans are clean and he's the picture of health, the most energetic 69-year-old I know. Bruce is a dear friend who was also making his third trip with me. He lives in Maryland and loves *Quetzal* as I do, and he has the sweat equity to prove it. A retired engineer, he's a terrific shipmate who can turn his hand to any task. His dreams of world cruising had taken a back seat to raising a family and pursuing his career, and he was thrilled at having the opportunity to make a genuine sea passage.

Marco, a friend of Rik's and a fellow dentist, was reserved but carried himself with quiet confidence and was always ready with a quick smile. He proved to be a fine sailor and a delightful watchmate as he and I happily chatted for three hours each night. He had recently bought a Rustler 42, a world-class sea boat that he kept in Falmouth, England. He hoped our passage would prepare him for his own voyage south across the Bay of Biscay to the Mediterranean.

And then there was me. Why was I still making long passages, taking on the challenges of a new boat and new crew? I make more money with shorter passages. Anyone who knows me also knows that my sailing has never been about money. In fact, I have always felt a bit guilty for taking money for doing what I love most and never forget what a privilege it is to make a living doing what I love. While my reasons for undertaking the passage were plentiful, in the end what I craved, what I needed, was the sense of joy and freedom that inevitably washes over me when I am sea. I was just as excited as the crew to embark on a passage that would take 15–20 days—precious time spent without phone service or 24-hour news updates. It was time, I knew from experience, that would unfold slowly, a blessed relief from the demands of and unwanted inputs from a hurly-burly world. We were not dropping out for a few weeks, we were dropping in, and we were the luckiest six people on the planet.

Ocean passages are exercises in management. You manage provisions, water, fuel, and, most importantly, your psyche. Early one morning I joined Chris in the cockpit. Clare, her dogwatch over, retreated to her cabin and crawled under her sleeping bag and extra blanket. It's cold in the North Pacific. Water temperatures hovered in the mid-50s Fahrenheit, and the air temperature was just a bit warmer by day and cooler by night. Once we cleared the trade winds we were bundled up with base layers and balaclavas. I made Chris and myself a cup of coffee and we chatted. One person was always perched behind the helm ready to take the wheel because the autopilot frequently, and without warning, would simply stop working.

I mentioned that we were, in a way, all pilgrims aboard *Lady B*, each looking for something different but joined in a common cause of crossing an ocean. Chris joked that the food was a lot better aboard *Lady B* than what the pilgrims on the *Mayflower* had endured, adding, "and I doubt the cook made two different menus each evening." I am always the cook aboard, for several reasons. One, I can produce a decent meal in any condition and have never accepted the notion that just because you're on a boat you can throw together sandwiches and call it supper. Second, I carefully manage the provisions; and finally, I like to have a little alone time, and do my best thinking in the galley. It didn't bother me in the least to prepare vegetarian options each day, especially because I was full of admiration for Rik. By the end of the passage most of us preferred a healthy meal of rice, beans, or potatoes and an assortment of vegetables to a heavy dose of meat and cheese.

Chris noted how a long passage transitions from the urgency of trying to get away from your point of departure to when the countdown to your destination begins. At some point we stopped measuring how far from Hawaii we were, and then the distance to the Strait of Juan de Fuca became our focus. Chris, like me, had no fixed schedule on the back end of the voyage and was quite happy taking each day as it unfolded. I knew that Tadji would meet me upon arrival and that we'd tarry in Seattle and visit friends in Vancouver. We were also liberated by having flexible plane tickets.

As happens on all passages, we had a few problems along the way. A week out we had a fire, which always gets my attention at sea. We were running the generator when Bruce smelled smoke. I immediately checked the engine room and then the electrical panel, but nothing was burning. Bruce tracked it down quickly, finding a smoldering AC outlet in the forward head. It had obviously been leaked on and saltwater had corroded the wires. We disabled it and aired out the boat. We also resolved to charge the batteries with the main engine. The mast partners, where the mast goes through the deck, gave us grief for much of the passage. The hard jibe on the outbound leg had blown out the polycarbonate ring that both supported the mast and kept water from pouring in. We had pounded it back in place before leaving Hawaii but it frequently popped out, especially when conditions were lumpy. Rik tackled pounding in new shims—whacking them with the precision and power of a dentist pulling a tooth—and Bruce designed a clever lashing system to keep them in place. This is what you do on passage—fix things—in addition to standing your watch, thinking a lot, sleeping when you can, and relishing the face-to-face communication with your shipmates. The fading but vital art of discussion is still alive and well at sea.

I was right, the winds did return and we all rejoiced when the westerlies arrived. Our mood brightened as placid seas quickly gave way to small waves, then white caps formed and I waxed on about how the waves are the winds' messenger, and boldly predicted that the winds were here to stay despite the fact that the GRIB files suggested otherwise. I am a good salesman and we all hoped that we'd be on a sweet reach all the way home. Alas, it was not to be. After a day of fast sailing, with the headsail poled out and the mainsail paid well out—to prevent a damaging jibe—the winds eased.

We had a dilemma. The winds were from the west but they were light to moderate, around 10 knots. *Lady B* was prepared to cope with strong winds and gales, but she was not well set up to keep moving in light air. Our only headsail was a high-cut yankee, around 100%, or the size of a standard working jib. It didn't provide much horsepower downwind. The mainsail furled into the boom, a nice idea in theory, and one that's becoming more popular, but it also had practical limitations. For one, it was tricky to execute a proper reef, especially off the wind, and required a highly coordinated effort of easing the halyard and taking up on the furling line. Second, all the battens had shattered during the jibe on the way out to Hawaii, so the sail, which is by design smaller and cut flatter than a conventional mainsail to allow it to furl in the boom, was even more underpowered than usual.

Our speed dropped to 3 knots. We would never make our flights at that speed, and we would also run out of vegetables!

Lady B sailed nicely from 50 to 100 degrees off the wind, easily topping 7 knots and sometimes more, so we chose a route that would offer a steady diet of close reaching instead of broad reaching, which violated my instincts and all the clever route planning we had done before the voyage. Instead of continuing northwest, into the heart of the westerlies, we pointed the bow right at the Strait of Juan de Fuca, tightened the sheets, heeled over, and made good speed. Many days we couldn't quite lay the strait, and aimed just north of it. Ironically, our new heading turned out to be the great circle track, the shortest distance between any two points on a sphere, and the distance to go dropped quickly. Rik and Marco might make their flights back to Holland after all.

Great circles are any circles that cut the earth into equal halves. The only parallel of latitude that is a great circle is the equator, while every meridian is a great circle, as meridians run through both poles. One degree of arc of a great circle represents 60 nautical miles, and each minute is a mile. It's beautiful and symmetric and that's why you always use the side of a chart, along a meridian, to measure distance. Great circle charts seem distorted at first glance because the meridians are angled and gradually get closer together as they run north or south of the pole. If you glance at a great circle chart of the North Pacific, it'll immediately be obvious that the quickest way across the ocean is via the northern route. The Aleutian Islands, the Kamchatka Peninsula, and the Japanese Islands are not very far apart. Your plane flies over Iceland on the way to Europe because that's the shortest route.

We are trained to look at the world via the Mercator projection, which, like all charts, represents a spherical world in two dimensions. Gerardus Mercator is referred to as the first scientific cartographer and is, arguably, the most underrated genius of all time. Bestselling books have been written about John Harrison and his chronometers that helped Captain Cook chart the world, and we all know that Isaac Newton used to the tides to help explain calculus. But 200 years earlier, Mercator came up with the idea of a cylindrical map projection that would become the standard for nautical charts because of its ability to represent course lines, or rhumb lines (technically, loxodromes), as straight lines with constant angles along every meridian. In essence, Mercator made meridians straight lines and extended them right off the edge of the world. While the Mercator projection distorts the size of landmasses as latitude increases from the equator to the poles, it made navigation dramatically more practical for great swathes of ocean where most people sailed. Greenland is the poster child of distortion, followed by Antarctica.

Mercator, who was Flemish, was also a Lutheran, and this nearly cost him his life when he was imprisoned by the court of the Catholic Inquisition after his village of Louvain, not far from present-day Brussels, was overrun. He was held for seven months and witnessed the brutal deaths of many of his fellow prisoners before he was mysteriously released. He kept his head down after that, quietly teaching at the university, and it was 27 years before he unveiled his famous projection. The incredible fact is that we still use the Mercator projection today. All the chart software in your plotter uses the Mercator projection, as does Google Maps, and even NASA's star charts.

Sixteen days out of Hawaii we could smell land, but it was nowhere in sight as we sliced through persistent drizzle and patches of fog. Welcome to the Pacific Northwest. We had put away our great circle and small-scale ocean charts, and plotted our position on the Juan de Fuca approach chart. We had turned the strait—named after a Greek navigator who had sailed in 1592 with a failed Spanish expedition in search of the fabled Strait of Anián, the original quest for the Northwest Passage—into a question. Juan de Fuca became "What the fuka" as the gray horizon sealed off any glimpse of land.

The morning of July 19, our seventeenth day from Hawaii, dawned clear, and those early hours are often the best time to spy distant land. Sure enough, just before sunrise, Chris spotted the mountainous coast south of Cape Flattery, and with the simple words "Land ho," everything changed aboard *Lady B*. We became land focused. Cell phones emerged and were constantly checked, everyone impatiently awaiting the magic moment when "we had service." We were excited about, and proud of, our passage, but there was a sense of a loss too. We all realized that our interlude, our time warp, our splendid isolation had come to an end. My shipmates and I would soon be immersed in our complicated land lives. At least I knew it wouldn't be long—it never is—before I would once again cast off the lines and escape to sea. It is my job after all.

Postscript

In late October 2017 *Quetzal* got moving again. We sailed direct to Grenada, an 1,800-mile passage from North Carolina that was an upwind slog most of the way. Our plans, like those of most sailors bound for the Caribbean last fall, were altered by hurricanes Irma and Maria. At least we had the option of making new plans. Many friends lost their boats and their dreams in the unprecedented storm winds that devastated the eastern Caribbean. From Grenada we soared across the bottom of the Caribbean, staying well offshore of the now-dangerous coast of Venezuela, a once-proud country spiraling into anarchy as its experiment with a populist strongman collapses, standing as a stark warning to other countries. We called at Bonaire before continuing on to Cartagena, the steamy, seductive former colonial capital on Colombia's jungle coast. A few weeks later we were underway again, heading north on a nonstop 1,000-mile passage to Isla Mujeres, Mexico, wrapping up a ridiculously quick jaunt around the Caribbean basin. Even though she spent the summer being a diva at the boatyard, by year's end *Quetzal* had added another 8,000 miles to her odometer, which stopped working long ago. More importantly, 59 crewmembers signed her logbook.

NEVER LOST–JUST HARD TO FIND

Time at Sea • The Promise of Ocean Voyaging • Freedom

"But what is security? It is death, a state in which nothing can happen."

—Alain Gerbault, *In Quest of the Sun*

"It is out there at sea that you are really yourself."
—Vito Dumas, *Alone Through the Roaring Forties*

The North Atlantic, Near Bermuda, July 2016

The shimmering turquoise shallows inside the half-moon-shaped reef that circles the northern edge of Bermuda like a security fence quickly gave way to serious, deeper shades of blue as we made our way out the Town Cut Channel under full sail. The anchorage was crowded and, I'll admit it, we were showing off, but the southwest wind was a perfect escort and *Quetzal* steers better under sail than under power anyway. Some ocean passages take time to develop, especially if your course parallels a coastline with land peering over your shoulder, or if you have to clear a continental shelf. I am no fan of coastal sailing and usually feel stranded, plodding along in green-gray waters that seem tethered to the shore. The voyage doesn't really commence for me until the echoes we launch from the depthsounder no longer find their way back to the boat. Bermuda is my kind of departure point: the island dispatches her nautical visitors swiftly, and with a refreshing lack of subtlety. In less than an hour *Quetzal* was soaring over a bounding sea with 5,000 meters of ocean beneath her keel and a cloudy sky, a deep-ocean sky filled with uncertain cumulonimbus clouds, overhead. Just like that, we were at sea.

Quetzal felt huge, with room to spare for a change, as Tadji and I made up the full complement of crew. Tadji was excited, nervous, and feeling a little unsettled as I prepared dinner. We had tarried in Bermuda until a near-perfect weather window became impossible to ignore. There was the prospect of squalls and gusty winds the first night, but after that the forecast called for pleasant southwest breezes that promised reaching conditions all the way to the New England coast. Naturally we treated the forecast with a healthy dose of skepticism, but summer voyaging in the Atlantic is generally good going. Low-slung Bermuda was out of sight astern and Martha's Vineyard was just under 600 miles off the bow. We were in the splendid in-between, a watery chasm that belonged to the three of us—*Quetzal* and her lackeys.

Tadji wasn't interested in any of my famous chicken stew. She was feeling fine, but playing it safe, not wanting to tempt seasickness on the first night offshore. My feelings were anything but hurt, as I hastily scarfed down her portion, mumbling with a full mouth, "You sure you don't want any?" She was harnessed up, on duty, and ready for me to stop stuffing my face and hit the sack. Our watch system is a bit unorthodox but it works well when we are sailing without crew. Tadji does not like getting up at set intervals, every 3 or 4 hours, so instead she takes the first watch, which begins after dinner around 2000, and stays up as late as she can. Sometimes she makes it to 0100, sometimes midnight, sometimes 1100 if things are really rough, and if they're going smoothly, sometimes 0200 or beyond. I lie down and sleep, knowing that she's paying attention despite the fact that she usually has a headphone in one ear and sometimes watches a movie on her iPad. Nothing escapes her and she peers about the horizon more consistently than I do. The new hard dodger standing guard over the cockpit was really her idea and I always know where to find her if I pop up for a quick visit, snug on the low side out of the wind beneath the dodger. I don't sleep with one ear open, far from it, I sleep like a man with a clear conscience and a trusted mate. When Tadji's finally ready for sleep she wakes me, and after making a pot of coffee, my nightly ritual, I take the watch until first light.

I almost never listen to music, and I find that I don't read as much as I used to, as I don't want to spoil my night vision. I listen to the ocean instead. It's a beautiful symphony, and *Quetzal* adds her own movements. Slicing and sluicing, she strings together a rhythm all her own. She's not interested in an adagio, slowing down only when I force the issue and shackle her with a reef in the main or a furl tucked into the headsail. And I think. Modern philosopher Alain de Botton writes, "Journeys are the midwives of thoughts." My thoughts are uncluttered at sea, but also ephemeral, blown away by the wind if I fail to write them down. I don't mind. I am not materialist about them anymore, I like the notion that they're riding a steady breeze and may land anywhere. I study the sea. I watch for waves angling off in another direction as they crest a swell, suggesting a wind change might be in the offing. I am amazed by how often dolphins, birds, flying fish, and occasionally whales visit me. I suppose they've always been there, but I seem to have missed the steady parade when I was younger, content with a sighting here or there. Maybe they're just paying their respects to a fellow ocean wanderer who's getting up there in years. I wonder if they recognize me, maybe thinking, "So you're still out here doing your thing, brother, pretty cool."

Tadji woke me at 0100. I was well rested, and knew that I'd slept well because the wind was up and it was time to reef the main. Down below, in the aft quarter cabin, it was as quiet as a library and I had not noticed the wind was steady at 20 knots. Tadji helped me secure the first reef, gave me a kiss, and went below. "Don't wake me unless you need me," she said with a last smile before she climbed into her bunk. The Hydrovane—a self-steering device that captures the wind via a small sail that in turns drives an independent rudder—was in control and thankful for the reduced sail area which eased its workload. We installed the Hydrovane a few years ago. In a case of reverse evolution it has consigned the electronic autopilot, which, as you know, is much praised in this book, to a backup role, like drafting a rookie quarterback and then benching Tom Brady. The Hydrovane takes a bit of tweaking and—like most equipment on a sailboat—works best when the sails are balanced, a desired state when the boat is sailing efficiently but without much heeling and the various loads are under control. The beauty of the Hydrovane is that it's completely mechanical, an anachronism from a time before we became utterly dependent on electrons: it requires no power from the battery bank, not unlike the act of sailing itself. I love that there's not any kind of digital readout on the thing. It's robust, reliable, and independent—good traits for offshore gear and offshore sailors—and it is something of a badge of honor perched on the stern of a serious cruising boat. It's also an emergency rudder, mounted and ready for action should the main rudder become disabled—not a small issue, considering that Jimmy

Cornell states that 75% of abandoned boats are abandoned because of rudder failure.

The clouds formed a dark canopy, eerily backlit by a crescent moon that was trying to squeeze into view but couldn't find an opening. *Quetzal* was sailing at about 80% efficiency. I was OK with that percentage as it translated into 7 knots of speed, a soft ride that made sleeping below manageable and steering easy with low stress levels on the hull, rig, and crew. I love sailing fast but also recognize that taking your foot off the accelerator, without slowing down too much, is good seamanship at times, and one of many reasons I admire *Quetzal*, because she thrives without being pushed, freeing my mind to wander a bit without the need for constant supervision.

I was not in a hurry for the hours to race by, relishing the motion as *Quetzal* cut a clean swath through gentle seas, leaving only a momentary trail of bioluminescence as a fleeting wake. This was my fourth Bermuda passage in less than two months, crazy maybe, but beautiful too, and I certainly felt I knew the way to and from the island and was testing the theory about the Bermuda Triangle—I had a target on my back. We had sailed north from St. Martin in late April, in mostly calm conditions, then a few weeks later, a new crew signed aboard and we made our way to Newport, Rhode Island. That passage was lumpy, especially at the end as we beat into 30-knot winds for two days to make landfall on schedule. From Newport we made our way back to Bermuda, an intriguing passage that saw us heave-to for a day to dodge a deep low that turned into a tropical storm. After my reunion in the Hebrides with *Gigi*, Tadji and I were headed back to New England, giving the ghosts of the Triangle one more chance to wreak havoc on us. I confess, I don't put much stock in the Bermuda Triangle theory, having sailed out to the island 25 times. I have had my share of gales along the way, and been rocked by a few serious storms, but I've also had a few drifters—calm trips—and plenty of exquisite passages too. Bermuda is in the crosshairs where fronts exit the North American continent—and as a result, the island receives its share of intriguing weather. We planned to spend July and most of August moseying about Martha's Vineyard, Nantucket, the Elizabeth Islands, and Buzzards Bay, a slothful summer in a lovely setting. In September, we'd make our way back to Solomons, Maryland, to prepare for the passage south to the Caribbean in November—just the regular commute for a working sailboat.

It was turning into a lovely evening as the clouds moved off to the east. I had no intention of setting up our tracking device, at least not for another day or so, and our AIS at that time was set up to receive signals, not transmit them. I didn't feel the need to broadcast our exact position to the world via my Facebook page. I wanted to relish our isolation. The slogan for my sailing business is "Never lost, just hard to find," but it is becoming harder to pull off both parts of that statement these days. Sailing in the dark, I could feel with my whole body that *Quetzal* wanted more sail, but I resisted. This night was mine. I didn't want it to end too soon. I remembered long-ago voyages during my delivery days when I would call my mother from a quayside pay phone, or write her a letter (believe it or not), to tell her that we were setting off on a passage and not to expect to hear from me for 20, 25, 30, 35 days. If she didn't hear from me after a couple months, she should start to worry a bit. The contrast to voyaging today is stark: now we are like prisoners with electronic bracelets mapping our every move.

The promise of ocean voyaging is unfettered access to one of the last great wildernesses on the planet, where time is measured naturally and not necessarily by clocks. I hear the snickers, and of course there's plenty of clock watching on a sailboat: the watch system, the noon sight, and that mother of all clocks, GPS, all rely on knowing time. If someone is five minutes late for watch, those minutes can be excruciatingly long. Captain's Hour starts at 1700 most days, and we plan our naps around that crucial hour. If the GPS loses its signal, Neptune forbid the consequences, as our vital data—course over ground, speed over ground, distance and course to waypoint, velocity made good, not to mention our position—all vanish too. And you know what? That's OK.

Historian Lewis Mumford claimed, "The clock, not the steam-engine, is the key-machine of the modern industrial age." He added that "the clock is a piece of power-machinery whose 'product' is seconds and minutes: by its essential nature it dissociated time from human events..." The clock owns us as never before, reducing everything to a schedule, measuring our value on a per-hour basis, sucking away the net worth of our human experience. It's hard to imagine life before the clock took control, but I know one sacred place where the clock does not define time and can be disregarded—on a sailboat far from land. You have control of your days, and nights, your minutes, and seconds, you can turn off the GPS, the satellite phone, and the all the other devices that demand you get down on your knees and pray to their time gods, who extract your offerings through monthly service plans. At sea, nobody can tell you when to open or when to close shop. Your schedule is dictated by your human needs, not those of some atomic clock overlord. I stand with Marilyn Monroe, who observed, "I've been on a calendar but I have never been on time." At sea, sunrise and sunset have a power that no clock can render obsolete—and this restores your humanity.

The challenges of ocean voyaging on a sailboat are what set it apart from other forms of sea travel. I want—no, I need—to be fully engaged in a voyage, and have no desire to peer from a porthole or pool deck, leaving the decision making to others—that's not going to sea for me. I want to be tested by the sea and accept all the consequences of my voyage. Storms and steady breezes, calms and breakdowns, they're all equals in the cast of characters waiting to join you every time you shove off. There's risk in ocean voyaging, but without it there's nothing, nothing but moving from one place to another in a slow, uncomfortable, expensive manner. Mitigating risks before a voyage and managing them along the way is a core element of seamanship, of being a sailor. Trying to eliminate them altogether turns a voyage into another humdrum day at the office. Why bother? Take a plane and leave the ocean to sailors who understand the risks and rewards.

I am not looking for risks when I go to sea, far from it, and I have pleaded for Neptune's mercy (and to any other gods that might be interested in helping, for that matter) during the seemingly endless hours of a deep ocean storm. And I have been terrified, wondering if maybe this time I might not survive the ocean's fury or my own stupid mistakes. I have pushed myself to the point of complete exhaustion—steering before breaking waves, frantically repairing a steering system, desperately jury-rigging a stay, bleeding an engine in a violent sea, conning my boat away from a rocky shore and hauling it off a coral reef. But I never expected ocean voyaging to be easy. These desperate events, shared with shipmates who have become my family, are carved into the lifelines on my palms. They're my story, our story—they're real and I wouldn't trade them for any amount of money or time.

Storms and stories dominate our memories of ocean voyaging, but the freedom starts as soon as you slip the lines and head out to sea. I feel a powerful release from the clutches of land life every time I shove off. I've been chasing this freedom my entire life, and for the most part,

I've been lucky enough to find it. I have never worked for "the man" and have lived by my wits and pursued my dreams with abandon—at times recklessly so. This freedom has demands and consequences. You must be willing to embrace a degree of self-reliance that is unnerving to some: there are times you have no one to rely on but yourself and your shipmates—everything depends on you and your resourcefulness. Freedom also means you can't cry for help when you no longer want to be free.

For some, the prospect of being trapped aboard a floating tiny house of about 300 square feet is anything but freedom—it's purgatory with seasickness thrown in to complete the misery. I understand. Ocean voyaging in small boats has never been for everybody. This life is the domain of a select few who are not willing to farm out the essential choices of how they want to live to others, and even more, it's something of a calling. I am not running from any particular evils ashore, and confess to following sports, politics, and all the overwhelming news of the day. Indeed, my stepsons Nick and Alex and I have been known to shout irrationally at the television while watching the Miami Heat play, and felt the collective pain of watching LeBron James abandon the Heat and return to the Cavaliers. I am not even close to being a hermit, or a recluse, or even a loner. I am just happy at sea. I love the community we create aboard *Quetzal*, and I have a strong desire to share what I have learned with other sailors who, as I was so long ago, are looking for the key to unlock the door to the freedom, for a few days, or a few months, of ocean voyaging.

First light snuck up on me. The eastern sky was aglow and the sun was about to make its entry. The hours of my watch had raced by and I heard Tadji stirring below. She joined me in the cockpit just as the sun nosed above the horizon. The promise of another nice day of sailing was in the offing. I didn't need assurances beyond that. We pulled the reef out of the main, and *Quetzal* surged in gratitude. Looking over my shoulder, toward the southeast, I thought about that young boy swimming for his life on the storm-tossed sea so many years ago. I looked back toward the companionway, where my beautiful wife was tucked under the dodger, content to be at sea with me. How had I managed to navigate to this point, to these very coordinates that placed us on the edge of time? What a distance I've traveled only to have fetched up back where I started.

APPENDIX

WRINKLES

Downwind Sailing Comfort • Security Concerns •
Vessel Awareness—The Walkabout • PFDs, Safety Harnesses,
and Jacklines

"A century ago a famous English seaman named S.T.S. Lecky
wrote a book on navigation called Lecky's Wrinkles to Practical
Navigation. *The book went through many editions, and Lecky's*
Wrinkles, *as it was soon called, became a handbook of the sea*
because of its practical usefulness. I have borrowed the key word
from Squire Lecky's title (Wrinkles) and present a few ideas that
I have found helpful, not on navigation, but on general sailing."

—Hal Roth, *After 50,000 Miles*

"The sail, the play of its pulse so like our own lives: so thin and
yet so full of life, so noiseless when it labors hardest, so noisy and
impatient when least effective."

—Henry David Thoreau, *A Week on the*
Merrimack and Concord Rivers

To begin this appendix with insights from Hal Roth and Henry David Thoreau is like comparing *Fortuna*, my old steel boat, a homebuilt but capable world cruiser, to a simple and graceful daysailer, maybe a winsome boat lovingly crafted by the late Tom Morris, that takes your breath away as she glides swan-like across the bay. They're both sailboats, and both harness the wind to achieve their objectives, but the similarities end there. Still, Roth and Thoreau would have been kindred souls as both were passionate about experiencing the natural world without blinders, and about living honest, fulfilling lives free of the shackles of mainstream expectations. Sailing, particularly deep-ocean sailing, is an art and a science, poetic and mechanical, and a full appreciation of a day at sea requires a deep, almost mystical connection to the environment and a mastery of skills and techniques that form the basis of seamanship and allow for safe, successful, satisfying voyaging. This appendix provides some insights into some of the seamanship aspects of ocean voyaging.

I have always been attracted by transcendentalism, the school of thought that flourished in New England during the early and middle nineteenth century. It celebrated humanism and the cathedral of nature, and stood in resistance against the storm winds of the Industrial Revolution. The transcendentalists used words, not weapons, to remind us of our precious individualism, and their legacy is preserved through a canon of literature that's an essential part of the American ideal, or at least the American mythology. Thoreau, a founding father of transcendentalism and best known for his classic book *Walden*, can make a gnarled tree stump seem like the lord of the forest, something we must not only respect but cherish. Nautically speaking—and Thoreau was a devoted sailor, albeit mostly in small boats on rivers and lakes— his soaring prose requires Roth's copper-bottomed wisdom to wrestle it into a plan of action, to translate it into a successful seagoing strategy. That pulsing sail that Thoreau describes as though it's a living creature needs a practical block-and-tackle rig devised by Roth to bring it under control in a rising wind.

Nobody would call Roth a poet—he writes in a straightforward manner—but even decades after his last books were published you can still stake important sailing decisions on his insights. His compiled observations, practical gems on boat handling and living aboard, were published in his book *How to Sail Around the World*, and it continues to sell well today. I've borrowed his borrowed word, "wrinkles," for the title of this appendix. I love the idea of touching on a variety of subjects, and this section wanders around the ocean, and around the deck, with stories that reflect hard-won knowledge, lessons learned from both good and bad decisions, and even a revelation or two from my place of worship, the cathedral of the sea.

I've been writing about time throughout the book and would love to be able to travel back to Walden Pond to talk with Thoreau, or better yet, go for a sail with him. Alas, I haven't discovered that point of sail just yet, but I did meet Hal Roth at the Chicago Boat Show several years ago. It was not long before he died and I was grateful to be able to thank him for his wonderful books that helped me unravel so many thorny details of offshore voyaging. I told him how the picture of his wife Margaret, smiling in the cockpit in a full-blown snow storm after they'd rounded Cape Horn, was iconic, and etched in my memory, right up there with the photo of Sir Francis Chichester's *Gypsy Moth* rounding Cape Horn.

Talking about the Horn seemed weirdly appropriate as we braved a bitter January wind whistling through narrow corridors between skyscrapers to walk to a nearby coffee shop and chat. Roth, who sailed around the world three times and was awarded the Blue Water Medal by the Cruising Club of America in 1971, was impressively humble and soon turned the discussion to me. An authority on WWII, especially the naval battles, he was intrigued by my name and wondered if I was related to the great German submariner Otto Kretschmer. He was disappointed that I wasn't sure, and later sent me reams of information about Admiral Kretschmer and concluded that we had to be related. He also researched my father's war history, and although I knew my dad's story intimately, in a kind and thoughtful gesture he told me in a handwritten note how my father and the other brave B26 pilots helped turn the tide of the war in 1944.

Roth's "Wrinkles" chapter, first published in his book *After 50,000 Miles*, touches on some topics that seem quaint today, like catching water with canvas tarps, adjustable boom topping lifts (rigid boom vangs have nearly rendered topping lifts obsolete), and tips on lighting kerosene stoves. Other topics have surely stood the test of time, including the need to have easy-to-deploy running poles for downwind sailing, the importance of aggressive nonskid for safe maneuvering on deck, and the never-ending battle to keep cockroaches off the boat in the tropics. (He recommends that you avoid bringing cardboard containers aboard at all costs, and use boric acid instead of nasty insecticides to kill the uninvited buggers.)

Downwind Sailing Comfort

I promised that I'd mention how to make the boat more comfortable when sailing before the wind, especially if the seas are large or lumpy. I also noted that most offshore cruisers don't fly spinnakers day after day, or more specifically, night after night, as the stress they create is usually not worth the spotty performance boost they offer. You must figure out a way to sail effectively downwind with your headsails. This is important because the most efficient way to cross an ocean, or sail through life, is with the wind at your back. A mental vision of just that, a handsome boat soaring before a distant trade wind, is the incubation chamber for faraway dreams. This is especially trenchant on cold, sleety, stressed-out suburban nights, when darkness falls too early and the thought of having your own sailboat anchored off a tropical island seems as improbable as winning the lottery. Downwind sailing is the stuff of dreams—you just have to figure out how to stop it from becoming a recurring nightmare as your boat rolls from gunwale to gunwale.

Quetzal's natural tendency is to *roll*—a side-to-side movement through the longitudinal axis of the boat—while running, and she's not unique. As I noted earlier, one of the advantages of multihulls is that they hardly roll at all when running. In my yacht-delivery days, I sailed several catamarans offshore and came to appreciate how they handle in following seas. They do *pitch*—an up-and-down motion that runs through the bow and stern—a bit, but it's less pronounced and much easier to accommodate because things, and people, don't unpredictably career from one side of the boat to the other. To prevent Tadji from mutinying to a roomy catamaran I have had to devise a system to cut down on *Quetzal*'s roll during long passages.

I have spent years talking with other sailors about this subject and experimenting with different sail plans. My brother-in-law Trevor, a circumnavigator whom you've met in previous chapters, carried twin-poled-out headsails on his 37´ cutter *Wandering Star* during solo crossings of the Atlantic and Pacific. Typical of that time, the sails had high-cut clews and were hanked on as most serious cruisers either didn't trust roller furling in those days, or, as Trevor says, couldn't afford it. He claims that this sail arrangement reduced rolling but definitely didn't eliminate it. It did, however, make self-steering more efficient, and his Aires windvane (which he and my sister Liz continue to use many years later) loved the balance provided by the double-poled-out jibs. In fact, early voyagers, especially singlehanders, used double headsail rigs with sheets tied to the tiller to make passages before the invention of self-steering gear.

Trevor experimented with flying a steadying sail off the backstay to cut the rolling but found it was not effective. The only consistent way he discovered to reduce rolling was to fly all of his sails—all the time. In addition to twin-poled-out jibs, he set the mainsail, either full or partially reefed, and prevented it off to leeward. He also flew the staysail, sometimes trimmed on the centerline or sometimes also boomed out. Trevor constantly sought the elusive balance that kept them full. "I looked like a clipper ship," he jokes now, "sails flying everywhere," but it takes a sailor of great skill and patience like Trevor to keep all those sails happy and not blanketing each other. When the world was working right he found that the wind bending around the mainsail helped fill the windward-side, poled-out headsail. And when it wasn't working just right, "it was loud."

There's no disputing that sailing with two headsails is a bit intimidating for many cruisers even if it does cut the rolling a bit, especially in beamy modern boats. It requires two poles, and in the old days at least, a second forestay, and a lot of other hardware that makes the process of getting the running sails up and down daunting. The idea of throwing up a poleless, asymmetrical spinnaker seems easier than fussing with all that gear. However, there's a good alternative today as more and more serious cruising boats are factory fitted with a solent stay, a double headsail rig that differs from a traditional cutter—or slutter—by having the aft stay set just a foot or so behind the forestay. Like many concepts in sailing, it's a fresh take on an old idea and has come into its own because of advances in roller-furling technology, especially on big boats. This arrangement allows the sail set on the solent stay to be larger than a traditional staysail, making it more effective as a running sail. By using two lightweight— often carbon fiber—whisker poles that are mounted on the mast and easy to set, the prospect of running with two poled-out headsails, and the reduced roll that comes with it, becomes much less unnerving. If you're considering retrofitting a solent stay, remember it's a serious project. The base of the stay must be anchored to a stout chainplate tied into the stem—the strongest point of any sailboat. A distinct advantage of a solent stay is that you don't need to fit running backstays (required on traditional cutters) because the top of the solent stay is mounted near enough to the masthead that the backstay can carry the load. Another option for twin headsails is to fly two equal-sized jibs on the forestay, utilizing a single halyard and the twin luff grooves in the furling gear foil extrusions. With this arrangement you can furl the headsails by flopping one onto the other, and then flopping them back into position for running with reduced sail area. You can also sail on a reach with the sails essentially lying on top of each other, taking care to sort out the loaded and lazy sheets.

I confess, I've tried all of these configurations with varying degrees of profanities and success over the years, including logging plenty of miles on boats fitted with solent stays. Left to my own devices, I still much prefer to drop the mainsail, pole out a single large genoa, and romp across the ocean with minimal fuss. I noted earlier, back in Chapter Two, that with the mainsail out of my life, I don't worry about jibes or squalls, and the loads are relatively easy on the rig and we roll off mile after easy mile, sailing at 80% efficient, that happy place that balances speed and safety. Roll is the key word—we do roll under this rig, but I don't even notice it anymore, like Melville's Ishmael, who proclaims as he rides the masthead, "There is no life in thee, now, except that rocking life imparted by a gently rolling ship; by her, borrowed from the sea; by the sea, from the inscrutable tides of God." In other words, it's just the motion of the ocean. When folks struggle with this downwind rollercoaster ride, part of me wants to scream, "Come on, people, deal with it, this is way better than beating into the wind." But that's the old, insensitive John Kretschmer. The new, kind and caring John Kretschmer does all he can to figure out how to reduce the roll while muttering under his breath.

The strategy that works best on *Quetzal* and other similar sea boats is to put a deep reef in the mainsail, usually the second reef, but sometimes the third, and take the time to make it tight and flat, sucking the draft out of the sail. Then we pay out the traveler as far as we can to leeward, and ease the sheet until the sail fills just off the aft lower shroud. We control the boom angle, aiming for horizontal with the sea, by applying a fair bit of vang tension. The boom is prevented with a Dacron high-stretch line that runs forward on the leeward side, and back to the cockpit for easy control to allow for a soft, mushy jibe should things go awry. The headsail is furled while the pole is deployed. Once the pole is ready for action, with fore-and-aft preventer lines and a topping lift keeping it in place, the headsail is then unfurled, and it takes some effort as there's plenty of load on the sheet as it makes a sharp bend from the pole end to the winch. The carbon sleeve of the pole is extended to flatten the jib and in effect raise the clew, allowing both main and headsail to stay filled while deep reaching. The main dampens the rolling dramatically and the headsail provides the horsepower to keep us moving smartly.

It is vital to keep the headsail from flogging. We have a no-flogging rule on *Quetzal*, one of the few rules we have, but I must say, enforcement is lax. It's also vital to keep the mainsail from riding up against the shrouds or mast spreaders. A sail lying against the rig will have a short life, and this is one of several good arguments against running wing on wing—that is, with the headsail poled to one side and the mainsail prevented on the opposite side—invariably sprawled against the shrouds and spreaders. This is a lazy technique we all use when daysailing, but it's no way to cross an ocean. The one drawback of the *Quetzal*'s "reefed mainsail – poled headsail" approach is that it does not allow us to sail dead downwind, which is often the most direct course to our waypoint. We can usually fill both sails with the wind 160–165 degrees off the bow, unless the seas are heaped up—then we need to sail closer to 150 degrees. Of course, by not sailing dead downwind our speed is usually better and our VMG (Velocity Made Good, or speed relative to a waypoint) is usually higher. It just means that at some point we'll have to jibe to get where we are going, and jibing is a big job that requires switching all the running gear to the other side of the boat.

A final comment on deep-ocean downwind sailing concerns split rigs: ketches, yawls, and to a much lesser degree, schooners. They offer the ability to fly a mizzen sail, which is the after-most boomed sail, and a poled-out jib on the same side. The separation between them usually prevents the mizzen from blanketing the headsail. The mizzen can be trimmed specifically for slowing the roll and assisting the steering vane or autopilot. This rig also allows you to set a mizzen staysail—a small, controllable spinnaker flown from the head of the mizzen mast and much less intimidating offshore. This is the sail plan we carried day after day on the Gulfstar 50 ketch that we delivered to Japan. It worked so well that I was free to let my thoughts wander and to observe and record seabirds, as you may remember from Chapter Six. (Also, from a recent rereading of my journal of the passage, I recalled that I read 22 books while crossing the Pacific. My favorites? According to my journal, #1 was *The Naked and the Dead*, by Norman Mailer. I agree, that's a weird choice, but #2, *Tinker, Tailor, Soldier, Spy*, by John le Carré, is a great book by any reckoning.)

Security Concerns

On to other reckonings and wrinkles. Let's assume you are 200 miles offshore, running before a gentle breeze and following sea with a carmine sun melting into the western horizon. The boat and crew are happy, enjoying Captain's Hour with minimal rolling, and suddenly you notice a small, unlit boat steaming directly at you. As it gets closer you can see that there are five men standing amidships and it doesn't feel right. It isn't right. What are their intentions? Could they be pirates? We encountered this very scenario sailing from the Galápagos Islands to Panama. There was very little time to make a plan—so quick action and clear thinking were required.

It was a few years ago, and I had chartered a 54´ steel ketch, *Blue Nomad*, and organized two month-long excursions to the Galápagos Islands. The usual motives inspired the passages—a desire to spend some quality time in the Galápagos, to make a little money in the process, and, most importantly, to be at sea, the place where I am always happiest. The offshore sailing community can be a bit incestuous at times—we are a small but devoted group of ocean wanderers, and the same people and same boats turn up year after year in all the cruising crossroads, and at all the sailing events. I was delighted to be able to find *Blue Nomad* for this adventure. Dear friends Roger and Myrna, whom you met in Chapter Five (and from whom I had borrowed that seabird identification book), had previously owned her and sailed from Europe to Vancouver and back to Florida, via Cape Horn. I remember talking with Roger when he was considering buying her in Spain back in the late '80s—he'd come a long way from the landlubber who missed the Bahamas on his first passage and sheepishly turned up at my navigation school. Another friend, Pam Wall, introduced me to Paul, *Blue Nomad*'s new owner. Pam and her husband Andy, and their two children, spent six years sailing around the world. Sadly Andy passed away much too soon but Pam carries on, and is a highly respected voice of experience and reason in the cruising community. She has been advising sailors at boat shows and in various seminars and workshops, including mine, for years. Paul had completely restored *Blue Nomad* and was enthusiastic about my idea of using her for a couple of expeditions to the Galápagos.

Built by the Van Dam Shipyard in Holland, *Blue Nomad* was more small ship than sailboat with a displacement north of 30 tons. She had a proud clipper bow, a sweet sheerline, and a long keel. A pilothouse by design, she also had a hard dodger that covered half the cockpit and protected a bewildering array of the latest electronic gadgets. Paul, a brilliant IT guy, loves technology, and his JET was off the charts. The interior was huge, and accommodated eight in three private cabins. Her main engine was an old Volvo and she carried 500 gallons of fuel, which, as it turned out, was not quite enough to cope with the dreadful calms that ply the equatorial seas between Panama and the Galápagos. She was not, as you might have surmised, a terribly efficient vessel under sail, especially in light air, but she was stout and inspired confidence in all who sailed her.

We were staged on the Atlantic side of the Panama Canal. Paul, Alan, and another friend, Sergey, had helped me deliver the boat from Fort Lauderdale, a lively test sail running before a stiff northeast wind. The Galápagos crew joined us in Panama, all *Quetzal* veterans and fine shipmates. Ron and Chris had been part of the notoriously challenging 2008 Atlantic crossing. Denise and Deb L. had sailed together in Newfoundland, and Don had sailed aboard in the Bahamas and the Caribbean. Paul, who had attended the State University of New York Maritime College as a young man, was delighted to be going back to sea and also joined us for both passages. The excitement began the night before we transited the canal.

Before loading five shopping carts' worth of provisions aboard, we went through the boat, scrubbing the lockers and tossing out all the old food and anything else unnecessary for the upcoming passage. Denise and I ruthlessly cleaned out the canned-goods locker as some cans looked as if they'd been there for decades. Shaking a tomato soup can—it felt empty—Denise looked at me curiously. Without hesitation I told her to toss it out. With the boat cleaned out, we stowed the provisions and then joined Paul and the rest of the crew at the bar of the Shelter Bay Marina. He'd been busy sorting out details with our canal agent and dealing with the mountain of paperwork required for a transit.

"All stowed?" he asked cheerfully.

"Stowed and cleaned up," Denise replied. "Some of those cans were ancient."

"I know," Paul admitted, then added with a smile, "but you didn't throw out my soup, did you?"

"What do you mean?" she asked, and it suddenly hit me like a flying fish to the head.

"Oh shit," I blurted out, remembering that Paul had told me earlier that he used the tomato soup can as a secret safe. He had $5,000 stashed in the can.

While Shelter Bay Marina is a nice place, the cinder-block compound behind the docks that houses the garbage dumb is utterly squalid. So much so that I stood back as far as possible when tossing the trash bags over the wall to lessen the chances of encountering any nasty creatures that might be prowling about. Now, the only choice was to go back and comb through all the bags of trash we had just thrown into that disgusting compound. And of course it was pitch black.

I wasn't exaggerating when I said we had a fine crew—none begged out of the ghastly search project. We entered the garbage dump through a rickety gate and by flashlight located our bags and went through them. It was extremely unpleasant work, made more so because we couldn't find the damn soup can. We spent several hours going through the entire compound, ripping open trash bags and chasing the rats and the more fearsome feral cats away, but the tomato soup can wasn't there. Depressed and feeling filthy to the dermis, we retreated to the marina and dove into what we hoped was a highly chlorinated pool, where we tried to wash the night's adventure away.

Back on the boat Paul was notably calm, and I assured him that I'd make it up in the charter fee, but he wouldn't hear of it. Then I noticed one small bag of trash that we hadn't carried to the compound. Glancing inside, I saw it—the Campbell's red-and-white logo, the can of tomato soup! The crew didn't know whether to cheer or to flog me for putting them through that ordeal. I told them that it had been a pre-voyage exercise in "extreme team building," and when they didn't buy that lame excuse I broke out the good rum, the 12-year Flor de Cana, to hold them at bay.

We transited the Panama Canal and then motorsailed to the Galápagos, dealing with 800 miles of calms and light headwinds. Eighty miles from San Cristóbal, our first landfall, a wayward red-footed booby landed on deck, a sure sign that the islands were ahead. We were awestruck, and crept about like *National Geographic* photographers. A thousand or so pictures later, the bird moved from the bow pulpit to the pilothouse; it clearly wasn't feeling well, and it was a messy transfer. Soon the bird was going with abandon, spoiling the decks and pilothouse. Paul and I, brooms and mops in hand, were guilty of environmental terrorism as we chased the damn red-footed booby off the boat. Things improved after that encounter and we explored the islands extensively, by land and sea. I had arranged special permits that allowed us to wander more or less as we pleased. We came to appreciate the bountiful biodiversity and Ecuadorian heritage of the Galápagos. The wildlife, ashore and afloat, is extraordinary, and lives up to expectations, but so are the people living in the islands, and they're dedicated to preserving one of our planet's treasures.

We carried on to Cocos Island, a Costa Rican national park 300 miles offshore. Renowned as a pirate hideaway in centuries past, it's a resplendent island with numerous waterfalls, and is famous for the many sharks that frequent its reefs and harbors. It was a joy to hike shady trails, swim in natural freshwater pools, and visit with the rangers, the only full-time inhabitants. Leg One concluded in Puntarenas, on the Costa Rican mainland. A month later, Paul and I did the same passage in reverse. We had left the Galápagos two days earlier, and were taking advantage of a rare fair wind and actually sailing, albeit slowly, when we noticed the fast boat approaching.

We had been watching a large offshore fishing boat off our starboard beam, about four miles away according to the radar, without concern as we'd seen several other trawlers earlier in the day. Our attitude changed abruptly when we noticed a boat charging our way. I had read about a few isolated incidents off the coast of Ecuador where fishing-boat crews had robbed passing yachts. This had all the makings of a similar incident. We were a crew of eight, with Hartmutt and Ellen from Wisconsin, my friend David, whom you have read about throughout the book, John and Cindy, who also turn up time and again, and Aaron, a geography professor from North Carolina.

I knew one thing—I wanted to speak with one voice, to assess the situation quickly as it developed, and respond without discussion. We immediately fired up the engine and I pushed the throttle forward for all speed. I wanted to make it as difficult as possible to board *Blue Nomad*, which was already challenging because of her high freeboard. I asked the crew to stand up to let everybody in the approaching boat see them, then go below and stay there until I gave them the order to return. I told them to arm themselves as best they could but to stay below until I gave the word. Paul was a bit miffed that I had demanded that he remove his specially-made stainless steel rifle from the boat before the passage, but its removal was part of the package for obtaining the Galápagos permits. No weapons were allowed in the islands. Plus, I knew that unless you were prepared to use it, a weapon was as likely to get you killed as to prevent it.

The boat was around 25′ with a proud bow and low freeboard. Often called a Mexican skiff, it was common along both coasts of Central and South America. Powered by a noisy outboard engine, the skiff paralleled our course, clearly sizing up the situation. There were five men aboard, unshaven and scruffy, which of course is the way most fishermen look, and, for that matter, is the way I've looked for most of my life. Tucked halfway behind the dodger, with a winch handle in hand but hidden from their view, I was determined to smack the crap out of them if they tried to board us without permission. They were not carrying guns, but there was a big tarp on the bottom of their boat and they were all eyeing it nervously. Something was under there that they didn't want me to see. A couple of the men carried machetes in their belts.

"*Que quieres?*" I asked in my gringo Spanish. What do you want? I wasn't friendly, but not obviously hostile either.

They tried to come alongside *Blue Nomad* and I said sternly, "*Nada, no, vete.*" No, go away.

"*Necesitamos gasoleo,*" one of them shouted. We need diesel fuel. But they looked confused, possibly wondering where the rest of the crew was. That was my hope anyway.

"Impossible," I said, "*tenamos poco.*" We have little. My Spanish was failing me. "We need it, every drop, sorry," I added in Spanish-accented English. It seemed unlikely to me that a commercial fishing boat needed to borrow fuel from a sailboat.

Fortunately, despite the light winds the sea was choppy—caused by the collision of wind and a strong south-setting current—and it was challenging for the skiff to come alongside. Twice they closed with our hull and tried to hold our rail but had to pull away as the boats bucked apart.

"*Vete, ahora,*" I said, firmly. Go—now. But I wasn't sure what my next move was going to be if they decided not to take my suggestion.

After a brief but animated discussion among themselves, which made me extremely nervous, especially when their boat rammed our hull when the guy steering the outboard momentarily lost control, they turned away from *Blue Nomad* and headed back toward the fishing boat at a slow but deliberate speed.

"OK, everybody," I shouted in a shaky voice, "come up."

The crew emerged, and we were all a bit shaken but also incredibly relieved. Everyone started talking at once. The incident had gone as well as we could have hoped for, with no violence or injuries to the crew, no real damage to *Blue Nomad*, and not even any precious diesel fuel lost. Did they really just need fuel? I began to doubt myself. "Maybe I overreacted," I ventured. "John," John chimed in, "they were NOT looking for fuel. And by the way, I think we should turn off all the lights." He was right, we needed to stay vigilant, and immediately turned off every light aboard, even the compass light, and shut down all our tracking devices. We altered our course significantly while maintaining full speed under power and sail. The fishing boat faded from view astern, but we kept a nervous eye and ear out throughout the night.

"What about pirates?" is one of the first questions land people ask when you mention that you are planning an ocean passage. Followed quickly by, "Do you carry guns aboard?" Later that evening, after the incident with the skiff, Paul—who is a dear friend, a lovely human being, and gentle in all ways—and I had a lively discussion about the pros and cons of having guns aboard. He contended that if we'd had his rifle we could have made a show of force and sent them on their way sooner. I strongly disagreed, and although I can't prove it, feel certain that they had weapons under the tarp in their boat. I argued that once a weapon was introduced things would have escalated, and nothing good would have come from it. I told him about a seminar I'd spoken at years before that was sponsored by my friend, the literally larger-than-life Bob Bitchin, and his former magazine, *Latitudes and Attitudes*. Bob and I were having a repartee, fielding questions from the audience about pirates and weapons. He was pro-gun and I was anti. We babbled on, with neither one of us being overly convincing, when finally an exasperated gentleman stood up and said, "Look, I admire both of you guys but it's obvious that neither one of you knows the first thing about handling weapons under duress."

Clearing his throat and collecting himself, he explained that he was a former marine, and a 30-year veteran of the Los Angeles Police Department. "There's only one reason to draw a gun, only one reason to fire a gun," he said, and the entire audience was under the spell of his quiet authority. "And that's to shoot to kill, to pull the trigger." He continued, "That's the question you have to ask yourself, are you capable of doing that?" He added, "It's harder than you can ever imagine to take somebody's life, especially at close range. Most cops can't do it the first time, that's why rookies are always paired with vets. Bad guys can shoot to kill, that's what makes them bad; good guys don't want to kill anyone, but if you hesitate it will be too late. The gun you just raised will get you killed. If you can answer that question yes, and know it in your head and heart that you will pull the trigger when the time comes, then go ahead and have a gun aboard. But just buying a gun doesn't do you much good, you need to be fully trained in the care and operation of firearms and practice frequently to keep up your skills."

To some degree, the guns-or-no-guns-aboard discussion mirrors the larger gun debate in the U.S., and it's not any easier to rationally discuss the matter afloat than it is ashore. I think the cop had it right—if you are trained and experienced with firearms, and feel that they make you safer, by all means carry guns. Tim, my mom's sailing partner, was a crack shot, a long-time hunter who felt that guns were a necessary part of cruising safety. He had a 30-06 bolt-action rifle, a sawed-off shotgun, and a long-barrel WWII sniper's rifle aboard *Epoch*. I sailed the boat back across the Atlantic for Mom after Tim died, and the arsenal aboard made me nervous. I clandestinely sold all three guns to the Agriculture Inspector in Santa Cruz de Tenerife, in the Canary Islands, my only transaction as an international arms dealer. I am not rabidly anti-gun, but I am also not convinced a gun will help you in an emergency. There is a large body of evidence that supports the notion that brandishing a gun is more likely to get you killed than anything else. The late Sir Peter Blake, the great New Zealand sailor and environmentalist, was needlessly killed when he tried to thwart a petty robbery on his yacht that was anchored in the Amazon delta when he charged up the companionway with a rifle in hand.

Just how likely are you to encounter pirates at sea? First, we need to define an act of piracy and how it differs from other crimes. The great majority of incidents that involve sailors occur when a boat is in harbor, usually at anchor. Just because an incident happens on a boat does not make it piracy. According to the United Nations Convention on the Law of the Sea, piracy is defined as "any illegal acts of violence or detention, or any act of depredation, committed for private ends by the crew or the passengers of a private ship and directed on the high seas." And what are high seas? It's a bit murky, but basically waters beyond the territorial limits of a country. So if your dinghy is stolen while at anchor it's not an act of piracy, just aggravating.

Noonsite.com, a website first developed by cruising guru Jimmy Cornell (whom you met earlier in the book), is a great resource for sailors, with up-to-date information about every country and harbor that cruising sailors visit. One of its most popular pages is "Piracy and Security," which tracks worldwide violent incidents directed against yachts. The recently published 2017 synopsis revealed 41 incidents for the entire year—that's it, 41 incidents from around the globe. And of those, four were acts of piracy, or crimes committed when yachts were underway, and of those, three were when yachts were less than 20 miles offshore. The rest were almost exclusively robberies. Admittedly the site relies on voluntary self-reporting of incidents—but still, the chances of bad things happening to you on your boat are very small. Another site that's popular with Caribbean cruisers is Caribbean Safety and Security Net (safetyandsecuritynet.org), which tracks every single crime-related incident involving yachts, from violent assaults to petty thefts. In 2017, there were 111 incidents involving yachts. The majority of crimes were onboard robberies committed when the crews were ashore, and dinghies and outboards are clearly the most desired objects. CSSN also reported the same four acts of piracy that Noonsite documented, and they all occurred off Honduras and Nicaragua. For the record, there were 11,741 crimes committed in my hometown of Fort Lauderdale in 2017.

The point of all these statistics is to suggest that the perceived need for security, especially as it pertains to offshore sailing and potential piracy, is a bit overblown. The areas where piracy may occur are well documented and easily avoided. However, if you do encounter pirates on the high seas, nefarious characters who make a living robbing vessels, the chances that you will be able to outgun them are unlikely, and your best chance for survival is to give them what they want. But what about defending yourself from robberies at anchor? A gun will surely come in handy then? Quite possibly, but the problem is that border authorities in all countries require that you declare weapons upon entry, and many then remove them from your boat to be returned only when you clear out. Other countries insist that your weapons be placed in bond and remain in a sealed locker aboard. Of course you can "forget" to declare your gun, and then if forced to use it, beg for forgiveness afterward, but as a foreigner you won't have a lot of clout. And speaking of foreigners, almost exclusively the only cruisers who carry weapons are American.

I always remember the time when a thief boarded *Fortuna*, my steel ketch that you've heard about in earlier chapters, while anchored off Livingston, Guatemala, at the mouth of the Rio Dulce. I was alone aboard, and it took me a moment to realize that someone was on deck and clearly trying to untie the dive tanks lashed to the stern rail.

Enraged, and without thinking, I threw open the hatch and leapt on deck, screaming, "Hey, what the f— are you doing?" The site of a large, naked, and apparently crazy gringo terrified the thief and he dove overboard and swam ashore like Michael Phelps. When I calmed down I realized two things. First, I'd been hasty and reacted in a Peter Blake–like manner by jumping on deck without first assessing the situation. And second, if I'd had a gun at that moment I might have killed the guy. Would I have wanted to kill somebody over a dive tank? For me, the answer was clearly no. I am not suggesting that you don't protect yourself and your loved ones, and I am not naïve, you can be vulnerable in a sailboat. I carry bear spray, which, if the wind is right, will drop somebody like a rock; a speargun with a nasty lionfish tip; and my secret weapon, a hunting slingshot. None of these "weapons" needs to be declared, although local authorities occasionally ban spearguns for fishing. Tadji teases me that I am going to turn up on deck with my slingshot as pirates with automatic weapons come aboard. "Your only chance is to hit them while they're laughing." She's right of course, a slingshot is not likely to deter bad guys with big guns, but I can really fire the thing. Stretching the three rubber bands to the breaking point, I release a very well-aimed marble with considerable force, accurate to about 20 meters or so. At least one of those bad guys is going have a hell of a headache.

Vessel Awareness—The Walkabout

Enough of guns and slingshots, let's get back to sea, to the unrivaled majesty of being far from land and its associated maladies and madness. As my friend Dan Moreland, the captain of the globe-girdling tall ship *Picton Castle*, says, "all the bad stuff happens on land." I agree and feel a palpable relief every time I shove off for a long passage. As land recedes astern, I am invigorated. It's not the destination beyond the horizon that draws me, it is the joyous sense of being underway. The subversive guilt that saddles us ashore, that insidious western belief that we should always be doing more, quickly dissipates as we lay down a course and trim the sails. To be going is enough; indeed, to be going is to be alive. Most of us can't resist taking one last look astern, especially at the beginning of a long voyage, and the curvature of the earth makes the land look as if it's sinking, or maybe being overwhelmed in a flood. John Huth speculates in *The Lost Art of Finding Our Way* that flood stories, a core plank in the creation myths of many early cultures, might have arisen from this very perspective, a sailor watching land recede behind her vessel. Peter Matthiessen describes a similar phenomenon in his lyrical novel *Far Tortuga*. As the Cayman Island turtle fishermen aboard the rickety schooner *Lillias Eden* head out to sea, one of the crew, looking astern, declares, "Land sunk out. All dese years I've seen dat Old Rock sink away, and still I be wonderin if I ever see her rise again." Søren Kierkegaard, the Danish existentialist philosopher, wrote that "life can be understood only backward, but must be lived forward," a sentiment sailors understand intuitively.

I love the first morning at sea. The awkward first night is behind us, there's no turning back for a forgotten part or because of a change of heart—we're truly underway and the natural routines that define a passage begin to fall into place. One of my at-sea rituals is the "walkabout," the simple task of making a thorough inspection of the deck every day. It might seem odd, but once you find yourself into the rhythm of a passage it's easy to become complacent and rarely venture from the sanctuary of the cockpit. That's one reason I am not a proponent of leading all sail controls aft. I like to work the deck, to instinctively know how to keep my balance and my center of effort low in a rough sea. I want to remind myself where the hand- and hipholds are, and where the safe places to operate from in an emergency are. There will come a time, most likely on a moonless night with a cap full of wind, when you will have to leave the cockpit to deal with an issue on deck. I guarantee it. This is not the time to be groping like a landlubber, looking for a handhold with the white light shining from a headlamp destroying your night vision, floundering about, wondering where you should park yourself to effect a critical repair.

The walkabout is a simple affair. I stroll about, or if it's rough, hang on for dear life and climb about the deck, and look at things. I also listen. As I've noted several times, your boat will talk to you if you bother to listen to her. Indeed, for several years before the near dismasting described in Chapter Two, when we lost the shroud off Ikaria in the Aegean, I had been hearing a weird, metallic clanking. It was especially apparent from the starboard pilot berth. I inspected the chainplate, and carefully examined the terminals, turnbuckles, and wires on deck. I peered up at the fittings aloft and inspected them every time I went up the mast. I couldn't see anything amiss and eventually just put it down to one of the many weird noises a boat makes. Alas, it turned out to be a very serious problem caused by a slight misalignment of the wire and upper swage terminal where it connected to the mast. The problem arose after we lost the mast in a tornado in Italy. The yard cut the stump of the mast and rigging away when they righted the boat. Without the old shrouds for a template I had to take precise measurements for the manufacture of a new mast and rig, and I was off just a fraction. Over time, the wires chafed on the terminal, making a distinct noise as they traveled down the 1x19 stainless wire, as if the shroud was crying out, "John, listen, something's not right."

On the walkabout I look for signs of chafe, make sure that the leads are fair, and that gear lashed on deck is still well secured. It's surprising how often I find evidence of things not quite right, and note them as needing attention. The sails, even new, top-quality sails, take a beating offshore as stitching fails, seams rip, webbing frays, and battens break.

My policy is simple. If I find a problem with the rig or sails, we repair it as soon as possible. Waiting is always a mistake, and among the most valuable spare parts to carry aboard are a few yards of sticky-backed Dacron, sail needles, twine, and a palm. Precut lengths of Dux, which is souped-up Spectra line, and incredibly strong, is ideal for emergency rigging repairs. Be sure to have spliced deadeyes in each end and plenty of small-diameter Spectra for lashing.

Your boat looks different from different perspectives. From the bow pulpit looking aft you can watch the wake and see how the helmsperson is steering. You can sense if the boat is balanced and literally feel if the vessel is tracking well. Glancing up, you can see if the mast is aligned and note if the rigging is groaning or seems overloaded, or maybe is too slack. I always find it rewarding to climb as far forward as possible, and while holding on, peer back at my boat. Just watching her slice through the water is reward enough. Despite what the sailing safety patrol insists, it's not against the rules to move around the deck, and, in fact, it just may be the safest thing you do all day.

PFDs, Safety Harnesses, and Jacklines

The walkabout is the perfect segue into the controversial topic of safety harnesses, jacklines, and overall deck awareness. Folks are always surprised when they come aboard *Quetzal* and we discuss safety. "I am not responsible for your safety," I explain, "you are. I can tell you what I think you should do, even how to do it, but ultimately you are responsible for your own life. There are no cast-in-stone rules—this isn't a hotel with NO DIVING signs posted around the pool. It's up to you to pay attention all the time." And I mean it. The power of an offshore passage is that we are privileged to visit the edge of time, a set of coordinates where we can't easily escape the consequences of our own decisions, where we are fully engaged and responsible for the choices we've made—and for those yet to be made—and we are able to embrace this ultimate freedom. None of us wants to perish at sea, and preventing situations that imperil my crew is my number-one job as captain. I always make it clear to my crew that it's not the fancy gear they bought at the boat show that makes them—and, by extension all of us—safe, but an awareness of what the dangers are, where they are, and how to avoid them.

It is standard procedure for offshore sailors to wear an inflatable personal flotation device (PFD) with an integrated harness, and be tethered to the boat any time they're on deck. I completely support the practice of wearing a top-quality, properly fitted inflatable PFD. If you go overboard your chances of survival are markedly better if you have flotation to sustain you while a rescue operation is mounted. The notion of being tethered to the boat at all times is, however, starting to be questioned, and some studies suggest that the tether might just be what does you in. That this alternative view is being put forward is a relief to me because for many years I've felt like a lone voice in the wind, questioning the design and use of both tethers and jacklines.

Let's start with PFDs. The old debate was whether to have an automatically inflated model or one that you deploy yourself. The automatic inflatable devices have soundly carried the argument and it is becoming difficult to find a high-quality manual PFD/harness today. The premise is that when you go overboard the last thing you need to worry about is inflating your PFD. The top models use hydrostatic releases that are activated by water pressure (that is, at a certain depth, usually less than 2 feet, they deploy), and these are a big, and expensive, improvement over automatic units that deploy when a water-soluble bobbin dissolves. These latter models were infamous for going off when a wave splashed aboard, leaving you sitting in the cockpit with an inflated harness and hoping that you have a spare CO_2 cylinder to rearm the suddenly useless PFD.

Not surprisingly, I fall into the other camp: I wear a manually deployed PFD/harness. Maybe it's the haunting memory of that long-ago swim I took early in the Cape Horn voyage, when an inflated PFD would likely have been the end of me. I don't think that's it, though—I believe it has more to do with the nature of what actually happens when you fall off a boat, something that I've been discussing and conducting drills about for years. If you are not a strong swimmer, and if the thought of being in the water terrifies you, and furthermore, if you know that you are likely to panic if you suddenly find yourself overboard, then wear the best automatic inflatable PFD/harness you can afford. Also, take swim lessons and attend safety seminars where PFDs and life rafts are deployed. Most fear is a result of ignorance and inexperience. You can overcome it.

I choose to wear a manual PFD/harness because my experience has taught me that once in the water, there's a good chance that I am going to have to do something to help save myself. I might be ensnared in a line, or in a piece of gear that came overboard with me, and need to free myself. I may need to push away from the boat so it doesn't run me over. If the boat is capsized, or just knocked down, I will need to be able to go deep in the water to avoid being crushed or drowned. And if I do fall and am arrested by my tether, partially overboard, or being dragged in the water, I have a much better chance of pulling myself, or of being pulled, back on deck without an inflated PFD. Trust me, I know the risks of this decision. If I am unconscious, my harness will not deploy and I will drown before I can be rescued. The reality is that if you're unconscious your chances of survival are minimal anyway, so I'd rather take the gamble that I'll be aware and able to impact the odds of my own survival.

With both types of PFD, once the inflation tube is deployed, swimming is no longer an option, and you essentially are left to bob in the water, especially if there's a sea running. I have conducted many offshore-sailing workshops, and one thing that sets ours apart is that we actually launch a life raft from a sailboat at sea. This is a fundamentally different experience from watching a raft inflate on a classroom floor or in a swimming pool. We then get wet and board the raft—from the boat, from the water, with foul-weather gear and sea boots on, and with harnesses deployed and, for the strong swimmers, with them not yet deployed. Boarding a raft from the water, especially a double-floored offshore raft, which is a very real likelihood in an emergency, is extremely challenging with an inflated PFD/harness. Rafts often inflate upside down and it's very difficult to climb on top in order to right them. Partially deflating your PFD helps. With automatic or manual PFDs, knowing where the deflation tube is and how to use it, and then how to blow back into it, is essential but something rarely discussed in safety demos. The fittest crew need to board the raft first, and then help others. We have observed over and over that the more aware you are in the water, even if you are out of shape, the better the chances that you will make it into the raft. The critical need for situational awareness is never more apparent than in an unfolding emergency.

In his recent book *200,000 Miles: A Life of Adventure*, under the subchapter heading "Safety Rules," Jimmy Cornell declares: "Swimming in the open ocean while on passage is never permitted." Barry, one of my crew on a recent tough passage from Maryland to Grenada, was reading the book and pointed this out to me a few days after we'd taken a refreshing swim in the Puerto Rican Trench, the deepest spot in the Atlantic Ocean. I have enormous respect for Jimmy Cornell but differ with him on this issue. If conditions permit, we do swim at sea, and I think it's an important safety drill as well as a lot of fun. Usually we drop all sails and let the boat drift, but sometimes, if it's breezy, we heave-to. We are extremely cautious and deploy safety lines buoyed with fenders, make sure the boarding ladder is lowered and secure, and appoint observers while taking turns in the water. It is eye-opening for the crew to see how difficult it is to keep up with a boat drifting at 2 knots, and I ask them to imagine a boat moving away from them at 6 knots. In just a few seconds the boat will be hundreds of feet away. Also, imagine being pulled along by a tether after falling overboard. It's unlikely you will be able to get back aboard—your only option may well be to pull the quick release on your tether, or to find your knife and cut the tether. It's also revealing to see how challenging it is to swim at all if a swell is running. Now imagine being overboard in a gale. Experience is always the best teacher, maybe the only real teacher, and knowing what it's like to be in the water, in a controlled but very real environment, can only help you if suddenly you find yourself overboard in an emergency.

The best way to resolve this debate about PFD/harnesses is not to fall off the boat in the first place. The way we discuss and practice man-overboard emergencies is ludicrous. It finally dawned on me a few years ago that we go about it completely backward. Just think of how you teach your children to cross a street and behave around busy roads. You don't say, "Now, honey, after the car hits you, do this…" We say, "Look both ways, pay attention, make eye contact with the driver, assume the driver is not paying attention. Don't get hit by a car!" Of course, if an accident happens an emergency plan is vital. But the same first principle applies on a boat: "Pay attention, assume gear will fail, don't fall off the damn boat!" That's the starting point for crew-overboard procedures.

This leads us to the subject of jacklines and tethers. I am not a quick study, I confess, and for most of my sailing career I have led jacklines, usually flat canvas webbing, down the side decks. Then, when I was using a tether, I hooked one end to the jackline, the other end to my PFD/harness, and sauntered about the deck feeling safe, or at least that I was being responsible and setting a good example for the crew. I always stressed that the tether needed to have a quick release on the end that attached to you, so that if you were dangling overboard you would be able to free yourself. But old dogs can learn new tricks, and today the jackline arrangement on *Quetzal* has been completely revamped.

We still use two lengths of flat reinforced canvas webbing, with loops secured by Spectra thread led to dedicated U-bolts for the jacklines. We route them as close to the centerline of the boat as practical and stretch them tight. Then, instead of attaching a shackle directly to the jackline, we loop it around the jackline and attach the highly-quality quick-release snapshackle to the D-ring on the harness part of the PFD. With this arrangement, it's almost impossible to fall off the boat—you just can't reach the deck edge. I demonstrate the technique and try, seriously, to throw myself off the boat, but my movement is arrested on the side deck. Had such an arrangement been in place, it may well have saved the life of Simon Speirs, who was tragically washed overboard in the 2017 Clipper round-the-world race. The top-of-the-line tether clip he was using was secured directly to the jackline on deck. The jackline was terminated to a cleat. Speirs, who was on the foredeck for a sail change in rough conditions, was clipped to the jackline. It seems that his tether clip was caught on the cleat, and when it was suddenly loaded as the wave carried him off the boat, it twisted and failed. Attaching the tether end directly to the D-ring on the PFD/harness makes it far more likely to load properly. Most importantly, jacklines that allow a sailor to be washed overboard in the first place are completely inadequate. The Clipper race organizers, and the sailing community in general, need to find a way to run the jacklines down the center of the boat. With the old system—jacklines on deck—you always ended up carrying the shackle that was attached to the jackline to prevent it from clanking along the deck, in essence leaving you with just one hand to work with. With the looped tether and jackline arrangement, you have both hands available to help you hold on as you move about. And, as anyone who has ever sailed with me will attest, I remind you over and over and over again to work the deck from the high side, the windward side, whenever possible. I'll also ask you to identify the danger points—i.e. the loaded-up fittings—and stress that staying upwind of these fittings is what makes you safe.

Even with this new and improved jackline design, you still have to be prepared to release from your harness tether if you go overboard. Tethers with locking shackles on both ends should be banned. After another tragic death—that of British sailor Christopher Reddish in 2012 when he fell overboard and died despite being tethered to the boat and wearing an inflated PFD—the U.K. magazine *Practical Boat Owner* conducted a series of tests to determine the safety of being tethered to the boat.

Using a realistic 180-pound dummy called Fred, they simulated tethered-man-overboard emergencies. Even with a full crew, it was extremely difficult to retrieve Fred as he dangled over the side, especially the low side. At more than 3 knots of boat speed, Fred's head was barely above water, despite the fact that he was wearing an inflated PFD. It was almost impossible to lift him back aboard. At 6 knots, poor Fred was not in good shape at all, being pulled along face down. Fred fared better when dragged on the high side, when the boat was well heeled, but it was a rough ride as he repeatedly smacked into the boat.

Ultimately they concluded that short tethers—corresponding to the new looped technique on *Quetzal*—are much safer than the standard 6´ tethers we often use, and that operating from the high side reduced the overboard sailor's chances of being dragged along the dangerous leeward side of the hull. They also found that if Fred was to remain tethered to the boat, it was critical to reduce boat speed as quickly as possible to be able to retrieve him before he drowned. Dropping all sail and immediately heaving-to were the best options. But even with the boat slowed down or nearly dead in the water, if the crew was unable to haul the sailor aboard, the overboard sailor must be prepared to release from her tether.

Another sobering finding was that the quick-release snapshackles on many tethers refused to open when under load. As a result, *Practical Boat Owner* suggested that a web cutter, or safe knife, like the ones used by SpinLok on their top-quality PFD/harnesses, should be mounted on your PFD/harness and easily accessed so that you can cut away if all else fails.

Hal Roth concludes his "Wrinkles" chapter with a brief description of safety harnesses. This was before the days of inflatable PFDs and personal AIS beacons, and looking at the black-and-white pictures of his simple canvas harness, I realized that the obsession with safety is a modern preoccupation. Clearly our safety devices have made us safer, in many cases dramatically so, but they do not absolve us from the need to be aware of our situation all the time. A sailor in shorts and a T-shirt with a keen sense of situational awareness is dramatically safer than a sailor dressed to the nines, wearing $10,000 worth of the latest safety gear, but oblivious to the fact that the boat is about to jibe, or that he's straddling the jibsheet while standing on deck or sitting on the low side with his head right in line with the throw of the vang should the mainsheet suddenly release. Safety and seamanship go hand in hand— you can't buy them—you need to practice them.

Those of us who ply oceans year after year find solutions to problems as they arise and try to prevent them by preparing our boats and ourselves before shoving off. Most importantly, we don't let the threat of a problem, be it a person overboard, an act of piracy, or failed gear, prevent us from making voyages. The risks associated with voyaging pale when compared with the rewards. As Annie Dillard reminds us, "How we spend our days is, of course, how we spend our lives." Ocean voyaging is best way I know of to spend my days.

ACKNOWLEDGMENTS

April 27, 2018. Latitude N 33° 56′ Longitude W 75° 54′. Speed Over Ground 9.2 knots. True Course 040°

It seems appropriate to be writing these last words from the cabin of *Quetzal*. We're on passage, hurtling toward Cape Hatteras with a poled-out genoa on a deep reach. Life is good. Naturally we're in the heart of the Gulf Stream, greedy for the 3 knots of extra speed and willingly accepting the lumpy ride that comes with it. I have a delightful crew aboard, a mix of first-timers and *Quetzal* veterans. We just reeled in a mahi-mahi—fish tacos are on the menu for lunch. We are bound for the Chesapeake Bay and then on to Solomons, Maryland, and Spring Cove marina. Familiar waypoints and staging points—we have a busy summer ahead and need to complete a few projects before heading across the Atlantic. We are destined for the Azores, Ireland, Scotland, and beyond—another crossing. We keep moving, always pressing on. It's what we do.

When I think of the many voyages that I have been fortunate to contemplate and complete, I am thankful and humbled. As a kid I dreamed of a sailing life and somehow it has worked out that way. These past 15 years sailing *Quetzal* have been immensely satisfying. My heartfelt thanks go to the many people who have worked on *Quetzal* over the years, professionals and volunteers—working long hours repairing and refitting the old girl in boatyards the world over—who have embraced her spirit and understand our need to be at sea.

Of course our passages have been made possible by the folks who have signed aboard: devoted sailors and adventurers who took a leap of faith, stood watch on the blackest of nights, and shared their dreams as we crossed oceans together. You are the lifeblood of *Quetzal* and I regret that I can't mention you each by name. Every one of you lives in these pages.

In addition to those mentioned in the book, I would like to thank a few dear friends who have been indispensable to *Quetzal* and her captain: Bob Pingel (who does appear in the book but who has done so much for *Quetzal* over the years, he needs mentioning again), Rick and Janie Thompson, and Tim Johnson. They have provided support and wisdom that has allowed us to keep sailing the oceans of the world.

I'd also like to thank my stepson Nick Rodriguez. He was an early reader of the manuscript, and also endured many stories in the breaks between our spirited games of one-on-one basketball.

Thanks to my magazine editors and publishers for sharing my story in their pages and granting permission for much of that material to appear in these pages: Greta and Erin Schanen at *Sailing*; Herb McCormick and Mark Pilsbury at *Cruising World*; and Peter Nielsen at *Sail*.

Writing a book is never easy and, in many ways, this is the book I've been writing my entire life, which only makes the job more demanding. My editor and dear friend, Molly Mulhern, is responsible for anything good about *Sailing to the Edge of Time* and the faults are entirely mine. This is the third book of mine that Molly has edited, and this one was the most challenging. I had ideas and stories but Molly had the vision, saw it as a book, and believed in my lofty ambition of trying to nail down the essence of the good life at sea. She was instrumental in helping me find my voice and keeping me on course. I can't thank her enough.

The sailors and publishing professionals at Adlard Coles/Bloomsbury have seen to it that we North American sailors have a home and a voice on their list, and I am profoundly grateful and appreciative of their expertise. Hats off to Janet Murphy and her entire crew, especially Penny Phillips for seeing to all the details of publishing *Sailing to the Edge of Time*.

Finally, my wife Tadji did what only she can do, finding intriguing places for me to write in between voyages, and keeping me inspired when I despaired. Parts of this book were written in the 11th arrondissement of Paris, the seaside village of Anavyssos, outside of Athens, Deia on the north shore of Majorca, the Giudecca district of Venice, Cape Town, Antigua, Guadeloupe, Isla Mujures and San Miguel de Allende in Mexico, and Placencia, in southern Belize. Tadji was my anchor that never dragged through the entire process. I must say, she seemed to enjoy our "writing" travels too. We are partners in sailing, travel, and life, and I love her profoundly.

John Kretschmer

Aboard *Quetzal*

At Sea

CREDITS

Photographs

James Braun: page 3 *top*

Walter Cooper: pages 4 *top*, 5 *top*, 6 *top left*, 8 *top left & bottom*

Alan Creaser: page 2 *bottom*

John Evans: page 1 *bottom*

Fred Grimm: page 3 *bottom*

Ed Kretschmer: page 1 *top left*

John Kretschmer: pages 2 *top*, 4 *bottom*, 5 *bottom*, 6 *bottom right*

Tadji Kretschmer: pages 6 *bottom left*, 7 *bottom*, 8 *top right*

Joe Murton: page 7 *top left & right*

Molly Potter: pages 1 *top right*, 6 *top right*

Text

The author and publishers gratefully acknowledge the following sources of quoted material:

page ii: *The Writing Life* by Annie Dillard, HarperCollins Publishers, New York, 1979

page ii: *The Fall* by Albert Camus, 1956

pages 1 & 54: *Zorba the Greek* by Nikos Kazantzakis, translated by Carl Wildman, Faber and Faber, London, UK, 2008

page 9: *Margins of Philosophy* by Jacques Derrida, translated by Alan Bass, Chicago University Press, Chicago, Illinois, 1982

pages 24–25: *The Long Way* by Bernard Moitessier, translated by William Rodarmor, Sheridan House, Dobbs Ferry, New York, 1995

page 41: *Tribe: On Homecoming and Belonging* by Sebastian Junger, Hachette Book Group, New York, 2016

page 70: "The Fray" by Chris DiCroce, 2014

page 95: *A Forest of Kings: The Untold Story of the Ancient Maya* by Linda Schele and David Friedel, William Morrow and Co., New York, 1990

pages 87 & 125: *Finding Your Way Without Map or Compass* by Harold Gatty, Dover Publications, New York, 2003

page 125: *The Lost Art of Finding Our Way* by John Edward Huth, Cambridge, Massachusetts; The Belknap Press of Harvard University Press, copyright © 2013 by the President and Fellows of Harvard College

page 147: *The New Founde Land* by Farley Mowat, McClelland and Stewart Limited, Toronto, 1989

page 183: *Wanderer* by Sterling Hayden, Alfred A. Knopf, New York, 1963

page 213: *Waterland* by Graham Swift, Heinemann, London, UK, 1983

page 233: *Alone Through the Roaring Forties* by Vito Dumas, McGraw-Hill Education, New York, 2003

page 263: *Far Tortuga* by Peter Matthiessen, 1975

Every effort has been made to contact the copyright holders of the extracts reproduced in this book. Any inadvertent omissions in acknowledging quoted material will be rectified in future editions provided that written notification is made to the publishers.